Praise for *A New Personal Pentecost*

In A New Personal Pentecost, *Professor Kanaga provides a passionate examination of the "Pentecostal Experience": its scriptural basis, its manifestations during the apostolic period, and its continued occurrence during subsequent church history, all in support of its authenticity and its relevance to events in the 21st century.*
–Dr. John Lackey, former Academic Dean of Southern California College (Vanguard University), Costa Mesa, CA

Rev. Kanaga gives a compelling argument for the place of Pentecostal Gifts and their manifestations in the modern church. Events leading up to, and subsequent to, the Day of Pentecost are written in such a manner as to make them understandable to the person in the pew.
–Dr. Raymond White, Education Department, Vanguard University, Costa Mesa, CA

There is no truth more relevant to the modern church than the work of the blessed Holy Spirit. To remove that work from the public square to the back room is not only blasphemous, but is a serious denial of the very power needed to confront Satan's 21st century schemes. Professor Kanaga's scholarly work encourages a new personal Pentecost.
–Rev. Vernon ("Cap") Marks, District Superintendent, Oregon Assemblies of God

Rev. Lynn Kanaga's book, A New Personal Pentecost, *should be required reading for all biblical students. It clearly and precisely presents the Pentecostal phenomenon as an experience that has biblical and historical roots. The message of this book cannot be ignored. It exposes the cessationist philosophy as a hoax that is based on poor exegesis. Kanaga's interaction between scriptural truth and historical fact builds a solid, irrefutable case that the Pentecostal experience is for the Christian today.*

–Professor Glen R. Robertson, Assemblies of God Missionary; Lecturer at University of Matej Bela Evangelical Seminary; Banska Bystrica, Slovakia

In a world desperately seeking answers and longing for help, the quest has begun for wells that are full and offer refreshment. The understanding of the fullness of the Holy Spirit as the answer to the human longing is provided in a clear and compelling manner in this outstanding book by Lynn Kanaga. Readers will find an intellectual look into history and a practical resource for "tapping in" to God's abundant supply. A "MUST READ" FOR THE STUDENT OF THE WORD.

–Rev, Scott R. Erickson, Senior Pastor of Peoples Church, Salem, OR

It has been my pleasure to watch the development of the manuscript of A New Personal Pentecost from an idea to a labor of love and to its finished form. I observed the struggles and the moments of triumph when ideas came together. Calling it a labor of love is very appropriate. The subject is one the author loves supremely and the product contains a part of his soul.

I am a chemist, not a theologian, and I sometimes struggle with concepts and terminology in theology. Professor Kanaga has written so that even the laity like me can understand and appreciate his work. His experience as a pastor is evident in his approach to the subject and his presentation. I have a great appreciation for his ability to use words to express his ideas, his love for the subject, and his concern for his readers.

I highly recommend Professor Kanaga's book to anyone interested in the history of the Pentecostal experience and its relevance in the twenty-first century. It is definitely "a must read."

–Dr. Donald Lorance, Professor and Chairman of the Department of Chemistry Vanguard University of Southern California, Costa Mesa, CA

I am writing in behalf of Rev. Lynn Kanaga and his book entitled A New Personal Pentecost. *Having spent the better part of thirty years in Nigeria and Ethiopia educating students of those nations to build the Church, I have often wished for a scholarly work of this nature to meet the student's needs to understand Pentecost. This work fills a unique niche in that it covers the historical and theological bases of the subject.*

Brother Kanaga is a qualified author, having spent twenty years as a pastor and twenty-five years as a professor at Vanguard University. He is able to bring these two backgrounds into the structure and content of his book, making it relevant to both fields. I sincerely recommend its publication.

–Dr. James W. Macauley, Asst Pastor, Peoples Church Salem, OR

This new book gathers in one place the personal testimony, the historical apologetics, and the biblical interpretation characteristic of classical Pentecostal authors. The book will appeal especially to those interested to sample how classical Pentecostal writers think and write. Not aiming to engage the newer, more technical analyses of Pentecostalism, the book rather reflects the spiritual and literary heritage of what is now the second largest sector of Christianity, after the Roman Catholic Church.

–Russell P. Spittler, Provost/Vice President for Academic Affairs (Interim), Vanguard University, Costa Mesa, CA

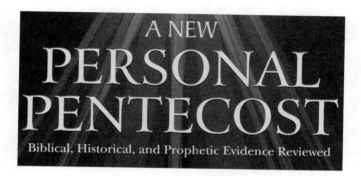

A NEW PERSONAL PENTECOST

Biblical, Historical, and Prophetic Evidence Reviewed

by
Rev. Lynn D. Kanaga

VMI PUBLISHERS

Partnering With Christian Authors, Publishing Christian and Inspirational Books

Sisters, Oregon

Copyright © 2005 by Rev. Lynn D. Kanaga
(All rights reserved)

Permissions to use previously published
material appear on page 271.

Published by
Virtue Ministries
Sisters, Oregon
www.vmipublishers.com

ISBN: 1-933204-12-5
ISBN 13: 978-1-933204-12-3

Library of Congress Control Number: 2005935224

Author Contact:
lkanaga@msn.com

Dedication

To my dear wife Marguerite,
Who has been my patient Encourager
In moments of my frustrations, and a
Proof Reader and Advisor on request.
May God bless her as much as she has blessed me!

Foreword

Lynn Kanaga has been an ordained minister of the Assemblies of God for over 50 years. He has served capably as a pastor and as a college professor. With one foot in the pastoral world, and the other in the academic milieu – he understands well the need to communicate Pentecostal vitality to a range of audiences.

In this book, he has written a defense of classical Pentecostalism. In a sense, Pentecostalism needs no defense. In 100 years, this Movement has grown from a handful to embrace perhaps as many as one billion followers of Jesus Christ. However, concerns still exist among non-Pentecostals that Pentecostal theology is rooted in experience rather than Scripture. This work by Lynn Kanaga affirms the Scriptural authority underlying Pentecostal experience. Additionally, he examines Pentecostal experience through the history of the medieval and reformation eras, as well as contemporary church history. He points to the prophetic ramifications of Joel's prophecy, cited by Peter, on the day of Pentecost.

This work will influence you through its strong conviction that the Pentecostal experiences described in the book of Acts, and the gifts of the Spirit displayed in 1 Corinthians 12 – 14, are not only meant for modern Christians, but also are given as a precursor to the return of Jesus Christ.

On a personal level, I was privileged to serve for a number of years as pastor to Lynn Kanaga and his family. They serve as sterling examples of Spirit-filled character. I commend this work to you.

Dr. George O. Wood, General Secretary,
General Council of The Assemblies of God

Acknowledgments

I am very much indebted to many colleagues, friends, and family members who, during the time I have spent researching this important subject, have encouraged and assisted my efforts.

Foremost in my recollections is the assistance and encouragement I received from my dear friend and colleague, Professor Ronald Wright of Vanguard University. Although I had graduated many years earlier with a Bible major from Bethany Bible College, Professor Wright allowed me to attend and participate in many of his Bible classes. Furthermore, we often had lunch together, and long discussions regarding the subject I dreamed of writing about. Professor Wright encouraged me to proceed, posthaste. It was Professor Wright, too, who reviewed the earliest stages of my manuscript, and was always both critically helpful and encouraging. I am sorry to say that my friend has gone on. Now he is with the Lord, there to fully enjoy the fruits of his labors, particularly his ministries among the students of Southern California College and Vanguard University.

But there are many others of Vanguard's faculty and staff who were more than willing to provide critical evaluations of my work as it progressed. Mel Covetta, a fine Librarian serving at our O. Cope Budge College Library, was always willing to locate texts that I needed, either from our own stock of books or by retrieving those books held in other depositories. Mel has always been wonderfully pleasant, regardless of the unusual requests I made of him. May the Lord add to Mel's store of blessings, in ways that I cannot.

In a more personal vein, I want to thank all the members of the "Friday Lunch Bunch," whose friendship and fellowship I cherish! This homogenous "Bunch" was an unofficial group who met for lunch after the rigors of college classes were over for the week, just to have a friendly, intellectual discussion about anything and everything. My friend Dr. Donald Lorance was the originator, and unofficially the continuing "supervisor" of that delightful group. I count each and every one as my dear friends. Thanks for your encouragement, for supporting me in ways that I cannot fully express!

Also, I wish to thank Dr Murray Dempster, President of Vanguard University, for always amicably including all of us in the activities of the College, and for maintaining a pleasant environment in college life. I also owe a debt of gratitude to many members of the Religion Department, Dr Bill Williams, Dr. Frank Macchia, and others, who were an encouragement and help along the way.

I must include in my expressions of gratefulness, special thanks to our two children and their spouses for their specialized help in numerous ways. Our daughter, Lynette Robertson, having worked for a law firm, has guided me through the perilous intricacies of word processing. Her husband, Rev. Randy Robertson, presently completing the writing of his Ph.D. dissertation, has offered helpful advice and encouragement. Yes, and, sometimes, we have commiserated about the occasional agonies of trying to write a scholarly document in an appealing manner. Our son, Valiant Kanaga, who is employed for a company which deals with the technical level of computers, has helped me keep my computer running in the right direction during my writing and revision work. And our dear daughter-in-law, Linda, has encouraged me often by her loyalty to our clan and her pleasant demeanor. Thank you all!

Lastly, but certainly not least, I am so very grateful to Bill Carmichael, CEO of VMI Publisher, Ms. Lacey Hanes-Ogle, Asst. Publisher, along with their efficient staff, for believing in the success of this book and encouraging me accordingly. May the dear Lord reward all of you richly!

Table of Contents

THE RATIONALE FOR THIS
IMPORTANT STUDY

The Gifts of the Holy Spirit, so prominent in the New Testament Apostolic Church, have been from the very beginning the center of controversy, through all of history to the present. The divergent responses to this God-ordained experience are likely caused by the general inclination of fallen human nature to run from God's awesome, holy presence. The first recorded response of Adam and Eve was that they hid from God, Him who sought longingly to commune with them. Why? Because they had disobeyed, and they were instinctively aware of fractured fellowship. Regrettably, mankind has been sinning—and hiding—ever since.

But our Creator God has continued to plan ways to restore that Edenic fellowship humankind once experienced. As a consequence, Jesus the Messiah came to earth to redeem fallen man, and to provide the Comforter, the Holy Spirit, to those who believe. Since the resurrection of Jesus Christ, the Holy Spirit's design is to restore that primeval fellowship which our progenitors once enjoyed.

However, even though our Savior made the restoration of fellowship possible, not everyone is willing to accept God's plan, which is salvation from sin by submission to Christ, and spiritual enablement by receiving the Baptism of the Holy Spirit. From the beginning, Christ's offer was disdainfully rejected by the religious leaders as the efforts of an impostor. Similarly, the initial outpouring of the Holy Spirit recorded in

Acts 2 definitely aroused its share of scoffers, even though it was the Lord Himself who was fulfilling prophecy to benefit mankind.

The Corinthian Church, too, was guilty of misusing the Gifts of the Holy Spirit so that the Apostle Paul felt compelled to offer correctional advice: ". . .*Never to* discontinue the Gifts of the Spirit, rather we are to use them wisely in a manner that would honor the Lord" (emphasis added). His admonition is just as applicable today as it was then: "Eagerly desire the greater gifts . . . [but] do not forbid speaking in tongues" (1 Cor. 12:31, 14:39, NIV). That statement is plain enough! This God-ordained instruction *is* still applicable to modern Christians because it is an integral part of God's inspired Word.

True, it can be a terribly unsettling experience to have a Sovereign God appear unexpectedly in the world of mundane, mortal men. This is probably because we humans do not have much of a reservoir of experiences to draw upon when faced with unexpected spiritual manifestations. The Bible records many examples of human overreactions (and in some instances, under-reactions) to such conditions.

The outpouring of the Holy Spirit on the Day of Pentecost was just such an unprecedented occasion in God's dealings with mankind. Ancient prophecies were wonderfully fulfilled! God was there to anoint and empower otherwise uninspired people, and to commune with them in a manner similar to His communion with mortals in the Garden of Eden. And yet in spite of all of these glorious events, there were those who scornfully rationalized that these manifestations were less than honorable.

Imagine! God's presence was attributed to human drunkenness! (Acts 2:13-15). Unbelievable! Some—perhaps even many—on that day reasoned wrongly and as a regrettable consequence totally missed the Lord's outpouring of grace. Unfortunately, similar mistaken reactions happen even today, because the narrowness of human nature has changed very little.

In whatever period of history God manifests Himself, some, of course, will respond as they should. But the responses are very likely to range from rationalized unbelief on the one hand, to awe-inspired overreactions on the other. For example, there were accusations leveled against Jesus as He was healing the blind and the dumb, alleging that He did so by the power of the devil (see Matt. 12:22-32). Such flawed thinking by the "doctors of the Law"—the theologians of that day— provoked a sharp rebuke from the very Messiah they claimed to know so much about.

By way of contrast, however, on the Mount of Transfiguration Peter apparently overreacted by offering to build three tabernacles to commemorate the glorious occasion (see Mk. 9:2-7). God's answer was, "This is my Son; Listen to Him!" (verse 7, NIV). Good advice! When unsure about what to do, "Listen to the Lord!" However, it is important to note here that Jesus sharply rebuked the error of the Pharisees, but He did not rebuke the exuberant error of Peter. One can justly conclude, therefore, that the most dangerous of the two extremes is to ascribe the works of the Holy Spirit to the devil himself (see Matt. 12:31-32).

It is still true that human nature hasn't changed very much. Early twentieth-century Pentecostals were frequently accused of being under the influence of the devil. For example, my own maternal grandfather, a respected medical doctor in our community, was soundly converted in a Pentecostal tent meeting, wonderfully delivered from the wicked life that would eventually have led him to ruin. Everyone in the town knew him well and were outspokenly surprised that "Doc" had "got religion."

So with his spiritual appetites joyously rejuvenated in that tent revival, my grandfather decided to attend another advertised evangelistic meeting, to be held in one of the local established churches. At the conclusion of that meeting, he was approached by the leaders and *sharply admonished* that while conversion was certainly acceptable, Pentecostal-like experiences were "of the devil" because "such things were no longer operational." "After all," they exclaimed, "the Apostles are now dead."

Ah, But God was not dead! They were too late. My grandfather had found reality at last, and the bubbling joy of the Lord. Needless to say, my grandfather did not follow their well-intentioned warning. He continued to attend Pentecostal services wherever he could find them.

Similar comments of unbelief were expressed to my wife and me many years later while we were pastoring. My grandfather, a scholar and writer on his own, and my dear grandmother gave me my earliest instructions in the Bible; and eventually I, too, received the Baptism in the Holy Spirit, demonstrated by my speaking in tongues. After that experience, I was ecstatic, "walking on air" for days. Wonderful!

Later, I felt called of the Lord to the ministry and eventually enrolled in Central Bible College (where my grandfather—late in his life—had attended in the days of "Daddy" Welsh and Myer Pearlman). There I met my lovely wife, Marguerite, also a Pentecostal, and after we graduated we became pastors. During our second pastorate, we applied for missionary appointment, and both of us passed our initial physical exams.

A subsequent exam, however, revealed that Marguerite had a "toxic" thyroid and a deficient red blood cell count. Further tests indicated she was afflicted with *melanoma cancer* of the bone marrow. Things became serious! Our faith was being severely tested! She was sent to Kansas University Medical Center because of her alarming weakness. Her red blood cell count had dropped to 4, when normal would be 12 to 15.

Oh, but there was still more to come! Things became even more serious. The KU specialist talked with me privately in the hospital hallway:

"She cannot possibly live more than a month—six weeks at the most. She is not making any of her own blood cells." I was awestruck!

Shocking! This trial had become *deadly* serious! What were we to do? We had two little children! We were in a situation we could do nothing about—except to pray for the Lord to rescue us. Suddenly, it became very, very obvious: we were not going to the mission field! And even more alarming, we faced the possibility of having to give up the pastoral ministry. We desperately needed a biblical miracle. We urgently needed the Lord's intervention—soon!

As we faced the hideous possibility of death, we had both been seeking courage from the Lord, earnestly—and often. During those times, the Lord gave both of us promises from Scripture which encouraged us again and again. Timidly, we began holding those promises before the Lord, reminding Him that these were His words, which He had confirmed to our hearts. Then, with increasing boldness, we began sensing that we were using these promises as a sword, hacking away at the devil's lies to believe otherwise. Yes, it seemed as though we were using the Sword of the Spirit. After many struggles of faith, eventually the Lord won! Marguerite was healed! And she lives, healthy still today.

Marguerite came to rely on a personalized promise from Hebrews10:35-39:

> "Cast not away therefore your confidence which has great recompense of reward. For you have need of patience, that after you have done the will of God, you might receive the promise. For yet a little while, He that shall come, will come. . . "

In addition, one day while I was praying earnestly, the Lord turned my attention to what would prove to be a very relevant promise. I had the sensation of God speaking directly to me. It was Psalm 128:3-6, an encouraging word which I do not remember ever noticing before:

Blessed is every one who fears the Lord. . . Thy wife shall be as a fruitful vine by the sides of your house: thy children like olive plants round about your table. Behold, thus shall the man be blessed who fears the Lord. Yes, you shall [live to] see your children's children.

Wow! The statement of that passage certainly seemed to fit our situation! So I accepted it as from the Lord, and held it often before Him as a reminder of what He had promised. Thus, while facing the crisis, we were sustained time after time by God's promises. Meanwhile, many of our Christian friends were praying for us as well.

At our most critical moment, something very unusual happened. While my dear wife lay in her hospital bed at KU, a man neither of us knew—a total stranger—entered her room one day. He was dressed in an off-white, cream-colored business suit—white shoes, white coat, off-white everything— and announced himself as an "evangelist." He said he had heard that Marguerite was very sick and needed prayer. So he stood quietly at the foot of Marguerite's bed and prayed for her healing. Then he walked from the room, and we never saw him again. And to this day we do not know who he was—or is. But from that moment, unusual things began to happen.

A day or so later, when the medical specialist and his entourage of interns were gathered around Marguerite's bed, one of the interns hurriedly appeared—seemingly surprised— and announced that Mrs. Kanaga's tests were showing she had started making her own blood cells. Subsequently, she was released from the Medical Center, and we returned to our parsonage and our wonderful, praying parishioners. That was about 1960.

Her health since then has continued to improve, and to stabilize. To this day, she receives a yearly survey from KU Medical Center, checking to see if she is still alive. On the survey request for 2005—over forty years later—Marguerite was able to report, without equivocation, that she is still in good health!

Do we believe miracles happen today? Of course we do! How could we believe anything else? I praise the Lord as I enjoy living with a miracle every day of the year!

But, in spite of our experiences, so obviously miraculous, some of our "cessationist" acquaintances have said recently, "Oh, Yeah, but she would probably have gotten well anyway."

So which form of "fanaticism" is the most damaging? Which claim brings the most honor to the Lord?

It cannot be denied that some revivalists, both past and present, in their longing to experience fully all that the Lord has for them, have indulged in occasional extremism. But Pentecostals are not alone in this kind of emotional response. Numerous other rejuvenated, revived church members in other denominations have not always behaved with the dignity expected of them.

For example, in 1741, when Rev. Jonathan Edwards delivered his most famous sermon, "Sinners in the Hands of an Angry God," many of his Enfield, Connecticut, congregation responded "with shrieks and groans and writhing." (McMichael, *Anthology of American Literature*, I. p.236, footnote 1) Their animated emotional responses caused Rev. Edwards great alarm, so much so—it is reported—that he sought to warn those so deeply convicted to calm themselves lest their emotionalism lead to madness. Some church historians have speculated that Edwards warnings may have limited the effectiveness of America's "Great Awakening."

Indeed, we must remember, too, that our emotions are a part of our tripartite human nature that must all experience redemption, just as much as does the soul and the intellect. Furthermore, we must hasten to notice that once the Lord reveals Himself to us in a special way, our learning to walk obediently with Him takes stumbling persistence and stubborn practice. It takes time and patience to learn to walk the path of Faith.

Paul's exhortation to the Ephesians seems applicable here: "Because of this light within you, you should do only what is good and right and true. Learn as you go along what pleases the Lord" (Eph. 5:9-10, TLB). The writer of Hebrews seems also to affirm this teaching in chapter 5:14: "But solid food is for the mature, who because of practice have their senses trained to discern good and evil." (NASB). No question about it, as we conscientiously follow the Lord, we do mature in our understanding of what pleases Him. Notice what the Apostle Paul advised about this process in 1 Timothy 4:7: " . . . Train yourself toward godliness . . . keeping yourself spiritually fit." (AMP).

But if over-enthusiasm has led some to improper behavior, then unscriptural preconceptions, hardened into some kind of "dogmatic theology," are profoundly more dangerous. Why?Because mistaken theological assumptions *will rob* us of God-intended blessings, especially stealing from those seeking the Lord for *more* of their spiritual inheritance. The narrative of John's Gospel, chapter 9, illustrates this:

Following a vigorous verbal exchange with the Jews in the Temple area (chapter 8), Jesus encountered a beggar, blind from birth, and He healed him. But the poor man, momentarily enjoying his dramatic deliverance, suddenly faced a storm of unbelieving questions, first from friends, then from citizens of the community, and eventually from the local theological society. The Pharisees asked the healed man to explain how he came to be healed—with the implication, of course, that this probably wasn't really a miracle.

The parents, too, were called, and the unfortunate man was "grilled" several more times, to his utter dismay. Eventually, Jesus was named as the healer, but He was immediately declared a "horrible sinner," because He had healed someone on the Sabbath. Further, the healed man, in spite of all his efforts to cooperate, was summarily thrown out of the synagogue. Such is the irrational behavior of codified, stultifying unbelief!

Does this sort of thing happen in Christendom today? Of course it does! And sadly so, human nature being what it is. Jesus' rebuke to those self-assured Pharisees was startling, to say the least:

I have come into the world to give sight to those who are spiritually blind and to show those who think they see that they are [in reality] blind. . . If you were [really] blind, you wouldn't be guilty. . . But your guilt remains because you claim to know what you are doing (Jn.9:39, 41, TLB).

In this context, it is incredible to observe that in spite of the overwhelming biblical evidence to the contrary—along with the amazing exponential growth of those who have experienced twentieth-century biblical Pentecost—it is incredible, I repeat, that there are still those who *insist* that these miraculous Gifts of the Holy Spirit are not available to believers today. How sad, indeed! It is *not* God who has changed. It is the faulty reasoning of theologians who try to put God into a prearranged "theological" box. But, in spite of men's inconsistent thinking, the Bible continues to declare, "Jesus Christ *is the same* yesterday and today, yes and forever" (Hebrews 13:8, NASB, emphasis added).

The purpose of the study which follows is intended as a prayerful and honest examination of (1) the first-century accounts of the Baptism in the Holy Spirit as recorded in the Bible; (2) the records of Pentecostal experiences in Church History; and (3) the reports of miraculous Gifts of the Holy Spirit occurring in modern times.

But, please understand my position. While the focus of this research is on the continuing manifestations of Holy Spirit Baptism, it is absolutely never intended to minimize the importance of Jesus Christ's substitutionary sacrifice on the cross. Never! It should be obvious that without Christ's miraculous gift of salvation, no other theological study would really matter, would it?

Nor is this study intended as a defense of any particular denomination. Instead, it is intended as a defense of biblical Truth, and the spiritual experiences the Lord intended for believers to have, even today.

Furthermore, just in case it needs to be stated here, it is also the position of this author that the Scriptures are unequivocally the inspired Word of God, absolutely without error in the original monographs, and with no significant error—if any at all—in today's modern translations.

This research project has taken the better part of three years, during which time I have examined various translations of the Scriptures, numerous Church histories, several different Bible Encyclopedias, in addition to a number of secular Encyclopedias, textbooks by other authors on the subject of Pentecost—some from both schools of thought—as well as a variety of scholarly theological documents. The research and writing have been most enjoyable, to say the least!

This process of gathering documented information, however, has only strengthened my conviction that the outpouring of the Holy Spirit, with the attending Gifts of empowerment, is still available for today's believers. Indeed, has not the Lord promised to be forever Faithful to the promises He made to His followers? Jesus once said, "If you, then, being evil, know how to give good gifts to your children, how much more shall your heavenly Father give the Holy Spirit to those who ask Him?" (Lk. 11:13, NASB).

So, without question, the weight of the evidence which follows emphasizes the premise that God has always intended the Gifts of the Spirit to continue—to continue until the

Lord's Return. While it is true that the frequency of *charismatic* experiences did severely decline during the Dark Ages, it is also true that virtually all—perhaps, all—the other important doctrines of the Bible suffered the same deterioration, among them the principle doctrine of salvation by faith in Jesus Christ. This doctrinal erosion happened because the whole moral fabric of the Church of that period suffered tragically. But even then, the miracle Gifts of the Spirit did not totally disappear!

The cumulative evidences, then, have provided strong support for the following:

(1) That the manifestations resulting from being Baptized in the Holy Spirit—as they are described in the Bible—have been continuously represented through the centuries, including our own time.

(2) That the phenomena accompanying present-day Spirit Baptism experiences are fundamentally the same as those occurring among New Testament believers (and sometimes including the problems that Paul had to correct in the Corinthian Church).

(3) That present-day outpourings of the Holy Spirit are— I have come to believe—essential components of the Lord's program to restore and revive New Testament doctrines which have been neglected, or have been distorted by the established Church's inclination to rely upon codified ritualism as a substitute for the absence of the anointing of the Holy Spirit.

(4) That the present-day revival of Pentecostal experiences, as prophesied by Joel in the Old Testament, and quoted by

Peter in the New Testament, is all part of the fulfillment of other "Last Day" prophecies being fulfilled in our own time.

Please read this treatise prayerfully; it has been researched and written prayerfully! May the Lord Himself guide all of us into an accurate understanding of His perfect will. I wish you all of God's best!

Rev. Lynn D. Kanaga

Author, and Fellow Believer in Christ as Savior.
Associate Professor Emeritus of Vanguard University,
Costa Mesa, California
July 12, 2005

Chapter 1

INTRODUCTION:
THE MINISTRY OF THE HOLY SPIRIT
FROM THE BEGINNING

In the beginning God created the heavens and the earth. The earth was empty, a formless mass cloaked in darkness. And the Spirit of God was hovering ["brooding"] over its surface. Then God said, "Let there be light," and there was light. And God saw that it was good. (Genesis 1:1-4, NLT)

The Bible's Creation narrative opens with a very moving portrayal of the Holy Spirit. These opening lines from the timeless past seem to underscore an important attribute of God, His loving and nurturing nature. The imagery here is that of a mother hen carefully watching over her incubating nest, making sure that the eggs are obtaining adequate warmth so that new life might be generated as planned. Thus, this opening narrative describes God as no other Creation story does: portraying Him as a Creator who manifests compassion and concern, a God filled with *agape* love, beneficently disposed toward a universe of chaos. Of course, that is precisely the portrayal of the God we Christians have come to know and commune with.

In sharp contrast to the earliest Genesis portrayal of a chaotic Earth—a formless and meaningless "mass"—the Holy Spirit is characterized as a "brooding" and attentive mother hen, "hovering" just above the chaos. This is a beautiful early expression of God's kind of love, the *chief* characteristic of the

Lord and also an important element of the *"fruits"* of the Holy Spirit's presence (see Gal. 5:22-23).

Thus, out of that primordial Chaos, the Holy Spirit contributed to fashioning a pleasing and fruitful earth environment. It seems perfectly in character, then, that God would pronounce repeatedly during the Creation "week" that everything He had spoken into existence "was very good . . . and that He approved it completely" (Gen. 1:31, AMP).Beauty and order out of chaos? How like Him to do that! He accomplishes spiritual transformation in much the same way today, taking even our disoriented, ruined lives and making them into something of Beauty and Fruitfulness.

The symbolic connotations of the Genesis passage are in many ways similar to that plaintive moment when Jesus wept longingly over Jerusalem, as He looked down on the City from the slopes of the Mount of Olives: "O Jerusalem, Jerusalem. . . How often I have wanted to gather your children together as a hen protects her chicks beneath her wings, but you wouldn't let me" (Lk. 13:34, NLT).

Here we find an interesting implication of Jesus' eternal existence: that ever since those moments in the timeless past, He had been trying to "gather" these wayward children to Himself, but they would not. It is regrettable, however, that God's chosen people of the Old Testament, so well-prepared to experience the Truth, could so effectively avoid the Lord's redemptive purpose for themselves. Certainly, the Lord was willing, but they were not. They could not get beyond their own systematized philosophy.

There is a lesson here for us, too: It is possible to be so precise in our efforts to create a well-organized theology that it would make the Lord Himself cry! Why? Because we often leave no room in our thinking for our God to be the Lord of our lives. That is really the implication of the term "godlessness"— not necessarily being an *atheist*, but living as though our eternal Father has no claims on our mundane existence. The Jewish leaders fell into that mental "trap," and sometimes modern rationalists are guilty of the same error.

But that same regenerating, "incubating" Holy Spirit still hovers caringly over His Church—itself often chaotic, disagreeing, sometimes even disagreeable—maturing in us by means of the wonderful *fruits of the Spirit* the very character of Christ: Love, Joy, Peace, Patience, Gentleness, Goodness, Faithfulness, Meekness, and Self-control. And then this God-inspired character-change created in us by the Holy Spirit is propagated into the lives of others by the ministry Gifts of the Holy Spirit.

This is the true message of 1 Corinthians, chapters 12, 13, and 14. Certainly, not *to terminate* the continuance of the Gifts of the Spirit, but to control them in a loving manner. Indeed, *agape Love* is so important in New Testament experiences that it is the basic characteristic of both the "Fruits of the Spirit" and the "Gifts of the Spirit." As the Scripture have said, "The greatest of these is Love"(1 Cor.13: 13).

Thus, the Holy Spirit has continued His transforming work even into the twentieth century. And this century has experienced phenomenal, worldwide manifestations of the Holy Spirit exactly like those events demonstrated in the book of Acts—and as predicted by Jesus Himself (see John

14:12).Those miraculous Gifts of the Holy Spirit, having never completely ceased in history—as some seem determined to prove—began to reappear in noticeably greater volume early in the twentieth century.

And by now that biblical phenomenon continues worldwide, and in ever-increasing volume. Thus by today, it has become very clear that the move of the Spirit in the twentieth century—and now into the twenty-first—is not something which occurred "in an obscure little corner." Not at all! In modern times, as the nineteenth century blended into the twentieth, these biblical manifestations of Pentecost reappeared explosively, exactly as they had been experienced in the book of Acts.

This modern "move" of the Spirit is, quite frankly, another in the sequence of rediscovered and revived biblical truths which have been in the process of re-emerging since the days of John Huss, the Waldenses, the Anabaptists, Martin Luther, John Calvin, and John Wesley, et al. Each of these Reformers represents a heartwarming story of their enlightenment and their pioneering ministries. As they became increasingly convinced of the truths as recorded in the Bible, they eventually proclaimed those truths so that the thinking, searching multitudes might be changed toward God.

Of course, we might wonder why God didn't restore all those neglected truths at once. The narratives of church history reveal the answer. Established "orthodoxy" *could not tolerate* even the limited number of renewed disclosures that *were* given them. Generally speaking, established "orthodoxy"— doctrinally, all neatly packaged—has a history of resisting the revival of Truth, often even resorting to violence in their determination to exterminate so-called "newness" Or they have lumbered on even further by labeling such a revival of Truth as "fanaticism."

Unfortunately, it is a flaw of human nature that after phenomenal religious experiences have been "fully analyzed," and then reduced to some sort of "systematized formula," events that upsets their "comfort zone" is viewed very suspiciously. Church History also discloses that all too often, this resistance by the world of orthodoxy has resorted even to torture and murder just to emphasize the supposed "accuracy" of their own faulty arguments.

Consequently, many of those Reformers—although bearers of renewed shafts of Light—paid dearly for their convictions. As our Lord was scorned, they too were mocked, maligned, mobbed, mutilated and even murdered—literally. Thus, believers of today have inherited delightful experiences which cost our reforming forefathers their very lives!

And yet, Church History indicates that most of those Reformers perceived only a portion of what God was systematically restoring to human experience. They had centuries of traditions to reexamine, and discard, in light of the newly translated Scriptures. Regrettably, too, many of those brave leaders behaved very narrow-mindedly, adamantly opposed to any other "newly discovered" Bible-based doctrines which had not occurred to themselves first. In those days of Reformation, a number of basic biblical doctrines— now so very fundamental to us—were often heatedly debated among our pioneering Protestants. But we must remember, they were trying to find their way as outlined in the Scriptures so long denied them.

So it seems the restoration pathway was paved for the revival of Pentecostal experiences in modern times. Yes, exactly like those experiences recorded in the Bible. They have been joyously proclaimed anew worldwide in recent centuries. Thus, the renewed emphasis on the Gifts of the Holy Spirit is actually a continuation of that powerful stream of restored truths, truths which have been progressively declared ever since the medieval Dark Ages. And so it is, the Pentecostal dimension of this on-going Spiritual Restoration continues into our own period of history.

Thus, these "prophets" of biblical truth, at great cost to themselves, expounded one after another those important doctrines which the Lord gave them faith to appropriate into their own spiritual experiences. And in conjunction with their preaching of those God-inspired doctrines, the Holy Spirit then reaffirmed their efforts. And in spite of these facts, now widely evident in church history, there are those who still insist that "God doesn't work that way anymore."

How unfortunate that this arrogant resistance occurs even today in our well-informed society! Those in this group of dissenters are reminders of the stubborn behavior in New Testament days of the wisdom offered to the Sanhedrin by Gamaliel: "So my advice is, leave these men alone. If they are teaching and doing these things on their own, it will be overthrown. But if it is of God, you will not be able to stop them. You may even find yourselves fighting against God. The Council [the Sanhedrin] accepted his advice" (Acts 5:38-40).

Today, those who argue that the miraculous Gifts of the Holy Spirit are no longer operational are usually referred to as "cessationists." By definition, they are that group of present-day Christians who are persuaded that Gifts of the Holy Spirit have not continued since the death of the last Apostle (c. 100 A.D.). Others of this persuasion, who may not be so sure of the 100 A.D. position have created yet another argument, namely that the Gifts of the Spirit ceased when the New Testament was at last formulated (c.300 A.D.).

A dominant voice for the cessationist doctrine appeared on the scene in the early twentieth century, about the time Pentecostal revivals were appearing in the United States. He was Dr. Benjamin B. Warfield of Princeton Theological Seminary. Although he wrote otherwise commendable defenses of conservative orthodoxy, he determinedly denied the possibility of modern miracles. His major treatise on this subject is entitled *Counterfeit Miracles* (1983, 1918). The title itself seems an indictment of—if not an insult to—a Sovereign, all-powerful God.

With the viability of a modern Pentecost now understood, this research project will proceed as follows:

(1) We will examine the role of spiritual Gifts in the spread of the Gospel as the record might reveal in the book of Acts. The Corinthian Letters and other epistles will also be examined.

(2) In addition, we will review the ministry of the Holy Spirit in the Old Testament, and evaluate the meaning of Pentecost in the Old Testament typology relevant to the three most important Hebrew festivals.

(3) We will look at existing records of manifestations of the Gifts of the Holy Spirit in the history of the Christian Church, from apostolic times to the present.

(4) And we will also do a comparative evaluation of the outpouring of the Holy Spirit in the twentieth -century revival of *spiritual gifts* as they relate to the fulfillment of end-of-the-age prophecy.

Thus, the underlying argument of this study is that Peter's reference in Acts 2 to the ministry of the Holy Spirit in the "last days" is a significant clue to the importance of events which have occurred in the twentieth and twenty-first centuries.

Virtually all Bible scholars agree—among them certain cessationists—that the time to which the Apostle Paul refers in 1 Cor.13:10—"When that which is *perfect* is come" (emphasis added)—is a reference to the last-day Revelation of Jesus Christ, rather than as some claim that it refers to final compilation of the books of the Bible. Indeed, what could be more "Perfect" than Jesus Himself? It seems fair, then, to observe that since Jesus, the "Perfect One" has not yet returned, the Baptism of the Holy Spirit, with the accompanying *charismata* or Gifts of the Spirit, certainly must still be available to all those who believe His every Word!

In this context, then, we will review the book of Acts to examine the profusion of miracles that accompanied the ministries of these first century believers, and we will ask ourselves why these miracles were so important then and why—as some suppose—they are not just as important now.

We will examine, too, the phenomenal burst of assurance and authority manifested by those ordinary fishermen after they had been Baptized in the Holy Spirit.

Indeed, we must ask, and seek to answer, whether modern-day evangelism might be encouraged by miracles. Is it possible that Gifts of the Spirit and miracles might intensify the effectiveness of the Gospel in our present-day, sin-ridden world? Are these experiences recorded only for us to admire, only for us to appreciate as an expression of the romantic past? Or are these experiences recorded so we might hope for, seek for, and actually receive a similar empowerment by the Holy Spirit? We hope that by employing these avenues of examination we will discover the Lord's real intentions for our own day!

Chapter 2

THE GIFTS OF THE HOLY SPIRIT
IN THE MINISTRY OF
THE APOSTLE PETER AND ASSOCIATES

Since the book of Acts is universally accepted by the faithful as an integral part of God's inspired Word, in this section we will examine the supernatural and the miraculous recorded in Acts so as to discover the Lord's purpose in recounting the many, many miracles cited there.

Did the Lord inspire Luke's account only to provide modern believers an exciting lesson in history? Or is Luke's account designed to encourage modern believers to expect similar miraculous events in their lives today? Since God has repeatedly characterized Himself as being forever faithful to His promises, it seems self-evident that we have legitimate justification for reviewing this book with the expectation that the Lord intended Acts as an outline for later generations to follow.

Furthermore, can we possibly expect anything less than the Lord's confirmation of His Word when we consider His promise that "greater works than these shall you do"? (John 14:12). The New King James Version states verse 12 as follows: "Most assuredly, I say to you, he who believes in Me, the works that I do he will do also; and greater works than these he will do, because I go to My Father." By close inspection of that verse, we are forced to observe two important points:

(1) That the context indicates this promise is of greater-than-usual importance. The NASB introduces the statement as "Truly, Truly...." Williams begins this passage with, "I most solemnly say to you...." The Living Bible declares, "In solemn truth I tell you...." Thus, the importance of Jesus' statement is underscored for believers both then—and now.

(2) It appears to be a prediction of the magnitude of the miraculous work which would be done by the disciples after Pentecost. And we also are His disciples. Time and time again throughout the book of Acts, we see the Holy Spirit choosing to accomplish His will through persons who were fully yielded to Him.

In the opening twelve chapters of Acts, the focus is primarily on events in the Apostle Peter's ministry. In the second part, chapters 13 through 28, the focus is upon the Holy Spirit in the ministry of the Apostle Paul. And, as we might expect, when the Holy Spirit is active among His people, the evil spirit (that is, the devil) will eventually find those who consciously—or even unconsciously—resist the work of the Spirit. This spiritual conflict is evident all through the narrative of the book of Acts. They were, as we are now, in a spiritual warfare!

Because the outpouring of the Holy Spirit on the Day of Pentecost was so unprecedented, the event aroused a firestorm of disagreement among the residents of Jerusalem. But the disciples had the advantage, having been alerted by Jesus that they were to "tarry in Jerusalem *until* they were endued with power. . . by the Holy Spirit" (Acts 1:4, emphasis added). So they were probably already anticipating that something unusual was about to happen in the Upper Room.

The disciples had been tutored by the Lord about Pentecost, and it seems likely that they had been referred to Joel's prophecy. In support of this hypothesis, we are told in Luke 24:13-33 that on the road to Emmaus, Jesus expounded the Scriptures to them, "Through *all* the prophets. . . explaining and interpreting to them in all the Scriptures the things concerning . . . Himself"(verse 27, AMP,). And as they reviewed this experience afterwards, they remembered that their hearts were greatly moved and burning within them as He explained the Scriptures (see verse 32).

On the bases of these Scriptures indicating that Jesus continued to instruct His disciples, it seems reasonable that His followers may have been informed specifically about what they might expect on the Day of Pentecost. This seems even more plausible when we examine Acts 1:2-4: "He returned to heaven *after* giving his chosen apostles further instructions from the Holy Spirit. . . And on these occasions He talked to them about the Kingdom of God. In one of these meetings He told them not to leave Jerusalem *until the Holy Spirit came upon them* in fulfillment of the Father's promise" (TLB, emphasis added).

Which promise? We immediately wonder exactly which promise is referred to here. Could it have been Joel's prophecy promising the outpouring of the Holy Spirit? The context in which this statement was made certainly does indicate that Joel's prophecy was indeed the "Father's promise." The passage is referred to in Joel 2:28-32. Thus, it is plausible that Peter was not so unaware as we might at first suppose regarding the events about to occur on the Day of Pentecost.

So whatever the specific subject of those discussions, when the power of the Holy Spirit did fall upon the 120 in Jerusalem, it unleashed a firestorm of reaction. Power and praise were followed by persecutions from many of the populace and—especially surprising—from the spiritual leaders, who were supposedly so well-versed in the very Scriptures which predicted the outpouring of the Spirit "upon *all* flesh" (emphasis added). Along with the power, praise, and preaching, immediately observable is the scornful response of some of the local residents, along with their visitors from other countries.

"These men are drunken !" they charged. Imagine! While the 120 were delighting themselves in the "wonderful works of God," others could see nothing but some sort of supposed misbehavior. It is startling that erroneous preconceptions can color one's judgment so severely.

But an even more determined, organized resistance was developing among the religious leaders. After the healing of the lame man at the "Beautiful" gate of the Temple (see Acts 3), the Apostles evidently were subjected to a threatening visit from some of the local dignitaries, who were "very disturbed," as Acts 4:1-3 informs us:

> While they [the Apostles] were talking to the people, the chief priests, the captain of the Temple police, and some of the Sadducees [who incidentally did not believe in any resurrection, much less that of Jesus] came over to them, *very disturbed* that Peter and John were claiming that Jesus had risen from the dead. They arrested them and since it was already evening, jailed them for overnight (TLB, emphasis added).

In contrast with these manifestation of cynicism, however, there were many who did believe—even some of the Jewish priests, the Scriptures tell us. Wonderful! And because of this event the number of believers was immediately increased to 5,000 (see Acts 2:4). Great vindication! Thus, even while many were coming to Christ, others were moved to resistance. Remarkably, the manifestations of the Holy Spirit were polarizing the population, a phenomenon that unfortunately still results when the Gifts of the Spirit are in operation among His people.

We will observe the high drama of these conflicts unfolding in the chapters that follow. For example, in Acts chapter 5, after the tragic incident with Ananias and Sapphira's attempt at deception, the Scriptures indicate that the Apostles were meeting regularly with the people in the Temple area. "Many remarkable miracles" (verse 12) took place among the people, with more and more believers being added to the Lord daily—"crowds both of men and women" (verse 14). Phenomenal! By any standard, an unprecedented revival was occurring!

The Living Bible records it this way:

Sick people were brought out into the streets on beds and mats so that at least Peter's shadow would fall across some of them. . . ! And crowds came in from the . . . suburbs, bringing their sick folk and those possessed by demons; and every one of them was healed (Acts 5:15-16 TLB).

Remarkable! Exciting, too. If such miracles were to happen in our own time, wouldn't they have a similar effect on the "Needy" and the "Lost" of modern society?

So the populace had obviously seen a sufficient number of real-life miracles to be convinced of their authenticity. And regrettably, in the face of these miraculous moments, for the most part the spiritual leaders of Peter's culture staggered on in their disbelief. How sad that they could be so close to the Truth, and then reject it! Thus, it is evident that the Holy Spirit's empowerment enabled Jesus' disciples to do miracles, and those miracles enhanced the credibility of the Gospel. The result? Many believed because the Word of God was "confirmed with signs following."

Shouldn't today's Christians consider the possibility that miracles would still serve the same purpose in bringing the unsaved to Christ? The answer to this question seems obvious. And this persuasion via the supernatural is happening often in Central and South America and in Africa, and the unsaved are coming to the Lord by the thousands! This astounding response has been statistically verified. One of my missionary friends, Rev. Paul Finkenbinder (aka *Hermano Pablo* in Latin America) and his wife Linda, attest to these phenomena occurring again and again. We live in exciting and momentous times, in spite of the naysayers who look critically at what they claim is an "impossibility" in modern times.

But in spite of God's miraculous visitations in Jerusalem, all was not at peace, even in the domain of the Holy Spirit. The despicably ulterior motives of the religious leaders are recorded for us in Acts 5:17,18, so that posterity might forever be warned. Exactly who were these unbelievers, trying so blindly to thwart the work of the Spirit? None other than the High Priest, his relatives and their friends among the Sadducees, all reacted with violent jealousy and arrested the Apostles, and put them in the public jail" (TLB). Unbelief is often notoriously unreasonable!

All of the modern translations consulted emphasize in these verses the intensity of the spiritual leaders' carnal emotions, here displayed for all to see centuries after their foolishness. It is evident, therefore, that the presence and power of the Holy Spirit does not insure that everyone will react favorably. People are still given the privilege of *free choice*, even when their choices are wrong. Those with hardened consciences, or preconceived theological speculations, may fail to observe the parameters of God's intended purposes. And we are all susceptible.

Yes, "Jealousy," ugly and perverse, caused the leaders to miss the grace of God; while at the same time "crowds" of desperately needy people continued to receive visitations of deliverance and healing from God's Holy Spirit. Unbelief is especially a tragedy when it is manifested among religious leaders.

But, as the Scripture declares, "Where sin does abound, grace will much more abound!" (Romans 5:20). And so it happened that an angel of the Lord came at night and released the Apostles from jail so they could continue to preach the Good News to the people who longed for divine intervention in their lives (see Acts 5:19-21). And the Apostles did exactly that!

It would be totally inaccurate to assume, however, that only the Apostles administered the Gifts of the Spirit in this primitive church. As we study the book of Acts, it becomes apparent that others than the Apostles also ministered under the anointing of the Holy Spirit, and God provided evidence of His approval with accompanying "remarkable miracles." For example, in Acts chapter 6, when it became necessary for someone to oversee the Church's ministry to the widows of the congregation, seven deacons were chosen, men "full of faith and the Holy Ghost," among them Stephen and Philip.

Notice that Stephen, "full of faith and the Holy Spirit's power, did spectacular miracles among the people" (verse 8). But as for those religious unbelievers, rather than being grateful that the needy were being helped, certain members of "The Freedmen" cult began bickering with Stephen. And soon these were joined by others, as well, so that a real "row" developed. But "none were able to stand against Stephen's wisdom and spirit"(verse 10). Fully frustrated at their own inabilities, the authorities arrested Stephen for trial. *Arrested* him? Really? This man who was helping so many people—arrested? Falsely exercising one's authority is always a tempting option for those who are losing the argument anyway.

So, as was true in Jesus' trial, lying witnesses carried the day, and Stephen was taken out and stoned until he was dead (verses 59-60). *"At last,"* they congratulated themselves, *"we have scored a major triumph over these uneducated, upstart preachers!Surely they will think twice before they ever again accuse us of causing the death of Jesus!"* The Guilty have short memories.

But little did they realize that God had already chosen a replacement, ironically someone from among their own ranks, a Pharisee like themselves. A dynamic, well-educated young Pharisee who had smugly held their coats while they stoned Stephen to death.

It is an irony of fate that from that mound of bloody stones and the mangled body of a faithful martyr would arise the great Apostle Paul, who would become an unflinching champion of the cause of Jesus Christ. Centuries earlier, God Himself had asked, "Why do the people imagine an empty scheme?. . . The rulers take counsel together against the Lord and His Messiah? He Who sits in the heavens shall laugh; the Lord has them in derision, and in supreme contempt He mocks them" (Psalm 2:1-4AMP).

But an Accuser was soon to become an Apostle. Paul, at that time, had no understanding of what God had planned for him! In the meantime, however, the evil one gave Paul a rationalized substitute: the attempted extermination of the Christian Church. Chapter 8 of Acts opens with the startling announcement that "on the very day Stephen was martyred ... a great wave of persecution" (verse 1) broke out against the Church in Jerusalem, scattering everyone except the Apostles to the outer provinces of Judea and Samaria.

Two facts are evident in the narrative of this chapter:

(1) Saul the Pharisee was a willing participant, perhaps even the actual instigator, of this wave of intense persecution.

(2) Although the persecution caused most of the believers to flee, those believers apparently did not adopt a victimized

attitude. Instead, they triumphantly carried the salvation message with them, sharing it with anyone who would listen—and even some who would not.

Acts 8:4 records their positive behavior: "But the believers who had fled Jerusalem went everywhere preaching the Good News about Jesus!" (TLB). So the "fire" within them, started by the Holy Spirit's baptism, was fanned to white heat, inspiring them to win others to their Savior. One thing is certain, the authorities in Jerusalem were losing the battle, and God was winning!

Remember that second deacon, Philip, mentioned earlier? Evidently he was one of those who fled Jerusalem, and having arrived in Samaria—some 35 miles north of Jerusalem—he began preaching the Good News about Jesus the Savior. Immediately, he had extraordinary success. The Scriptures indicate remarkable miracles, many conversions, and numerous people who were baptized in water. God, through the Holy Spirit, had won again, in spite of the opposition of the authorities.

A modern English translation puts it this way:

Philip [the deacon] . . . went down to the city of Samaria and proclaimed the . . . Messiah to the people. And great crowds of people . . . heeded what was said by Philip, as they heard him and watched the miracles and wonders which he kept performing. . . .For foul spirits came out of many who were possessed by them, screaming and shouting with a loud voice, and many who were suffering from palsy or were crippled were restored to health. And there was great rejoicing in that city (Acts 8:5-8, AMP)

This chapter also provides us insights into the character and personality of Saul (Paul). For one thing, he was a very dedicated Pharisee. Prior to his becoming a devout Christian, he had terrorized the believers of the area, continuously laying waste to the church with all kinds of cruel tortures and violence. The Scripture indicates that he even went so far as to enter house after house of the Christians in Jerusalem, arresting those he captured and committing them to prison (see Acts 8:3).

Meanwhile, Saul's supposed success in Jerusalem must have excited his vanity because we read in Acts 9:1 that he was "*breathing hard*" with "murderous desire" (AMP) against the disciples of the Lord. Let us face facts here, Saul was a "terrorist." It was in this state of mind that he acquired letters of authority from the high priest in Jerusalem to arrest any Christians, men or women, whom he might find in Damascus and to bring them back bound to Jerusalem. He seems not to have known about—or had conveniently forgotten—the advice given to the Sanhedrin by Gamaliel, "Men of Israel, beware if this is of God, you may find yourselves fighting against God Himself"(Acts 5:35-39). Wise advice! But Saul, the Pharisee, had his own agenda, so he set out toward Damascus to accomplish the murderous task he had planned.

Since, in those days, it was several days' journey from Jerusalem to Damascus, Saul had plenty of time to reconsider what he was about to do. Did his conscience ever bother him during that lengthy journey? Did he ever, during his journey to Damascus, reconsider the horrendous murders he had planned? Because the Jews and the Samaritans had so little respect for one another, it is not likely that Saul and his "posse" would have traveled the route through Samaria. So Saul and his party must have taken the traditional road to Damascus by first traveling eastward down to the ancient city of Jericho, through the very wilderness where Jesus' baptism in the Holy Spirit was tested for forty days. Then they traveled generally northward along through the Jordan Valley.

But evidently Saul's rage and determination continued on—unabated. From Jericho Saul's party would have passed by the site where John the Baptist had baptized Jesus in the Jordan. Then traveling further northward parallel with the Jordan, Paul would have viewed Mt. Gilboa and Mt. Tabor on his left, famous sites in the history of Israel, perhaps causing Saul to remember his namesake king, Saul, of long ago, who had disobeyed God and suffered severe punishment for his arrogance.

Further on, he would have arrived in the ancient city of Beth Shan, "modernized" as it had been by the Romans, but still pregnant with historical memories of the gruesome display of the bodies of King Saul and his family on the walls of that Philistine city. Still further north, they would have viewed the city of Tiberius on the western shore of the Sea of Galilee. Then rounding Galilee's north shore, perhaps even through the streets of Capernaum, they would have turned northeast toward Damascus.

Ahead of them lay snowy Mt. Hermon and the headwaters of the great Jordan River, near the city of Caesarea Philippi, located at the foot of the Golan Heights. As they ascended eastward to the "Heights," Saul would have been able to view the Sea of Galilee behind him and eventually the city of Damascus clearly visible some twenty-five miles to the northeast. (This information is based on a 1996 lecture tour of the Jordan Valley, conducted by Dr. George O. Wood and his Israeli associate, Mr. David Asael.)

But still persistent through all of this journey of memories, Saul's demonic obsession continued unabated. In spite of his persistence, within view of Damascus God prostrated Saul to the ground—and his arrogant plan ended. God Himself had other plans for Saul! Saul, the Determined Executioner, was about to be transformed into the Dedicated Evangelist. Saul the Arrogant was destined to become Paul, the Apostle. Yes, the story of his conversion is classic by now, but it remains wonderfully dramatic just the same. For while Saul was on his way, nearing Damascus, a bright light from heaven flashed around about him; and, overwhelmed, he fell to the ground. Suddenly, he heard an authoritative voice challenging him, "Saul, Saul, why are you persecuting Me?" And Saul answered, "Who are you, Lord?" The response: "I am Jesus, Whom you are persecuting."

What an alarming disclosure it must have been for Saul to discover that he was offending the very God he supposed he was defending! And so, blinded, rebuffed, and reborn, he was led into Damascus where a "disciple" named Ananias had been instructed in a vision to find Saul and "lay hands on him" so that he might have his sight restored and "be filled with the Holy Spirit" (Acts 9:8-17). Significantly, later in his career, Paul confirmed to the Corinthians that he often spoke in tongues (see 1 Cor. 14:18). Saul's astounding conversion on the road to Damascus, and his subsequent Baptism in the Holy Spirit, opened the door to a new life of evangelism. And

Paul's message was confirmed by God, again and again, by miracles of the Holy Spirit.

With the preceding information in mind, it seems clear that the Apostle Paul's "tongues" experience began in Damascus on a street called "Straight." Paul seems to allude to this experience as he was defending his Apostleship to the Corinthians (2 Cor. 4: 6-7) where he writes:

> For God who said [at creation], 'Let light shine out of darkness,' is the One who shone in my heart, to give me the light of the knowledge of God's glory, reflected on the face of Christ. But I am keeping this jewel [treasure] in an earthen jar, to prove that its surpassing power is God's, not mine (Williams).

And Paul's subsequent activities indicated further that he had been marvelously transformed by his confrontation with Jesus Christ and by his Baptism in the Holy Spirit. For example, we observe that almost immediately after his conversion and Baptism in the Spirit, he began to fellowship with the Christian believers of Damascus and to preach emphatically that Jesus is the Messiah. Paul's dramatic conversion is made so obvious because his previous terrorizing reputation had made Ananias very uncertain about the Lord's assignment to go "lay hands" on Saul. And when Saul (Paul) returned to Jerusalem, the believers there thought his "alleged" conversion was all a deception.

But as for the believers of Damascus, there is no indication that they had any reluctance to accept Paul as a brother. Even the local Jewish leaders, recognizing his conversion as authentic, were quick to attempt silencing him by assassination.

There must have been something uniquely convincing about the authenticity of his conversion and his being filled with the Holy Spirit. After all, his conversion was very dramatic, witnessed by members of his entourage. Surprising? Especially so because when Paul arrived in Jerusalem later, we read that the Christians there "were all afraid of him, for they did not believe he really was a disciple"(Acts 9:26, AMP). What a thrilling conversion, even when reading about it so many centuries later.

A second indication of the genuineness of Paul's conversion is recorded in Acts 9:21-25; for Paul, while still in Damascus, evidently wasted no time declaring the scriptural evidences that Jesus Christ was without question the Messiah so long expected by the Jews (see verse 22). And as the Scriptures indicate, his public preaching went on for a "considerable time"(verse 23). In fact, his arguments were so convincing that the Jewish leaders in Damascus became increasingly angry and plotted ways to silence Paul's testimony.

So those obstinate religionists finally decided that the most effective method of disposing of Paul would be to lie in wait for him at the city gates day and night—and when he was captured, "kill him!" They wrongly supposed such action would please *their* God; for Paul's message of the Risen Christ wrecked havoc with their "well-ordered," long-established, systematized belief system. Unfortunately, those deceived by the devil can also be very "dedicated."

Very often the Lord surprises us by introducing us to some new approach which *had never occurred* to our finite minds. As Isaiah 55:9 declares: "For my thoughts are not your thoughts, neither are your ways my ways , saith the Lord." But Paul, not without his own informants, learned of this sinister plan, and counter measures were soon made. When his fellow Christians learned of this, they arranged to lower Paul down in a basket outside the city wall so that he could return to Jerusalem—or perhaps to the Arabian desert.

When he arrived in Jerusalem, however, he experienced yet another disappointment: the Christians of Jerusalem, still unnerved by Paul's notorious past, were not so sure that he wasn't pretending, so that he could find them out. But another believer with a more compassionate heart intervened. Barnabas (the "son of consolation") took Paul "under his wing," just to prove—at his own risk—that Paul was indeed a brother in Christ. Thank the Lord for those with enough spiritual courage, both then and now, who are willing to be instruments of "consolation"! In the next chapter we will read more of Paul's dynamic ministry.

Meanwhile, in Acts chapters 9-12, the Apostle Peter— under the power of the Holy Spirit—was experiencing magnificent miracles as he ministered to others. Momentary freedom from persecution and peace in the congregations of Judea, Galilee, and Samaria allowed Peter to visit many of the new congregations. In the words of Scripture, "The church . . . had peace and was edified. . . walking in . . . reverential fear of the Lord and in the consolation . . . of the Holy Spirit, and [the Church] continued to increase and was multiplied"(9:31-32, AMP).

During Peter's itinerary among the congregations, three notable miracles are recorded for our edification and consideration. During his visit in the town of Lydda a bedfast man was raised from his afflictions; and as a result "all the inhabitants of Lydda and the plain of Sharon saw what had happened to him and they turned to the Lord [Jesus]." So did miracles make a difference in winning people to Christ? Of course they did! And they are equally important now. The Bible indicates here and elsewhere that miracles from the Holy Spirit are important because they are a manifestation of God's great mercy and compassion for the human race. And, additionally, because miracles do awaken people to the presence of a concerned and loving God. So, think about the arguments of the cessationists for a moment. Would the beneficent Lord "cripple" His own eternal purposes by causing miracles to cease, as some theologians are claiming?

If miracles sometimes happen less frequently, it certainly is *not* because God has changed. Indeed, the decline of the miraculous may be caused by a personality much closer to home— the archenemy of God—and those who "swallow" the lies of that enemy. Any failures to experience all of God's provisions in our lives today are likely because the condition of our faith has seriously declined, or because we have "digested" too much of the teachings of the "dispensationalists/cessationists" who are more inclined to accept the speculations of naturalistic sciences than the clear promises of the God of heaven

A second notable miracle occurred at Joppa where Dorcas lived. She was a kind, benevolent lady, who "abounded in good deeds and acts of charity." But she suddenly fell sick, and then died—much to the alarm of her friends and loved ones. And since Joppa was only ten miles northwest of Lydda where Peter was at the time, the believers sent two men to Lydda to ask Peter to come quickly to their aid. When Peter arrived in Joppa, he found many of Dorcas' friends mourning her death—and her expected burial. The occasion demanded serious and immediate action. So Peter put everyone out of the room so that he could pray for the dear lady's resurrection.

Having sought the Lord, Peter then commanded her to arise, and immediately she opened her eyes to see Peter and her friends once more (see Acts 9:40-41). But that is not the end of the story! Magnificent results transpired, as recorded in verse 42: "And this [miracle] became known throughout all Joppa, *and many came to believe on the Lord. . . as their Savior*" (AMP).

Some may wonder why miracles of this magnitude happen so infrequently in modern Christian circles. First of all, if we are honest in our thinking, we cannot possibly ignore the reports of fully-documented miracles occurring in our own time, miracles similar to the incident with Dorcas. But, we must also admit that miracles do occur less frequently in so-called "civilized, Christian" countries, probably because moderns have such a predilection for disbelief, or feel more secure with events that have some more rational explanation.

Secondly, however, miracles are in fact occurring in Third World countries much more frequently nowadays. It is a verifiable fact that there are life-changing revivals occurring in the Third World. Multitudes are coming to Christ, as proven by the official statistics from these countries. Could this phenomenon be because they are also experiencing many of the same miracles as those recorded in the book of Acts?

Researched statistics indicate miracles are playing a significant role in the world's Revival.

The real cause could well be that in "civilized" countries the prevailing attitude is to overanalyze every unexpected incident that God does. Unfortunately, in our present-day, scientific answers have become a fetish, the "only possible phenomenological explanation," when in fact there may be other more supernatural explanations. On the one hand, we either find ourselves doubting from the start whether miracles could possibly happen in our time. Or on the other hand, we try to reduce every miraculous experience to some preconceived notion that fits our present frame of mind. Perhaps we ought to try a different approach, that is to recognize there are some phenomena that cannot be explained in purely rational terms.

So without discarding every vestige of rationality, perhaps we should try accepting the Bible in simple faith as the wisdom of the ages. Indeed, when we have to evaluate the unusual, sometimes we become our own worst enemy. After all, we should remember, even Jesus' miraculous power was greatly limited by the unbelief in Nazareth. The reason? Because its citizens had rationalized that Jesus was really only a local carpenter boy, not a worker of miracles, and certainly not the Messiah.

They reasoned, *"After all, we've known this guy ever since he was just a baby, when the family moved into the community thirty years ago. He grew up like the rest of our children. He can't be the Messiah! We have known this guy for years and years. He must be a little crazy to be parading around as he has been lately."*

Thus, when he returned years later to preach God's Word, they considered Him an imposter. So they escorted Him to the cliffs outside of town to throw Him down to the rocks below. But what they *thought* they knew was *not* accurate at all! God had long-standing plans for this lowly Carpenter's Son.

A third occasion involving Peter happened in Caesarea (see Acts 10), located about thirty-five miles north of Joppa where Peter was residing at the time. About noontime, Peter was praying on the rooftop veranda where God gave him a vision which resulted in his visiting Gentile believers. *"Gentiles? Really, Lord, are you sure? I have never. . . ."*

So later, after the Lord had altered Peter's thinking, he took the Pentecostal message to that devout Gentile group in Caesarea. According to Luke's narrative, Peter had barely started his sermon, when suddenly the Holy Spirit fell upon all the worshipers. And they began to speak in tongues, just as the Jewish congregation had done in Acts chapter 2. Everyone in Peter's party was greatly amazed, for apparently the Lord had opened the door to include Gentiles in His plan of salvation, *including* the Baptism in the Holy Spirit.

Time and time again, while reading the book of Acts, we are moved to admire those believers who so obediently laid aside their life-long prejudices because the Spirit of the Lord had instructed them to do so. And speaking of prejudices, in Acts chapter 11, the Jerusalem brethren required Peter to give a detailed account of his rather "annoying association with those Caesarean Gentiles." But after hearing Peter's report, the Jerusalem brethren agreed that this obviously was the

Lord's doing, and they all rejoiced that God was including "even Gentiles" in His magnanimous plan.

But what was it that convinced them so quickly that this was all ordained of the Lord? Obviously it was that the six Jewish brethren accompanying Peter had heard the Gentiles praising and glorifying God *in tongues* (Acts 11:15-17, just as they themselves had done earlier. These early Christians recognized quickly that the Holy Spirit had planned far in advance of their narrow-minded prejudices.

They are to be commended for their extraordinary open-mindedness. It becomes evident that those first-century believers had a wholesome awe, a holy reverence, for the reliability of the Holy Spirit's direction! From this point on in Acts, then, the narrative further displays the work of the Holy Spirit—primarily in the ministry of Paul. These dramatic events will be considered in the chapter which follows.

Chapter 3

THE GIFTS OF THE HOLY SPIRIT IN THE MINISTRY OF THE APOSTLE PAUL AND HIS ASSOCIATES

We have been reviewing Peter's ministry. In the course of observing the Holy Spirit in Peter's ministry, we have reviewed Paul's dramatic conversion as narrated in Acts chapter 9. From this point in Acts we will read of Paul's ministry, made always more exciting by the accompanying Gifts of the Spirit. After his conversion, the great evangelistic Apostle was immediately active in declaring the Gospel in Damascus (see Acts chapter 9). However, the persistent opposition by the Jewish leaders would eventually cause the Apostle to turn his soul-winning efforts to the Gentiles. This new direction, ordained by the Holy Spirit, begins in chapter 13.

THE SPIRIT'S MINISTRY IN PAUL'S FIRST MISSIONARY TOUR

From among the prophets and teachers in the church at Antioch of Syria, five members are identified by name (see Acts 13:1), among them are Barnabas and Saul (subsequently referred to as Paul). Although we will learn a great deal more about Barnabas and Paul in the Acts narrative which follows, we actually know very little about the other three, except that these men were notably active as prophets and teachers in the church at Antioch.

Just the same, we sense a kinship with them because of their devotion to the cause of Christ. The indication of this passage is that they were a part of the team who tarried, fasting and worshiping, with Barnabas and Paul when the Holy Spirit revealed that Paul and Barnabas should be "set apart" (ordained) to be sent out as missionaries. By means of the gift of prophecy, the Holy Spirit said, "Separate now for Me Barnabas and Saul for the work to which I have called them" (Acts 13:2). And after fasting and praying, the group laid hands on these two and sent them away to minister (see verse 3).

Almost immediately Paul and Barnabas departed from the seaport city of Seleucia on their way to the island of Cyprus located approximately 150 miles west of the mainland. Arriving in the island's seaport city of Salamis on the eastern shore, they began preaching the message that Jesus Christ is indeed the long-awaited Messiah. As they traveled westward from city to city, they arrived at last in the city of Paphos on the western coast of the island. There, as a result of their anointed preaching, the ruling proconsul of the area named Sergius Paulus, a "sensible man of sound understanding" (verse 7, AMP), requested a private audience with the two evangelists.

But when they arrived, they discovered there was immediate opposition from Elymas, a self-proclaimed "wise man" (the actual meaning of the title which he apparently bestowed upon himself). Ironically, his real name was Bar-Jesus, which translated, means "son of the Savior." And instead of behaving wisely in accordance with his title, Elymas's terribly flawed "wisdom" motivated him to resist Jesus the Savior, whose very name he bore—probably without his being aware of the name association.

Paul, writing later to the Corinthians, warned that mere human wisdom can actually lead to very erroneous conclusions. Addressing this very subject, Paul quoted from Isaiah 29:14:

> I will . . . render useless . . . the learning of the learned and the philosophy of the philosophers and the cleverness of the clever and the discernment of the discerning. I will frustrate . . . [them] and bring them to nothing. Where is the wise man—the philosopher? Where is the scribe—the scholar? Where is the investigator—the logician, the debater—of this present time and age? Has not God shown up the nonsense and the folly of this world's wisdom? (1 Cor.1:19-20, AMP)

By way of contrast, the Psalmist reminds us, too, in Psalm 111:10, "The reverent fear and worship of the Lord is the beginning of Wisdom and skill. . . a good understanding . . . have all those who do the will of the Lord"(AMP).

But Paul had the anointing of the Holy Spirit and the spiritual weapons of warfare ordaining him to be the master of the moment. Thus, according to Acts 13:9 Paul turned and looked intently at Bar-Jesus, declaring that the intruding sorcerer would immediately become blind for a time, because of his resistance to Sergius Paulus' inquiries. In fact from that very moment, Bar-Jesus "groped about seeking someone to lead him by the hand" (verse 11), unquestionably symbolic of his spiritual blindness.

So what was the result of this manifestation of one (perhaps even more than one) of the miraculous Gifts of the Spirit? The proconsul was so impressed by the power of the Lord that he himself believed, and because of the Gifts of the Spirit in operation, Sergius Paulus became a Christian (see verse 12). So did miracles matter in this situation? We are inspired to believe that miracles, along with the preaching of the Word, would serve the same purpose today.

But if we expect those results, we must begin by believing that the Lord not only *can do* the same today, but that He *will do* the same today! The overwhelming evidence of Scripture is that the Gifts of the Spirit are still available to Christian workers even in our own time! To believe otherwise casts doubt upon the integrity—yes, even on the credibility—of a merciful and Sovereign God. Hebrews 13:8-9 states with emphasis, "Jesus Christ . . . is always the same, yesterday, today, [yes] and forever [through all the ages]. Do not be carried about by different and . . . alien teachings; for it is good for the heart to be established and ennobled . . . by means of grace of God" (AMP)

Rejoicing over these recent victories, Paul and Barnabas departed from the seaport of Paphos (modern *Pafos*) in western Cyprus, sailing 150 miles northwestward toward the mainland, docking at the village of Perga in the province of Pamphyllia (now southern Turkey). But disappointment was brewing. It was at Perga that John Mark, the nephew of Barnabas, decided to go back home to Jerusalem to visit his mother (see Acts 13:13).

A lonesome boy wanting to go see his mother did not sit well with Paul, who had only the business of the Lord in mind. The event later caused a sharp disagreement between the two evangelists. However, having sent Mark on his way, the two evangelists departed Perga, journeying northward approximately 100 miles to Pisidian Antioch (near the present village of *Yalovach* in central Turkey). The province of Pisidia was located immediately east of the famous Bible cities of the book of Revelation.

Antioch of Pisidia was an important city on the trade route between Ephesus (then a seaport city) and the Far East. Thus, it becomes evident why Paul did not tarry long in Perga, and instead traveled on north to Antioch. The former was little more than a village; the latter was a bustling trading center, entertaining people from many countries. Paul and Barnabas were dedicated evangelists! (*Unger's Bible Dictionary*)

The arrival of Paul and Barnabas in Antioch was initially very successful, for when they visited the synagogue on the Sabbath, Paul was given opportunity to exhort the orthodox Jews and their Gentile converts. Paul's exhortation (see chapter 13) outlined God's dealings with the Jewish nation through the centuries, culminating at last in the arrival of Jesus Christ of Nazareth, their expected Messiah. Paul reminded them, too, that the Jews of Jerusalem had recently crucified Jesus, who was later resurrected and seen by many.

This news, of course, introduced elements of the miraculous, and all who heard this message were greatly moved. As a result the Gentiles "earnestly begged"(see verse 42, AMP) Paul and Barnabas to tell them more about this matter on the following Sabbath. The evangelists agreed. So at the appointed time "almost the entire city gathered" (verse

44). What an exciting response! Genuine revival seemed imminent. Or was it really?

But the devil was not going to give up without a fight! Not without some designed countermove. And who better to employ in this skullduggery than the hardheaded religious leaders who, "filled with envy and jealousy, . . . contradicted and abusively slandered" Paul and Barnabas (13:45 AMP)? The evangelists responded by declaring that while it was necessary that this Good News be offered first to the Jews, their rejection of God's offer rendered them "unworthy of eternal life"(verse 46, AMP). A startling word of prophecy! Indeed, a frightening pronouncement, to be declared "unworthy of eternal life."

As a result, Paul and Barnabas, from that moment on, vowed to turn to the Gentiles. Deeming their decision appropriate, "the Apostles shook off the dust from their feet" (verse 51, AMP), and went further down the road to Iconium. And in Iconium, once again the apostles "spoke with such power that a great number both of Jews and of Greeks . . . became Christians" (Acts 14:1, AMP). Indeed, the Savior will win Himself a people in spite of devilish opposition! But if Paul's previous warning had any effect on the orthodox Jews, one would never know it by their subsequent behavior, because they continued the same disruptive actions against the Gospel in Iconium, embittering the minds of the public against the brethren (see 14:2).

But this time Paul and Barnabas refused to be daunted, for they stayed in Iconium "a long time, speaking . . . fearlessly and boldly in the Lord," and the Lord "continued to bear testimony to the Word of His grace" by "granting signs and wonders to be performed" (14:3, AMP) by the hands of the Apostles. Once again, God's miracles confirmed the preached Word to the public! But the insults and abuses of the Jewish leaders against Paul and Barnabas only increased dramatically in Iconium, even to the point of a threat of stoning. As a consequence, the evangelists decided to move on southeast, down the road to Lystra and to Derbe, cities in the province of Lycaonia.

One day as Paul was preaching in Lystra, he compassionately observed a man in the crowd listening very intently to his message of hope. The man was a cripple, lame from birth, as it turned out. But Paul, looking directly at him, discerned that the man had faith to be healed, so Paul shouted to the man, "Stand erect on your feet!" Nothing secretive about this command! Immediately the man leaped to his feet and began walking (see Acts 14:8-10).

Indeed, if any of us observed a man known by everyone as lame suddenly jumping and running, we, too, would be excited. The results that day were really amazing! The local residents were moved nearly to a riot because they were convinced that Paul and Barnabas were "gods" who had come down among them. It is significant that the locals immediately recognized that something supernatural was occurring. After all, a well-known lame man was now walking and leaping in their midst. But, regrettably, the crowd's response was turning the Lord's good intentions into idolatry.

To the consternation of the Apostles, with great excitement the crowd prepared to make sacrifices to Paul and Barnabas, a shocking turn of events for the two evangelists. The devil's tactic this time was not abuse and slander as before, but rather to offer unwanted acclaim, a subtle move not unlike the fiendish alternative the devil offered to Jesus in His wilderness temptation. And, it was only with great difficulty that Paul and Barnabas were able to restrain the local citizens from doing this foolish thing (see 14:11-18).

It is evident, then, that even though these pagans arrived at wrong conclusions about what God was really doing, they accurately recognized that God's power had visited them that day. And all because a man lame from birth had been completely healed. Think of it! They had observed a miracle with their own eyes. Thus, a lame man, whom they all knew, was healed by the Gifts of the Spirit. And eventually, the miracle caused these unconverted people to turn to the Lord. Again, we observe that miracles did make the difference. Without a doubt, miracles would have a similar effect even today. Why? Because they confirm the preached Word, as promised in Mark 16:17-18.

But the spiritual contest was not yet ended (Is it ever?) Those antagonistic Jewish leaders from Antioch and Iconium arrived in Lystra—as they had before—and inflamed the people against the two evangelists. Feelings ran high. Shouts and insults followed. A mob attitude soon took over! Because Paul was the chief spokesman for the team, he was judged guilty of sacrilege and severely stoned. In fact, he was so badly mauled, they thought he was dead. While still in this heat of anger, the crowd dragged Paul unceremoniously out of the city, and left his broken body for the birds to devour.

But then an amazing thing happened. The stunned disciples "formed a circle around Paul's supposedly lifeless body (See 14: 20, AMP). Undoubtedly some wept, while others prayed. After all, what goes on when believers form a circle around a crisis? Somebody prayed through. Suddenly, Paul got to his feet and determinedly strode back into the town, a "gutsy" move, indeed! Could a man, just stoned nearly to death, suddenly rise and boldly return to the scene of his brush with death? He could if he had the same anointing as Paul. Miracles continued as a confirmation of the Truth of God's Word.

There must have been shouts of victory and praises to God! We may never know exactly what occurred when that circle of believers implored the Lord for mercy, but it is the "stuff "of miracles for a man supposedly dead suddenly to stand to his feet and boldly re-enter the belligerent city that had intended to kill him. What commendable courage and boldness, a notable characteristic of those Baptized in the Spirit! It was this kind of courage that eventually brought the Gospel to us.

But there is yet another indication that this involved the miraculous, also found in verse 20: "The next day he left with Barnabas for Derbe." What? No time-out for recovery from his stoning the day before? After such a life-threatening experience, it seems incredible that Paul would feel well enough to travel the very next day! Besides that, Derbe was quite a distance down the road, approximately thirty miles beyond Lystra, certainly more than one day's journey in Bible days. So, the circumstances of this event indicate that the Lord intervened in some miraculous way to bring all this about. Even though men may try to control the Lord's plans, God still insists on being Sovereign!

When Paul and Barnabas finally arrived in Derbe, they continued preaching the Good News and thereby they won "many disciples"(TLB) in Derbe also. It was, however, time for them to return to home base in Antioch of Syria, so they retraced their steps to Lystra, then to Iconium, and then to Antioch in Pisidia, "strengthening the . . . hearts of the disciples . . . and appointing elders . . . in each church, with prayer and fasting and "encouraging [everyone] to stand firm in the faith" (14:21-23, AMP). From Antioch they then traveled the 100 miles south to the coast, stopping in Perga to preach, and then on to the seaport of Attalia (*Antalya* in present-day Turkey) to board a ship sailing back to their home church in Antioch of Syria.

"Arriving there, they gathered the church together and declared all that God had accomplished with them, and how He had opened to the Gentiles a door of faith"(Acts 14:27, AMP). Thus, Paul's first missionary journey came to a close, and this section of Acts ends by informing us that the evangelists stayed with the disciples in Antioch for quite some time (see 14:28), "teaching and proclaiming the Word of the Lord"(Acts 15:35, AMP).

And what had happened to the Christian population during this time? About the time Paul concluded his first missionary journey, the messages of Salvation and the Baptism of the Holy Spirit had spread beyond estimates. Because of the those earliest persecutions in the city of Jerusalem, the message had gone to Samaria, then to Cyprus, then to the cities of Asia. And soon Paul and his colleagues would be taking the Gospel to Europe.

It is interesting to observe that the *number of believers* won to Christ by the Pentecostal outpouring was initially recorded several times. As long as the count occurred in Jerusalem, the 120 soon grew to 3,000, and that to 5,000. But once the Pentecostal explosion had spread beyond the capital to surrounding provinces, estimates could no longer be accurately recorded. Undoubtedly, the number of Christians had grown beyond estimates. We only know that the evangelizing disciples were accused of "turning the world upside down" (Acts 17:6). How can anyone evaluate the effects of a spiritual *explosion*, as the Gospel is spread miraculously under the influence of people Baptized in the Holy Spirit?

It is estimated that Paul's first missionary journey concluded approximately twenty-five years after Pentecost (c.55 A.D.), and the number of Christians was inestimable. In much the same way, the modern-day explosion of numbers of Spirit-filled believers has had a world-wide impact. Even in these days of fairly accurate statistical counting, the precise number of Pentecostal believers in the world's societies escapes imagination. We will review some official statistics in a later chapter of this book.

The Spirit's Ministry in Paul's Second Missionary Tour

After a time of ministry in Antioch of Syria, Paul suggested to Barnabas that they return again to minister to the churches they had established in various cities north of Syrian Antioch. Barnabas agreed, but insisted once again that they take John Mark (his close relative) with them. But Paul objected. After all, Mark had abandoned them on their first missionary tour! The disagreement (see "a sharp disagreement," Acts 15:39, AMP) became so serious that the two parted company, Paul teaming up with Silas (Acts 15:40), and Barnabas chose Mark (15: 39) to accompany Barnabas back to Cyprus.

Meanwhile, Paul and Silas traveled northward overland through Syria and the province of Cilicia where his hometown Tarsus was located (15: 41). From there, these evangelists traveled overland through the mountain pass northwest to Derbe, where they had ministered before, then to Lystra, then Iconium, and finally once again to Antioch in Pisidia (Acts 16:1). Paul saw the importance of doing "follow-up" work, checking on the spiritual condition of every church he had helped to establish (15:41). Excellent! Paul understood the sound principles of pastoring! "So the churches were strengthened . . . in the faith, and the believers increased in number day after day" (16:5 AMP).

Paul and Silas must have sought the Lord about where to minister next, for they passed by Phrygia, the province on their left. And Bithynia, on their right, was also bypassed for the moment. The Scriptures tell us the Holy Spirit had *forbidden* them to minister in these Asian provinces. That would happen later. And when they sought to enter the province of Mysia, the Holy Spirit once again did not permit them. The reason soon becomes evident. Because the Holy Spirit had other plans, such as opening Europe to the Gospel.

Thus, their only other option was to travel on northwest to the seacoast city of Troas, where Paul had a vision of a Macedonian pleading for him to "Come over and help us!"(Acts 16:9). At this point, the narrative shifts to the pronoun "we" in 16:10, so apparently Luke had joined Paul's group. And because of the urgency implied in Paul's vision, they immediately set sail for the island of Samothrace in Macedonia (approximately 100 miles northwest).

On the day following they set out on land for Neapolis (16:11), then they traveled down the coast to the city of Philippi (verse 12). There the evangelists met a noble and godly businesswoman, a seller of purple cloth. But once more Paul found his God-appointed efforts challenged by the devil.

One day, while they were on their way to their private place of prayer, they found they were being mockingly hounded" by a slave girl, possessed by an unclean spirit. For "many days" she kept shouting derisively, "These men are the servants of the Most High God! They announce to you the way of salvation!" (16:16-18).

Of course, her words were accurate enough, but her attitude was contemptuous and a distraction to God's work. So, Paul "sorely annoyed" (verse 18, AMP), and feeling no obligation to remain tolerant, Paul turned and said to the evil spirit, " I charge you in the name of Jesus Christ to come out of her!" Whereupon, the Scripture declares, "And it came out of her at that very moment" (verse 18).

But not everyone is so interested in delivering those in bondage, at least not when their monetary profits are so badly affected. For some, their wallet is their god, and that principle was evidently relevant in this incident. The young slave girl—now delivered—no longer proved profitable to her owners, and they blamed those intrusive "Pentecostal" evangelists for their momentary inconveniences.

So Paul and Silas were accused of "throwing our city into great confusion," and—because they were Jews—of "causing us Romans unlawful distractions." It is too often true that when people find their comfortable "nest" disturbed, even though it might be the Lord Himself who is doing the disturbing, they consider it is too big a price to pay. In any case, Paul and Silas were thrown in jail, and since they were thought to be such "horrendous criminals," they were beaten and locked up tightly in the "inner prison" (i.e. the dungeon) with their feet in stocks (16:19-24). All of this because they had been instrumental in bringing deliverance to a young girl held in bondage by a couple of swindlers in illicit business practices! Such a value-system is declared in the Word as "the love of money, . . . the root of all evil" (1 Tim. 6:10).

But God was not finished with this situation. He was about to reveal His mighty power in another awesome display! Undeterred by their tenuous circumstances, Paul and Silas were praying and singing hymns to the Lord—at midnight, yet. Really? It is heartwarming to observe two men of God, who, with their friends who had done nothing but good, rejoicing in their Lord, even at midnight. In addition to other injustices, Paul's party had been illegally arrested and severely beaten.

And the Lord, moved by their devotion and worship, showed to others His approval of their ministry by sending an earthquake to rattle the smug complacency of the whole community. In addition—just for good measure—God shook the prison doors open and the Apostles free from their chains. God, in His Sovereign way, showed everyone He was in agreement with delivering souls from bondage.

In the meantime, the Jailer was thrown into dismay and despondency. He was convinced by that time that all the prisoners had escaped, and that his own employment was ominously in jeopardy. What in the world to do? In great despair, he prepared to "snuff out" his own life. But Paul, still in his own cell, called out to the Jailer, "Do yourself no harm; we are all here!"

What a relief it must have been for the Jailer! The whole incident had the feel of a miracle; God was in this! And what was the result? With fear and trembling, the Jailer pleadingly asked what he might do "to be saved." The answer was that he should "believe on the Lord Jesus Christ, and he would be saved, along with his whole house"(Acts 16:31). So, God's supernatural intervention had totally reversed the negative spiritual powers in the community, and His purposes were wonderfully accomplished. Once again, the miraculous intervention of God had *confirmed* the intent and the power of the Good News.

The next morning the community magistrates, rather unceremoniously, sent word to the Jailer that Paul and his friends could leave, if they wished. But Paul, the spirited fellow that he was, would have none of it. After all he, a Roman citizen, had been shamefully insulted, so he adamantly refused to leave the jail unless the magistrates would come to the jail themselves and lead Paul and his friends outside. Wow! This Apostle had "spunk"; none of this "milk-toast meekness" for him!

Consequently, the magistrates—suddenly alarmed that they had unwittingly mistreated a Roman citizen—arrived quite apologetically to discuss the matter with Paul and the disciples. The Amplified Bible reads, "So they [the magistrates] came themselves . . . and apologized to them [to Paul's group]. And they brought them out and asked them to leave the city. So [Paul and Silas] left the prison and went to Lydia's house, and when they had seen the brethren they . . . consoled and encouraged them and departed the city" (16:39-40). Once again the miraculous intervention of the Lord had won the day, and new souls were brought to conversion because the God of heaven had intervened.

Leaving Philippi of Macedonia, they traveled southwest through Amphipolis and Apollonia to enter Thessalonica (present-day *Salonica*) a distance of about eighty miles (17:1AMP). There, as Paul reasoned with the citizens concerning Jesus Christ, numerous Jews and "a great number of devout Greeks" believed in Jesus as their Savior (17:3-4). The tragic part of this story, however, is that the same "unbelieving Jews" showed up again, adamant in their error.

The narrative of Acts indicates they were "aroused to jealousy" (17:5, AMP). They arrived on the scene, and mistakenly supposing themselves to be doing the work of God, they gathered a mob of "loungers"—according to the Amplified Bible—hired from the marketplace. These were persons whom these proud Jewish leaders would normally never associate with. In modern terms a "lounger" would be a "loafer," or "a ruffian, a rascal,"(*The Great Encyclopedic Dictionary*). Unbelievable! A double-dealing act by these supposedly "honest" Jewish "religionists," is recorded for centuries of readers to stare at—because the unspiritual, malevolent attitude of those dishonest Jews is here fully revealed for all to see.

In the mob's attempt to find Paul and Silas, they set the whole town "in an uproar" (17:10), a situation so dangerous the Christian brethren sent the evangelists away by night to the neighboring city of Berea, about thirty miles to the west. Of course, as we might expect, Paul preached the Good News there, too, and some of the Jews and many more Greeks believed in Christ as their Savior (17:12, AMP).

Obviously, in spite of the best efforts of the "religious" opposition, the work of the Holy Spirit was going forward anyway—"mightily." Very many were committing themselves to the cause of Christ. Indeed, in the words of Scripture, "The Lord was continually adding to the Church daily."

After all, God was, and still is, the Sovereign of His Church, even though some spiritually blinded authorities might choose to resist the Lord's activities. In spite of the miraculous work of the Holy Spirit, however, the hard-headed and hard-hearted religious opposition from Thessalonica once more appeared on the scene to do their evil work, inciting the masses to violence (17:13).

It is a puzzle indeed: we wonder if they ever realized it was the devil causing them to resist God's work. And as a consequence, in order to protect Paul's life, the brethren immediately spirited him away to the city of Athens, leaving Silas and Timothy behind to join him later (verse 14). Paul and those escorting him sailed down the east coast of Greece to Athens, about 200 miles to the south of Berea, where Paul found a new form of spiritual challenge.

Athens was the capital city and the cultural center of *Achaia*, or Greece as it is now known. That ancient city is usually thought of as the innovator of "democracy," a word derived from the Greek language, meaning "the rule of the people." Greece's best-known landmark in Athens is the Parthenon, located on a huge marble hill that looms 150 feet above the city streets, an edifice already there when Paul visited the city.

In the historical past the Acropolis was thought to be the home of the gods. This belief led ancient architects to build the Parthenon as a temple to their goddess Athena. Modern architects are even today in the process of reconstructing that ancient building, using, as much as possible, the original marble blocks of that beautiful structure. The Parthenon would likely have impressed Paul, for he visited the Aeropagus to dialogue with the Athenian Senators. Just below the summit of the Acropolis is "Mars Hill," the site of the amphitheater, where Paul gave his famous oration to the assembled Greek philosophers. I am always so impressed by Paul's tremendous courage, displayed here as he went "right to the top."

When Paul walked through the streets of Athens, he was deeply "grieved" to the point of "anger" by the overwhelming presence of idols here, and there—everywhere his eye turned (17:16, AMP). In verse 22 Paul is reported to have said to those philosophers, "I perceive in every way—on every hand and with every turn I make—that you are most religious"(AMP).

In fact, the Athenians were so careful not to offend any of

their imaginary gods, they had, sometime in their past, dedicated a special altar to "the unknown god" (verse 23). According to an ancient legend, this altar was originally built because a plague was devastating the city, and the Athenians were at their wits' end trying to determine which god to appease. As a consequence, they built a sacrifice altar to the "unknown god." This became Paul's point of reference, as he reasoned with the Athenians concerning the mercies of God and salvation through the resurrected Christ. "For in Him we live and move and have our being; as even some of your [own] poets have said, 'For we are also His offspring'"(verse 28 AMP).

But when Paul spoke of "resurrection," those self-assured intellectuals began to mock him. The Epicurean and Stoic philosophers scorned Paul's arguments by saying, "What is this babbler with his scrap-heap learning trying to say?" (17:18, AMP). In spite of their arrogance, Acts 17:34 indicates that there were some converts, after all, among them was a woman named Damaris, and even one of the judges of the Aeropagus, Dionysus, who, according to church tradition, became the first pastor of the Athenian church (Faussett's *Bible Encyclopedia*).

While the Lord does expect us to develop our intellects, if we become vain about our "wonderful" intelligence, our intellectual pride can greatly hinder spiritual perceptions! We are expected to be learners and thinkers, and to reason with the unconverted in the power of the Spirit. How can we possibly be His "disciples" if we refuse to be humble learners? That is exactly what it means to be a disciple. But when mankind's intellectualism seeks to rearrange the principles of God and godliness, it becomes a form of foolishness. As 1

Cor. 3:19 declares, "The wisdom of this world is foolishness with God." Intellectual foolishness is ruinous to the very persons who indulge in it, not to mention those unsuspecting souls whom they influence.

It is most unfortunate that only a few Athenians accepted the Lord as Savior. Their intellectual *vanity* inhibited their ability to accept Truth. Regrettably, most of those intellectuals remained unbelievers (17:34). Is it possible that intellectual pride obstructed their ability to believe? Could that same malady affect modern thinking? That possibility seems likely! This is one of the subtle dangers inherent in *unaided* human reasoning. Too often unsanctified rationalism is not sensitive to the spiritual or supernatural dimensions of life. The Bible observes numerous times that "Reverence for the Lord is the beginning of Knowledge"(Proverbs 1:7; 9:10).

Thus, because of the lack of a wholesome response in Athens, Paul left to go to Corinth. Corinth was a notable trade center in the ancient world, located about forty miles to the west of Athens, on the northwestern coast of the Peloponnesus, the largest peninsula of southern Greece. It was there the Lord spoke to Paul in a vision informing him, "Have no fear,. . . do not keep silent, . . . for I have many people in this city" (18:9-10 AMP).

Because of the Lord's direction, Paul "settled down among them" for a year and six months, establishing a community of believers (18:11). And to those believers he later wrote two epistles of instructions, 1 and 2 Corinthians, which make it immediately evident that Paul taught those Corinthians about the Baptism in the Holy Spirit and the value of the Lord's spiritual Gifts, even though they later misused their spiritual heritage.

After his disappointment in Athens, what a prize it was for Paul to win "many" to the Lord in the most notoriously wicked city of the ancient world. Corinth was so important to the commerce of that time because it was situated near a narrow isthmus connecting Greece with the Peloponnesus and lying between the Ionian Sea on the west and the Aegean Sea on the east. In that ancient period, ships arriving at Corinth would unload their wares on the Ionian side, transport the cargo over land, and then load it on another ship on the Aegean side. And, of course, commerce in reverse order took place as well.

Many rulers, both ancient and modern, dreamed of digging a canal through the narrow isthmus, but the task always proved to be too intimidating, until modern times. That canal was finally completed in the late nineteenth century, and functions flawlessly to this day. But all of this agitated business made the city of Corinth very affluent, cosmopolitan, and very corrupt morally. In the language of Paul's day, to be "corinthianized" meant a person was thoroughly corrupted by this olden "sin city," exactly the opposite experience of being "christianized."

It was this very city, then, into which Paul arrived, to be an evangelist for the Lord Jesus Christ. God was not daunted by their wickedness and, consequently, neither was Paul! Many years of archaeological restoration have uncovered the very streets of the Corinthian "marketplace" (the "Agora") through which Paul walked and preached. Even the "judge's seat," also known as the "Bema" judgment seat, has been uncovered. It is the Bema which is referred to in the riotous episode of Acts 18:12-17.

After his eighteen month ministry in Corinth, Paul boarded a ship bound for the province of Syria and the city of Antioch. They docked first at Ephesus, then on to Caesarea, a seaport city on the Palestinian coast, then inland to Jerusalem for a short visit, and then back by land to Antioch, his home church (see18:22). Thus, Paul's second missionary journey was concluded, rife with many miracles to confirm the authenticity and the authority of the Word they preached.

This chapter (Acts 18) closes with a very interesting parenthetical sketch about a Jewish believer named Apollos. Verses 24 through 28 indicate he was a native of Alexandria, Egypt, a well-known center of learning in the ancient Mediterranean world. He is further characterized as "a cultured and eloquent man, well-versed and mighty in the Scriptures"(verse 24, AMP). Moreover, "He had been instructed in the way of the Lord, and burning with spiritual zeal, he spoke and taught diligently and accurately the things concerning Jesus"(verse 25, AMP).

Really? With that kind of zeal, what could possibly be lacking in such a zealous Christian worker than to know Jesus and be proclaiming Him Lord? We are first introduced to Apollos when he arrived in Ephesus, where he began speaking "fearlessly and boldly . . . in the synagogue"(verse 26, AMP). He was a good man, evidently very tireless in the things of God, even expounding the Scriptures regarding Jesus Christ, the Savior. But still it seemed to Aquilla and Priscilla that he needed at least *one thing more*, the Baptism of "fire" which John the Baptist had reverently predicted.

This "deficiency" was perceived by this faithful Christian couple, who sat in his audience listening carefully—but not critically. Observing that he needed further instructions in "the way of God more definitely and accurately," they "took him [aside] with them," and patiently instructed him in the deeper life in God (see 18: 26, AMP). What could possibly be his deficiency? Verse 25 gives us a clue. "He was acquainted *only* with the baptism of John." (AMP) Of course, there was not a thing wrong with that, especially since he had been preaching that Jesus is the Messiah.

But still, something more was needed, no doubt about it! As we learn later, Paul was to have a similar experience with John's disciples in Acts 19. At that time, Paul's discussion with those loyal "Baptists" (see Acts 19) gives us a further clue regarding Apollos' deficiency. He needed to be Baptized in the Holy Spirit. And to his great credit, he was willing to accept the additional instructions.

Something really dramatic occurred, for Apollos left Ephesus, even more "on fire" than before. With that church's blessing he was sent to Corinth—of all places. Arriving there, he spoke "with great 'power'" (Cp Acts 1:8) and "refuted the Jews in public [discussions], showing and proving by the Scriptures that Jesus is . . . the Messiah"(18:28 AMP). Absolutely wonderful! Now Apollos had "greater power" than ever before because he was now Baptized in the Holy Spirit.

THE GIFTS OF THE SPIRIT IN PAUL'S THIRD MISSIONARY TOUR

Meanwhile, Paul was beginning his third missionary journey. After staying for some time in Antioch, Syria, Paul traveled by land "from place to place in "an orderly journey" through . . . Galatia and Phrygia, establishing the disciples and imparting new strength to them"(see verse 23 AMP). Marvelous courage, and genuine devotion to the work of the Lord! On this journey, Paul was obviously returning to dangerous territory, to cities and provinces where he had nearly died for the Gospel. All because he loved the Lord and the Gospel message.

Eventually, he arrived in Ephesus, that great seaport city that rivaled Corinth for wanton wickedness. It was there he met the twelve disciples of John the Baptist (19:6-7), and laid hands upon them so they might receive the Holy Spirit. And they did receive! How do we know? They began to speak in tongues and prophesy, the recurring New Testament evidence that believers were Baptized in the Holy Spirit.

As was his custom, Paul preached persuasively in the local synagogue about the Kingdom of God. And he continued discussing spiritual matters with the Jews for three months (verse 8). In verse 9 we observe the inherent danger of continually resisting the revelations of God. The Jews had hardened their hearts so frequently before that now it was an intellectual habit. Thus, they became increasingly belligerent, openly mocking Paul and his message of hope (verse 9)—a message of hope especially intended for the Jews—but they continued to reject it.

The result? Paul moved his discussion group to the lecture room of Tyrannus and continued there for two years (Acts 19: 9-10), ministering to other inquirers. There were good results, too! We are told that all the inhabitants of the province of Asia heard the Word of the Lord concerning salvation through Jesus Christ (verse 10). Furthermore, as indicated in verses 11-12, God did extraordinary miracles by the hands of Paul: physical healings, and evil spirits cast out of those in bondage. Yes! The Lord was continuing to confirm His Word with miraculous "signs and wonders."

Then an event happened that was both tragic and humorous. These miracles in Paul's ministry were so impressive that the seven sons of Sceva wanted to get in on the act. Sceva was the local Jewish chief priest. This ministry of power looked exceptionally appealing to these "budding" religionists. *"After all"*—they reasoned among themselves— *"why should Paul have all the public acclaim? Paul is Jewish, but so are we. And we also believe in a Holy Spirit. Besides, we've watched how Paul does this sort of thing, and we can do it the same way! Remember, too, Dad is the Chief Priest. We can rely on him to back us. So why not start our own 'deliverance ministry'? Sounds great! Let's do it."*

So they decided to visit one of the local rowdies they knew who was besieged by an evil spirit. Confronting the "Rowdy," they boldly commanded, "I solemnly implore you . . . by the Jesus Whom Paul preaches!" (verse 13, AMP) Nothing happened for a minute or two. Then the evil spirit answered cynically, "Jesus I know, and Paul I know about, but who are you?" Then the man with the evil spirit leaped upon them. . . and was so violent against them that they dashed out of the house in absolute fright. Surprisingly, too, they emerged from the encounter "stripped naked" (19:16, AMP). Well, there is the *real* thing, and there are also "frauds." So much for the impotent, impoverished rituals of unanointed exorcism. Public embarrassment pretty much scuttled their plans to be great evangelists. The Scripture is not without its humorous moments!

So what was the result? Did this event hinder the continuance of the Gospel? Did this untoward incident bring reproach on Christianity? Quite the contrary! The Scripture indicates exactly the opposite effect: "This became known to all who lived in Ephesus, both Jews and Greeks, and alarm and terror fell upon them all; and the name of the Lord Jesus was extolled and magnified"(19:17, AMP). Great results! God had won once again!

And there were additional results, too. Many of the believers, perhaps still entertaining elements of their former life, came making full confession, and many who had practiced magical arts, publicly burned their books, one by one. The total value of these was the modern-day equivalent of about $9,300 (see verses 18-19, AMP). So did the miracles and the negative news about the "frauds" make a difference in Ephesus? The answer is obvious to all who believe in the authenticity of the Scriptures. These Bible accounts do instruct us in righteousness! "Thus the Word of the Lord . . . grew and . . . intensified, prevailing mightily" (19:20, AMP).

More problems arose, however (see Acts 19:24-41). The local businessmen began to notice a dramatic decline in their income. People were not buying their miniature idols. Of course their pretended concern about the deterioration of religious life in Ephesus masked their real concerns about their personal income. Really, their hypocritical warnings arose from an inordinate "love of money"(see 19:26-27). One of the most influential, a man named Demetrius, got his whole guild upset. They in turn succeeded in agitating the community into a riot. The demonstration grew and grew so that the crowd finally retreated to the local amphitheater in Ephesus, because it held larger crowds—up to 25,000 people, according to historical records.

Paul became so concerned about the turmoil, he suggested he would go speak to the crowd, but his fellow believers, and some of his local politician friends restrained him, warning that if he did so the mob would kill him. Paul finally acquiesced. Eventually the rioters were dispersed by warnings that their noisy behavior might cause the area governor to quell their disturbance by force. After the uproar had ceased, Paul called the disciples together and consoled them, encouraging them to remain faithful to the Lord. Then he embraced them and departed to visit the Christians in Macedonia and Greece (20:1-2).

The primary purpose of Paul's third missionary journey seems to have been to encourage and strengthen the churches he had already established in Macedonia. But miraculous events occurred, even then. Later, we are told, that Paul also traveled back to Greece to do the same, spending an additional three months in that field. However, the Jewish leaders (we have heard much about them before) arrived to heckle Paul again following him from place to place. In fact they "hatched" still another plot to kill him, as he was about to board a ship bound for his home church in Antioch.

It is always so sad to see people such as Paul's antagonists, apparently so motivated by theological convictions, but so terribly, woefully wrong before God. From our historical vantage point, we look back, aghast at these religious zealots for being so intent on *murdering* their opponents, especially since that behavior was so emphatically forbidden by the very Law they espoused.

At about this very time, Paul wrote to the Corinthian Church, "[We are] not ministers of . . . the legally written code—but of the Spirit, for the code [of the Law] kills, but the [Holy] Spirit makes alive" (2 Corinthians 3:6, AMP). We should not be surprised, however, for Jesus Himself warned, "But an hour is coming when whoever kills you will think . . . that he has offered service to God" (John 16:2, AMP). And Church History confirms Jesus' prediction. The Scripture declares that these things are written for our admonition. And, of course, following our Lord faithfully, often involves self-examination and suffering.

So Paul carefully considered his antagonists' plan to murder him, and decided it was wiser to travel by land back through Macedonia. He was accompanied by some of his converts from Macedonia and from Asia (Acts 20:3-4), trophies of his ministry through those foreign lands. The travel plan was that some go on ahead and that all would eventually meet in the seaport city of Troas. Meanwhile, Paul with Luke as his companion, set sail a little later from Philippi, leaving, we are told, about the time of the Passover celebration, only fifty days before Pentecost. The trip across the Aegean Sea took five days, after which they met their friends at Troas, and then spent a week visiting with the local Christians (20:5-6). Paul, however, had his heart set on worshipping in Jerusalem by the time of Pentecost, so he pressed on.

But from this point on in his journey, Paul received repeated prophetic warnings that his life would be in jeopardy if he went on to Jerusalem. As Jesus the Savior had done before His crucifixion, Paul "set his face determinedly to go up to Jerusalem." But in spite of the predicted dangers, Paul's response was, "But none of these things move me; neither do I esteem my life dear to myself, if only I may finish my course with joy and the ministry . . . [entrusted to me by] the Lord Jesus, faithfully to attest the good news . . . of God's grace"(Acts 20:24, AMP). Paul's dedication is awe-inspiring! Indeed, the Gospel has come to all of us at a tremendous sacrifice by our spiritual progenitors. And in light of their pioneering devotion, we are moved to re-examine our own level of dedication.

Paul's statement above is a portion of one of his discourses to the assembled disciples at Troas. Luke records the event with occasional overtones of his own personal opinions, some hinting at humor and others at miraculously averted tragedy. Apparently, Paul and the local believers were all gathered in a third-story "upper room" on "the first day of the week" to have communion together (Acts 20:7), and to hear Paul's message.

In spite of Paul's intention to leave the following morning (Cp verse 7), he "kept on" with his sermon until midnight, and even beyond. All the while, one of the young men— Eutychus by name—was sitting in an open window. At first he became drowsy during the "long" sermon—and then fully asleep. Eventually, totally relaxed as he napped, the poor young man fell out of the third-story window and was killed (see verse 9). To attend to the crisis, Paul quickly stopped his sermon, rushed to the ground floor, embraced the boy, and then delivered him to his family fully alive (verses 9-11). An amazing experience! In the course of a few minutes, Eutychus enjoyed an anointed sermon, fell sound asleep, died, and was revived back to life again.

But, unshaken by the event, Paul then returned to the third-story room and continued his sermon—until daybreak—even though he was to leave Troas that very morning. It is an unavoidable temptation to wonder how acceptable Paul's sermonizing might be in modern times, even among the most dedicated.

The next morning as planned, Paul's companions boarded ship for the port of Assos, about twenty-five miles south of Troas. But for some reason Paul did not go aboard with them. Instead, he agreed to join them later in Assos, after he traveled the twenty-five miles by land. Why? Did he walk all the way to Assos? And if so, for what purpose? Did he evangelize at villages on the way? Luke does not inform us. At any rate, Paul did meet his group in Assos as promised, and they sailed on to Mitylene, bypassing the islands of Chios and Samos. They arrived three days later in the seaport city of Miletus (20:13-17), approximately 200 miles below Troas. Paul was hastening the journey so that, if at all possible, he might be in Jerusalem by the first day of Pentecost. Nevertheless, at Miletus he summoned the elders from the Ephesian congregation to meet him there, and his admonition to them is recorded in the closing verses of Acts 20:18-35.

As they parted, some very emotional goodbyes ensued (Cp verses 36-38) because Paul had told them they would very likely never see him again, since the prophetic messages he had been receiving indicated his visit to Jerusalem would result in his arrest and imprisonment. After leaving Miletus, Paul and his friends sailed by the island of Cos to Rhodes, and then to the seaport city of Patara on the southern shoreline of Asia (now Turkey).

THE HOLY SPIRIT GUIDES
PAUL TO ROME

By this time they had traveled nearly a thousand miles since leaving Greece, and they still had over 200 miles of open sea before arriving at Tyre, fifty miles or so above Caesarea, and Jerusalem beyond. Paul had come at last to the end of his third missionary journey. From this point on in his life, he would serve as "a prisoner of the Lord" (Cp Philemon 1:9). As had been prophesied, he was arrested in Jerusalem and then sent to Rome at the expense of the state (Acts 21:15-28:31). Many life-threatening experiences awaited him, but his triumphant joy in the Lord prevailed, and he would be a witness for Jesus Christ before rulers, and kings, and Caesars all the way from Caesarea to Rome.

The final chapters of Acts provide us with the account of Paul's arrest in Jerusalem, his two-year imprisonment in Caesarea, his miraculous sea-journey to Rome, and his house-arrest in that city. According to Acts 28:23-31, Paul lived in Rome for two years (Cp verse 30), in relative quiet in his own rented house, ministering to all who visited him "without being hindered" (Acts 28:31).

Historian Dorothy R. Miller (*A Handbook of Ancient*

History in Bible Light, 1937) postulates that Paul probably arrived in Rome in the Spring of 61 A.D. During the two years that followed, he wrote the epistles to Philemon, Colossians, Ephesians, and Philippians (p.256).

The phraseology in Acts 28: "for two entire years . . . without being hindered," (verses 30-31 AMP), certainly suggests that the Roman government did not oppose Paul's ministering during his arrest. Furthermore, "for two entire years . . . *without being molested"* (AMP) also indicates a cordial relationship, making Paul's eventual release from his first imprisonment entirely possible. So we can assume with relative accuracy that Paul was released about 63 or 64 A.D. (Miller, p.256). And these assumptions agree with the prevailing Church traditions regarding the remainder of Paul's life.

So, according to the traditions, *after his release* from Rome, Paul visited the churches he had established, as was his practice prior to his first imprisonment. And still anxious to evangelize new territory, he eventually traveled to Spain, fulfilling a desire he expressed in Romans 15:24, 28: "I hope to see you in passing [through Rome] as I go [on my intended trip] to Spain ... I shall go on by way of you to Spain" (AMP). In fact, the Catholic Church in Spain insists to this day that Paul did evangelize in their country.

Eventually, however, so oral traditions report, he was rearrested by Caesar Nero, some think at Troas because of Paul's request in 2 Timothy 4:13. Troas is located on the northwestern coast of modern Turkey. According to the legend, Nero was accused—and most likely guilty—of setting the fire that burned Rome, merely for his own sadistic reasons.

Documented historical Roman records indicate that a devastating fire happened in July of 64 A.D. Over half of the city was reduced to ashes.

But Nero, having had some dealings with Christians before, it is alleged he tried to escape the accusations by blaming the Christians for the fire. Many Christians were arrested during that time, tarred with pitch, then impaled and torched, making them a spectacle for public entertainment in his "Circus" Gardens. The famous Coliseum of Rome had not yet been built. Paul was by then widely renowned as a Christian leader, even well-known in the city of Rome because of his prior imprisonment and ministry there. He was, therefore, an obvious person to serve as Nero's "fall guy."

Thus, four years after having been released, Paul was apparently re-arrested about 68 A.D., probably at Troas, taken back to Rome, and thrown in a dungeon until his court trial referred to in 2 Timothy. Even today, tour guides in Rome will show you the *Incarcerea* where Paul (and supposedly Peter) was confined until his execution in the Spring of 68 A.D.

But all of Nero's efforts to protect himself by blaming others came to naught. In the same year Paul was executed, Nero, by then hated by all the Romans because of his cruelty and wanton lifestyle, was condemned to death by the Roman Senate. Fearing a painful, tortured execution, Nero committed suicide late in 68 A.D.

The epistle of 2 Timothy is generally recognized as Paul's final letter before his execution, and this letter does seem to have an atmosphere of finality about it, more than any of his other prison epistles. (See Philippians as a more hopeful example.) It seems likely, then, from reading 2 Timothy 4:16-17, that Paul had a preliminary trial ("my first trial," 4:16) where he acted in his own defense. Having been left to stand alone by his friends in the ministry ("all forsook me," verse 16), he stood at the last before the Roman tribunal all by himself.

In 2 Timothy 4:17, there is an implication that Paul's own Spirit-anointed defense may have saved him from crucifixion, or something worse than might normally be expected for a "common criminal." It may seem incredible to most modern readers that decapitation was considered a more honorable form of execution than crucifixion. But that's the way it was in those days. Could this mean, then, that Paul's defense before Caesar Nero had won him some new-found respect, and perhaps some concessions regarding his execution?

Regardless, Church tradition has it that Paul was beheaded outside Rome after witnessing for Christ before the despotic ruler Nero. If the traditions are accurate, Paul was probably about sixty-five years old when he "finished his course" (Cp. Intro. Notes on 1 and 2 Timothy in NKJV, "Expanded Edition"). So, it would seem that the Lord allowed Paul to retire—in heaven.

The Purpose for This Review of Acts

In those moments before Paul was executed, he wrote to his spiritual "son," "All Scripture is given by inspiration of God, and is profitable for doctrine, for reproof, for correction, for instruction ["training," marg.] in righteousness, that the man of God may be complete, thoroughly equipped for every good work"(2 Tim. 3:16-17). This statement is universally accepted by conservative Christians as applicable to God's Word, as to the degree of reverence we should maintain towards both the Old Testament and the New Testament. Does this apply to the book of Acts as it does to other Scriptures? It does, of course. And if so, then we are obliged to see Acts as *more* than just a history book. Rather, Acts—as is true of other books of the Bible—is inspired to instruct Christians in Righteousness.

It is in this frame of reference that we have taken the time to survey the abundance of supernatural events that accompanied the preaching of the Word in that early Church. Indeed, Acts is made profoundly different from—let us say— 1 and 2 Kings, because here, we see the presence of God personally active in the propagation of the Word and the conversion of the unsaved. These manifestations are described as the Gifts of the Holy Spirit. And it is obvious that there are still unsaved who need God; that is the same now as then. The Word still must be preached; that, too, remains the same. The enemy of our souls, perhaps now even more evil than ever before, still resists the Word of the Lord; that condition also remains the same! Since the Apostle Paul warned Timothy that the final days of the Church Age would be "hard to deal with and hard to bear" (2 Timothy 3:1, AMP), are we not as much in need of the supernatural intervention of the Holy Spirit as our spiritual forefathers?

Furthermore, there is not the slightest hint in the biblical prophecies preached by Peter and Paul that would suggest that the "Gifts of the Spirit" were to cease while there were still unsaved to be won. We have a God-given right to expect our preaching of a Savior to be under-girded by supernatural power (Gk. *dunamis*)! In fact, these final words of an Apostle condemned to die (Cp. 2 Timothy 3:1-7) conclude with the words describing the spiritual atmosphere of the very end time. In essence the passage says, "People will be lovers of pleasure more than lovers of God. . . having a form of godliness, but denying the power (*dunamis*) thereof" (2 Timothy 3:4-5, KJV and others).

Chapter 4

THE SPIRIT DIRECTS:
"THEY CONTINUED STEADFASTLY IN THE APOSTLES' DOCTRINE"

A number of important Christian doctrines are emphasized in the teachings of the Apostles in the book of Acts. In fact, some of our dearest beliefs began in that period of the history of the Church. This fact will be immediately obvious to any serious Bible student.. There are those, however, who have raised the rather weak argument that the book of Acts is a *historical* narrative, which—according to them—is not reliable for defining biblical doctrines. Such a position is hardly tenable when we observe that many historical sections of the Bible are already accepted as the sources of doctrines central to our Christian faith.

One such example immediately comes to mind: the Gospels are primarily history, especially the synoptics, and they provide the bases of many precious doctrines of our Christian faith. Why then should the book of Acts be excluded? Could it be that Acts is being singled out as an "untrustworthy" source because of its strong Pentecostal message? The book of Acts challenges modern theologians to consider Luke's account of the Baptism of the Holy Spirit as a legitimate element of systematic theology.

It seems appropriate here, therefore, to examine the doctrinal implications of the book of Acts. Indeed, this procedure seems especially valid since Acts so dramatically portrays the beginnings of the primitive Church, and since many contemporary beliefs have their roots in the events so studiously set forth in this book. Besides all this, we must agree that the book of Acts is a significant part of the inspired Word of God and should be respected for its contribution to our Christian experiences. In fact, all believers—because they are believers—have an implied mandate to examine Acts carefully for their own admonition and direction.

So what did the Apostles believe and teach? Certainly, many events portrayed in this book have become foundational to the teachings of the modern evangelical church. Let us review several of the most important Christian doctrines alluded to in Luke's narrative:

1.

THE APOSTLES TAUGHT THAT JESUS OF NAZARETH IS THE LONG-EXPECTED MESSIAH, THAT HE WAS CRUCIFIED FOR THE SINS OF THE WORLD, AND RESURRECTED BECAUSE HIS SACRIFICE WAS ACCEPTED BY GOD.

The doctrine that Jesus of Nazareth is the long-expected Messiah is so central in today's teachings of the Church that it may seem unnecessary to cite its emphasis in the book of Acts. However, the primary importance of this doctrine in the formation of the apostolic church is evident in Acts because virtually every chapter makes some reference to the supernatural person Jesus is: the *Messiah*, or *Jesus Christ*, or our *Savior*, or our *Redeemer*, or some other equivalent reference. Not only that, but frequent references to the purpose of His coming are also to be found in Acts: his suffering, his crucifixion, his resurrection, and his present intercessory ministry before God on our behalf. In addition, his eventual Return is often referred to as an unquestioned event, expected in the immediate future.

While it is true that the Jews believed in the coming of the Messiah, their theology apparently did not include the concept of a suffering Savior. And in addition, Jesus' declaration that His Kingdom was "not of this world" did not enhance their acceptance of Him either. On the contrary, they expected a Messiah who would dominate their political enemies and, in the process, restore Jewish dominance over the Gentiles. In other words, the Jewish mindset was largely political. But God had larger plans!

And it is true that their Messiah and our Savior—one and the same Person—will return someday to impose ultimate punishment upon the enemies of both God and the godly. But the Jews failed to perceive God's interim plan to "call out" believers from among the Gentiles. The Jewish theologians had made no provisions in their thinking for "the time of the Gentiles" (Luke 21:24; Romans 11:25), that this age of grace would be extended to *both* Gentiles and Jews. In other words, their dispensationalist views caused them to misjudge the redemptive purposes God was expecting to accomplish.

It was their misinterpretation of God's plan, therefore, that caused the Jewish leaders to resist so violently the New Testament preaching regarding the significance of Jesus' death and resurrection. And this became a particularly sensitive point because all the Jews of Jerusalem had been largely instrumental in causing Christ's crucifixion. In a mob-like moment, the Jewish leaders and their followers had loudly exclaimed, "Let His blood be upon us and our children!" But now, they did not appreciate being reminded of their arrogant statement nor of their political maneuvering to cause Jesus' crucifixion. In this context, then, it is understandable, although deeply regrettable, why the Jews resisted so determinedly when Paul stated the following in Antioch of Pisidia (present-day Turkey):

> Brothers—you sons of Abraham, and also all of you Gentiles here who reverence God—this salvation is for all of us! The Jews in Jerusalem and their leaders fulfilled prophecy by killing Jesus; for they didn't recognize him, or realize that he is the one the prophets had written about... When they had fulfilled all the prophecies concerning his death, he was taken from the cross and placed in a tomb. But God brought him back to life again! ... And now Barnabas and I are here to bring you this Good News—that God's promise to our ancestors has come true in our own time, in that God brought Jesus back to life again... For God had promised to bring him back to life again, no more to die. This is stated in the Scripture... Brothers! Listen! In this man Jesus, there is forgiveness for your sins! Everyone who trusts in him is freed from all guilt and declared righteous— something the Jewish law could never do. Oh, be careful! Don't let the prophets' words apply to you. For they [the prophets] said, "Look and perish, you despisers [of the truth], for I am doing something in your day... that you won't believe [even] when you hear it announced" (Acts 13:26 TLB).

Here it is obvious that Paul's preaching is loaded with "doctrine." Obviously, it was not especially designed to make friends. Rather, his message was intended to declare the Truth! And it is little wonder that the Jews reacted so belligerently (see Acts 13:45-50). It is evident that they had a much better opinion of themselves than Paul was declaring. This and other passages in Acts demonstrate the doctrinal emphasis in the early Church on the preeminence of Christ as the Savior of *all of mankind*. Of course we, along with those early converts, believe that Jesus of Nazareth is our Savior, that He died on a cross to redeem us from sin, and that He was resurrected from the grave because of our justification (see Rom. 4:25).

2.

The Apostles were committed to the premise that the Bible is the inspired Word of God and that the Bible is the final authority guiding us to faith and godly behavior.

The Scripture cited in the preceding section not only emphasizes the centrality of the doctrine that Jesus Christ is the Messiah, it also demonstrates the strong position the New Testament believers held regarding the divine inspiration of the Scriptures. This passage, in addition to many others in Acts, indicates the whole Church accepted without question the assumption that the Bible is the inspired Word of the Lord, and that the Word will continue to be important as its prophecies are fulfilled in centuries to come.

The earliest example of this is found in Acts chapter 2. When Peter was challenged regarding the behavior of the believers on the Day of Pentecost, he turned to the Word of God—the prophecy of Joel 2:28-32—to cite the scriptural basis for the outpouring of the Holy Spirit. When the Spirit fell upon them, the resulting expressions of joy and praise dramatically impacted the Upper Room congregation—and the populations visiting Jerusalem. The resulting response of all, even those foreign-born Jews visiting Jerusalem, was to cry out, "What then must we do?"(Acts 2:37). They were immediately convinced that prophecy was being fulfilled, and that God was truly visiting the people of Jerusalem.

In a similar way, Scripture was instrumental in bringing about the conversion of the Ethiopian eunuch. As Acts 8:35 discloses, "Then Philip opened his mouth, and beginning at this Scripture [Isaiah 53], preached Jesus to him [to the Ethiopian]"(NASB). In addition, the importance of Scripture is evident in Peter's message to Cornelius and his household in Caesarea (Acts 10:43): "To Him [Christ] all the prophets [give] witness that through His name, whoever believes in Him will receive remission of sins."

And Peter's statement to Cornelius and his friends was followed immediately by the supernatural visitation of the Holy Spirit as It fell on Cornelius' group, exactly as had occurred in Jerusalem on the Day of Pentecost. When the Holy Spirit fell, they all began to speak in other tongues, just as the believers had experienced in the Upper Room.

In like manner, Paul and Barnabas emphasized the inspiration of Scripture during their journeys of missionary evangelism. Arriving in Cyprus, the narrative reports, "And when they arrived in Salamis, they preached the word of God in the synagogues of the Jews" (Acts 13:5). This same power of the Scripture is repeated again and again throughout the narratives of the book of Acts, indicating that the Apostles were teaching that the statements of the Bible are divinely inspired and intended as a guide to righteous living.

To reinforce the argument for the Apostles' teachings about the divine inspiration of Scripture, we read later from both Paul and Peter on this very subject in their Epistles. For example, in his final days before he was martyred, Paul, facing immediate execution, declared with unshaken resolution in 2 Timothy 3:14-17:

> But you must keep on believing the things you have been taught. You know they are true, for you know that you can trust those of us who have taught you. You know how, when you were small child, you were taught the holy Scriptures; and it is these that make you wise to accept God's salvation by trusting in Christ Jesus. The whole Bible was given to us by inspiration from God and is useful to teach us what is true and to make us realize what is wrong in our lives; it straightens us out and helps us do what is right. It is God's way of making us well prepared. . . to do good to everyone (TLB).

It is generally believed this was Paul's very last message to the world and to his protégé Timothy. It is believed on good authority, too, that this was written about 68 A.D., the year of Paul's execution. But the tone is remarkably positive for a man chained in a dungeon, facing certain death any moment. Obviously, then, Paul found that no greater assurance can be achieved when one is facing death—or life—than the certainty of the "sure word of prophecy" conveyed by God's Word.

In much the same way Peter—traditionally just before his own crucifixion in Rome—made decisive statements about the authenticity of God-breathed Scripture. This is found in 2 Peter 3:16-21, where Peter refers to his momentous experience with Jesus on the Mount of Transfiguration. And using that as his basis, he emphasized that Scripture is the declaration of God Himself:

> For we did not follow cunningly devised fables when we made known to you the power and coming of our Lord Jesus Christ, but were eyewitnesses of His majesty. . . We also have the prophetic word made more sure, which you do well to heed as a light that shines in a dark place, until the day dawns and the morning star rises in your hearts; knowing this first, that no prophecy of Scripture is of any private interpretation, for prophecy never came by the will of man, but holy men of God spoke as they were moved by the Holy Spirit.

No wonder, then, that modern believers find such assurance in the Word of God, just as was experienced by those New Testament believers. Why? Because those Words were spoken by an eternal and Sovereign God who is in control of our destinies. It follows, then, that the inquirer after things spiritual, who is genuinely sincere in his search for truth regarding modern-day manifestations of the Spirit, that person *can know* the truth. If those experiences of ancient believers sustained them in the Lord, then those experiences will certainly be available to moderns, too. If Jesus promised it in His Word, then we too can rely on His "sure Word of Prophecy."

In John 7:16-17, Jesus made a remarkable statement, "My doctrine is not Mine, but His who sent Me. If anyone wants to do His will, he shall know concerning the doctrine, whether it is from God or whether I speak on My own authority"(NKJV). Furthermore, Jesus said on another occasion, "If you abide by what I teach, you are really disciples of mine, and you will know the truth, and the truth will set you free" (John 8:31-32, Gdspd).

Unfortunately, to the contrary, apart from the direction of Scripture, people are inclined to create rationalizations which agree with what they *want* to believe. Following that, they arrange their ideas into some acceptable, scholarly framework. The book of Acts is replete with examples of human reasoning apart from the mind of God. For example, Ananias and Sapphira (Acts 5); Simon (Acts 8:18); Bar-jesus (Acts 13:6-10); the Greek philosophers listening to Paul (Acts 17:23-32) . It is no wonder the prophet Isaiah warned the wayward Israelites: "For My thoughts are not your thoughts, neither are your ways My ways, says the Lord. For as the heavens are higher than the earth, so are My ways higher than your ways, and My thoughts than your thoughts"(Isaiah 55:8-9, AMP).

Consequently, we can be sure that faulty logic lies behind all heresy. The processes of reasoning—whether the reasoning is accurate or not—function pretty much as follows: rationalization, whether inductive or deductive, relies heavily upon some generally accepted presuppositions, called the *a priori*. These concepts are accepted by the "reasoner" as accurate, as if they are already proven, or that they will stand as fact without the need for further evidence.

But presuppositions developed apart from the wisdom of God are always susceptible to the possibility of personal bias, prejudice, or human error. After all, when considering any concept, accurate thinking must begin somewhere, and it must be governed by standards beyond ourselves, because human reasoning without God's control is always a little suspect. It is obvious that personal biases do distort clear thinking. Therefore, if any of our presuppositions are inaccurate to begin with, the whole logical system we may formulate will prove to be embarrassingly wrong. In other words, each and every rationalist must *begin* correctly in order to *end* correctly!

An example of *flawed* reasoning might go like this: "My puppet has a face that looks human; I have a face that looks human; therefore, my puppet must be human." By contrast, an example of accurate reasoning begins with a premise that is unquestionably truthful, in other words, a statement that is universally accepted as fact. Thus, accurate reasoning might be stated as follows: "God said, 'If I believe in Christ as my Savior, I will go to heaven'"; I do believe in Christ as my Savior; therefore, I will go to heaven."

This is not to suggest that there will *never* be anyone argue the major premise, no matter how accurate it is. It does mean, however, that sound reasoning is based on a premise with exceptionally high probability of accuracy. As for inductive reasoning, its major weakness is the tendency to state a conclusion based on inadequate corroborating evidence; for example, the accusations of "drunkenness" (Acts 2:13).made by "others" against the 120 baptized in the Holy Spirit.

Hence, in Bible times the prevailing, but inaccurate, Jewish world view was that when the Messiah eventually did appear (and they definitely were looking for His arrival), He would—so they thought—immediately restore Israel's independence, and severely punish the influences of the *Goyim* nations. But what the Jews conveniently forgot was that Gentiles also have souls that need to be redeemed. God loved the *Goyim* too! The Jewish mindset was, at that time at least, notoriously self-centered. But be assured of this: if the Jewish leaders had a rather limp opinion of the worth of Gentile souls, God had a plan that included salvation for "all flesh" (Joel 2:28). Thus, this latter doctrine was widely taught by the evangelists of Acts.

As a consequence, it is little wonder that Jesus' passive submission to crucifixion made little sense to the Jewish leaders, for their inaccurate reasoning was that their Messiah would appear to conquer, perhaps even to decimate, all of Israel's "enemies." And because of this erroneous mind set, the Jews could not make sense out of Jesus' declaration, "My kingdom is not of this world." That is not what they expected to hear, or wanted to hear. The problem hinged, then, on their inaccurate presuppositions, which twisted their conclusions out of sync with God's larger plan to include Gentiles.

Consequently, in this context of Jewish rationale, it is understandable that in the beginning days of the Church the major opposition was from the *Jewish* leaders, rather than significant resistance from the Gentiles. But that would come soon enough, full force! So about 66 A.D., Caesar Nero initiated Roman persecutions against the already suffering Church. Nero, widely accused of setting the fire that devastated Rome, decided to blame the Christians, and the most horrible forms of torture ensued.

The overwhelming irony was that those volatile Jewish leaders suddenly found themselves allied with the vicious leaders of Rome, each entertaining a simmering hatred for the other. Fate—or is it the devil?—arranges weird companionships at times. But just the same, the inspired Word of God sustained those thousands of Christians as their faith in Christ was "tried by fire" for more than two centuries

3.

THE APOSTLES TAUGHT THAT THE BAPTISM IN THE HOLY SPIRIT IS A NEW TESTAMENT PHENOMENON DESIGNED TO EXALT JESUS AND TO EMPOWER ALL BELIEVERS FOR SERVICE.

As Jesus communed with His disciples after His resurrection, He instructed them to tarry in Jerusalem *until* they were empowered by the Holy Spirit (Acts 1:8). Why? After all, they were already His disciples. Wasn't their faith in Him quite enough? Well, evidently not! As for themselves, they now understood all too well their own innate weaknesses, not the least of which was their embarrassing disloyalty to Jesus at the crucifixion. Furthermore, they sorely needed spiritual enablement to accomplish the assignments of the "Great Commission."

But let us consider for a moment a modern example and then apply it to our own Christian experience. A soldier can be drafted, trained, and commissioned for battle; but if he is not provided weapons, he will not be an effective soldier at all. In fact, it would be cruel for a Commander to send a well-uniformed soldier to the battlefront without appropriate weapons. Believers become soldiers of the cross when they accept Christ as Savior. Indeed, the immense suffering Jesus endured did work its miracle of Redemption. But if the newborn Christian is without weapons, he is of all people most miserable.

So, our Savior *has not* left us without weapons to defend our faith in Jesus Christ. Indeed, it is a matter of spiritual survival. We *must* discover what those weapons are and how to use them. Does the Bible provide us with any clue? Of course, we are appropriately informed in Ephesians 6:10-18. Verses 10 and 11 encourage us with these words. "Finally, my brethren, be strong in the Lord, and in the power of His might. Put on the whole armor of God, that you may be able to stand against the wiles of the devil." Then Paul describes each part of the armor in the context of spiritual defense, concluding his instructions with, "And having done all [having overcome all, see KJV margin], stand [your ground victoriously]."

But these weapons are, for the most part, designed for defense. So, what further weapons are we to employ when we take on *offensive warfare* in our effort to accomplish the Great Commission: "Go ye into all the world"? This is not just "standing our ground"; this means invading the Enemy's territory with the intention of complete conquest! So what additional weapons will we need in order to become "more than conquerors"?

I believe the answer is found in 2 Corinthians 10:4-5: "For the weapons of our warfare are not physical [weapons of flesh and blood], but they are mighty before God for the overthrow and destruction of strongholds"(AMP). Again, Paul observes that the weapons cited here are beyond the physical. They are supernatural. The imagery employed is that of catapults, battering rams, and scaling towers, all intended to level rock-walled fortresses supposedly protecting those people who are hardened in their resistance against God.

These weapons are more sophisticated than those cited in Ephesians 6. After all, as useful as a sword and shield might be, they could not be very effective against a stonewalled fortress. But in this passage the Apostle Paul speaks as an aggressor, confident of victory, even citing the usual ancient practice of parading captives before the victorious king (see verse 5). Could it be that Paul is referring here to the supernatural Gifts of the Spirit? Are these the "weapons" Paul is citing? I am persuaded that is what Paul intended here: a supernatural kind of weapon such as the Gifts of the Holy Spirit which can accomplish much more than our natural abilities can possibly do.

It must have been in their thoughts, too, that it was Jesus Himself, their Teacher and Guide for three years, who had commanded them to wait in prayer in Jerusalem for the outpouring of the Holy Spirit. For since we believers serve as soldiers of the Cross, it follows then that Jesus is the Captain. As for the disciples, at that moment they hardly felt capable of "turning the world upside down," action which was later attributed to these very same disciples (Acts 17:6)—but only *after* they had been Baptized in the Holy Spirit.

John the Baptist, and later Jesus Himself, had predicted the disciples' "Baptism in the Holy Ghost and fire"(see Matt. 3:11 and Lk. 3:16). That dramatic experience would transform them into fearless messengers of the Good News. Of course by now it is quite obvious to us that their *fiery* anointing changed the course of history. Furthermore, that heavenly anointing has been extended to present-day believers with the same kind of empowerment which the New Testament disciples experienced. Why wouldn't it be? Modern Christian workers are faced with just as many devilish obstacles as our spiritual forefathers were! Perhaps even more severe.

Notice also that because of the outpouring of the Holy Spirit, Peter was transformed so as to be both courageous and effective. For in Gethsemane, in his moment of fruitless militancy, he had managed to cut off a servant's ear, trying vainly to defend Jesus. And later when a maiden recognized him (Matt. 26:69-74), he traitorously denied even knowing Jesus. His "fleshly" efforts led to his destructive retaliation and blasphemy. But by contrast, after he was filled with the Holy Spirit, he captured the ears of 3,000 new believers as he [Peter] exalted the Name of Jesus Christ. What a marvelous transformation!

Paul is a similar example of change. As Saul the Pharisee, he found "pleasure" in the stoning death of Stephen (see Acts 8:1, AMP); but as Paul, the Redeemed and "filled with the Holy Spirit" (Acts 9:17, AMP), he "[persuaded] many to believe in Jesus"(Acts 19:8, TLB). Indeed, Paul understood better than most of us the depth of meaning in his declaration in 2 Corinthians 3:5-6: "Our sufficiency is from God, who also made us sufficient as ministers of the new covenant, not of the letter but of the Spirit; for the letter [of the Law] kills, but the Spirit gives life" (NKJV).

And so repeatedly throughout the book of Acts the outpouring of the Holy Spirit, as it happened on the Day of Pentecost, perpetually exalted Jesus and empowered believers for the cause of Christ. That same spiritual empowerment is just as necessary today. Furthermore, that same empowerment is equally available for Christian soul winners today!

4.
THE PREPONDERANCE OF TEXTUAL EVIDENCE INDICATES THAT THE EARLY CHURCH BELIEVED AND TAUGHT THAT THE INITIAL EVIDENCE OF BEING BAPTIZED IN THE HOLY SPIRIT WAS SPEAKING IN TONGUES.

If we accept the declarations of the book of Acts at face value—as we certainly should do—and if we accept those declarations without superimposing on them some sort of present-day theological rationalization, then we must conclude that in the New Testament Church "speaking in tongues" was considered the *normative experience* for those receiving the Baptism in the Holy Spirit. Even for the prejudiced Jewish brethren accompanying Peter to Caesarea, speaking in tongues was the phenomenon that convinced them that the Gentiles were truly children of the Lord. This point is emphasized in both Acts 10, at Caesarea, and Acts 11, in Jerusalem when Peter and his company were "called on the carpet" for associating with Gentiles. The record of the event reads as follows:

> While Peter was still speaking these words, the Holy Spirit fell upon all those who heard the word. And those of the circumcision who believed [i.e. the Jewish believers] were astonished, as many as came with Peter, because the gift of the Holy Spirit had been poured out on the Gentiles also. For they heard them speak with tongues and magnify God. Then Peter answered, "Can anyone forbid water, that these should not be baptized who have received the Holy Spirit just as we have?"(Acts 10:44-47 NKJV, emphasis added)

It is very interesting that after the event at Caesarea, Peter was challenged by the Jerusalem Jewish brethren to give an account of his visit to a Gentile community. The implication of the request was that he had "stepped over the line." But when he explained, it was the Gentiles' speaking in tongues that convinced the Jerusalem believers this was of God. That is how relevant "speaking in tongues" was to those early believers!

And from our present-day vantage point, their Jewish prejudices are almost shocking to behold. But then, it does take awhile for anyone to learn God's way of doing things. So Peter related the experience in Acts 11:15-16: "And as I began to speak, the Holy Spirit fell upon them, as upon us at the beginning. Then I remembered the word of the Lord, how He said, 'John indeed baptized with water, but you shall be baptized with the Holy Spirit'"(NKJV).

Three things become apparent as we review this event among the Gentiles: (1) that as the New Testament Church matured, the manifestation of *tongues* was continuing even after the Day of Pentecost; (2) that the six Jewish believers (see Acts 11:12) who accompanied Peter were also readily convinced that the Gentiles' experiences of speaking in tongues was adequate evidence of their being baptized in the Holy Spirit; and finally, (3) that Peter and his friends accepted it as authentic without further question because they had heard the Gentiles speaking in tongues and magnifying God (Acts 10:46, NKJV).

As a consequence, when the experiences of the Gentiles were further examined, and then finally verified, the leaders at Jerusalem could only conclude with Peter, "Who was I that I could withstand God?"(Acts 11:17, NKJV). Could it be that those today who question the significance of *speaking in tongues* in modern Christian experience are "withstanding God"? The *tongues* experience was sufficient evidence for the leaders of the early Church. Shouldn't it be considered equally relevant to modern leaders?

The scriptural evidence in Acts also shows that Paul held much the same theological position as Peter. This is demonstrated in his dealings in Ephesus with the twelve disciples of John the Baptist. Although they were already "believers" that Jesus is the Messiah (see Acts 19:2, AMP), those twelve had not yet received the Baptism in the Holy Spirit.

What's this? How could it be? And how did Paul know they had not yet received the Holy Spirit? Of course, when they were asked, they admitted they had not even heard that there was a Holy Spirit (see verse 2). Whereupon, Paul laid his hands on them, and the Holy Spirit came upon them, and they spoke with tongues and prophesied (verse 6).

Two significant points are evident here:

(1) That only being "believers" in Christ—although that experience is of paramount importance—was perceived by Paul as their living below their privileges. In other words, being filled with the Holy Spirit is even more fulfilling than conversion. It is the more complete experience in the Lord.

(2) That these twelve disciples received the Holy Spirit *after* water baptism therefore water baptism does not insure that the believer is baptized in the Holy Spirit. Even the great prophet John the Baptist distinguished between the two baptisms. And so it was that when John's twelve disciples were filled with the Holy Spirit, they, too, spoke in tongues and prophesied.

Thus, if we are absolutely honest about what the Scriptures teach, the final conclusions we must draw are: first, that the Baptism in the Holy Spirit is an additional experience above and beyond being *born again*; and second that those who receive the Baptism in the Holy Spirit *speak in tongues* as the initial evidence of their infilling. The word "initially" here means that this is just the beginning of even better things as we mature in Christ.

What do we mean by all this ? The Epistle to the Corinthians teaches that the Gifts of the Spirit are given so that all the Church might be profited thereby (1 Cor.12:7); and since the individual believer is indeed a member of the Church fellowship, he or she is *personally* profited by speaking in tongues. However, when *tongues* occur in a public meeting and are accompanied by an interpretation, then the whole Church fellowship is benefited thereby.

5.

THE APOSTLES TAUGHT THAT EXPERIENCING THE BAPTISM OF THE HOLY SPIRIT, AS IT HAPPENED ON THE DAY OF PENTECOST, WOULD CONTINUE UNTIL THE FINAL REVELATION OF JESUS CHRIST.

From the moment Jesus ascended from among the disciples on the Mount of Olives, the disciples must have heard, continually ringing in their memory, that profoundly meaningful prophecy from the angels: "This same Jesus, who was taken up from you into heaven, will so come in like manner as you saw Him go into heaven" (Acts 1:11, NKJV). This message would have given them an important prophetic focus on events which would eventually culminate at the end of the age, the very age in which modern Christians are still functioning.

For the 500 watching the ascension, it meant that Jesus would indeed return for His own just as they had seen Him go. That must have strengthened their tremulous hearts, troubled by memories of all kinds of their own failures in the past, and thereby assuring them of God's plans for the future. In fact, all their writings indicate that they expected the "last days" would probably conclude in their own time, with Jesus reappearing in their time—as they supposed—just as the angel had promised. Furthermore, the earliest Church fathers, inheritors of the Apostles, gave no indication from their understanding of prophecy that spiritual Gifts would cease before Christ's Return.

Following the Ascension, Peter, under the anointing of the Holy Spirit, preached a prophetic message on the Day of Pentecost. Careful consideration of his sermon is important here because it outlines the progressive phases of Jesus' ministry as the Messiah, from His first coming to His second, culminating at the end of the Age. Peter introduced his message with a reference to the "last days," so he obviously was considering those dramatic events of Pentecost in terms of the very *end* of the Church Age. And the prophetic progression of his inspired message makes that very clear. Thus, Peter's sermon demonstrated that the ministry of Jesus Christ was both sequential, and continuous, even to the time of Christ's Return. This is how Peter portrayed it:

(a) During Christ's *earthly* ministry, He worked miracles to help suffering humanity (verse 22).

(b) Next, His redemptive sacrifice *on the cross* was to provide salvation for all of sinful humanity (verse 23).

(c) Then, *His resurrection* from the dead (verses 24-32) was done to demonstrate that His sacrifice was an accepted propitiation to save humanity (Cf. Romans 4:24-25).

(d) Finally, His ascension to the right hand of the Father (verses 33-35) occurred so that He could continue to *make intercession* for the redeemed of struggling humanity (Cp. Hebrews 4:14-16).

Peter quoted lengthy passages from the Old Testament to prove his argument, so the Old Testament prophecies are in full agreement. Jesus the Messiah will continue to intercede for us at the right hand of the Father until our heavenly Father finally brings Christ's enemies into complete subjection, making them the Lord's footstool (Cp Phil. 2:9-11).

It is certain, then, that the overwhelming emphasis of Peter's message is that after the Resurrection of Jesus from His burial and the outpouring of the Holy Spirit which followed, the era of Grace would continue—as far as God is concerned—to function as it did in the book of Acts. And there is no indication either in Peter's outline that those Gifts would ever be discontinued, not until Jesus' Returns. (see Joel chapter 3).

Peter's exposition also fully agrees with Joel's outline of the fulfillment of the End of the Age! Thus, in these and other prophecies, there is never the slightest hint that after God had poured out His Holy Spirit upon *all flesh* (see Joel 2:28-32; 3:1-18) that He would then cause this beautiful Gift to mankind to cease. Furthermore, if the experience was to be poured out "upon *all* flesh" (my emphasis), how, then, could that experience be available to millennia of humankind which the early Christians could not foresee, if that experience were to be discontinued after the Apostles all died?

Humankind has a long history of restraining those blessings of God which they do not understand, or cease to understand. Yet Jesus invited His disciples (and we are included, too) to consider, "He who believes in Me, as the Scripture has said, out of his heart will flow rivers of living water"(Cp. Isa. 44:3). "But this He spoke *concerning the Spirit,* whom those believing in Him would receive" (John 7:38-39, emphasis added, NKJV). The Amplified Bible adds the words "shall flow *continuously.*" Thus, in view of Peter's revelation of God's prophetic map, as outlined above, it seems an arrogant affront to God even to suggest that any of the phases of the Lord's plan would be arbitrarily discontinued.

In fact, since when has God ever chosen to give *less* rather than *more?* Oh, it is true those events initiated at Pentecost will someday be concluded. But *only after Jesus returns* the second time! Yes, as the Scriptures declare, the Gifts of the Holy Spirit *will cease* at an appointed time, when "that which is *perfect* is come," and without a doubt "perfection" has not yet come.

In other words Jesus will definitely return to gather the redeemed to Himself and soon thereafter He will deal authoritatively with all those forces arrayed around Jerusalem, against God and His people, during the last of the "last days" (Cp. Psalm 2 and Joel chapter 3). On the basis of Peter's dissertation, then, it seems appropriate to conclude that the conditions of the dispensation of grace, including the Gifts of the Spirit—one of which is tongues—will continue until the Messiah's triumphant Return!

Indeed, the conclusion of Peter's Day-of-Pentecost sermon (Acts 2:37-39) clearly indicates that the miraculous events of

Pentecost were to continue to be available to believers to the very end of the Church Age. Notice, as Peter was completing his message, those listening were so deeply convicted that they cried out, "Men and brethren, what shall we do?" (verse 37). Peter's answer was obviously intended to be applicable to all those who ask the same question, even today. That promise is most certainly designed for *everyone* to the end of time. Conversion is here assured; water baptism is expected; and certainly the Baptism in the Holy Spirit is not here excluded.

Thus, the repeated emphasis in Peter's conclusion regarding the length of time this Pentecostal outpouring would be available is very dramatic. It would last as long as there are unsaved souls inquiring about conversion. And surely no one will deny that the experience of conversion to Jesus Christ is included in the scope of Peter's statement. But one must also accept the fact that all of the explosive events of the Upper Room were in everyone's mind when they asked, "What then shall we do?"

If Peter's response refers to the experience of salvation for all time—and it certainly does—then it must also refer to the outpouring of the Holy Spirit for all time. If one is obligated to accept the first—and he is—then he is also obliged to accept the second—and he must. The context of this passage demands hermeneutical honesty.

Therefore, it seems reasonable to request that if any present-day theologians claim—for whatever imagined reason—that the Gifts of the Holy Spirit have ceased to be available, it seems incumbent upon those dissenters to *prove* their assertion to the rest of Christendom, by citing Scriptures specifying as to when God changed His mind. This is especially an important consideration since the Apostle Paul reasons in the entirety of Romans chapter 11 that God is unremittingly committed to fulfill His promises—to *both* Israel *and* His Church. Indeed, God's promise to faithfully keep His promises is His very nature—forever. Psalm 138:2, speaking of God's faithfulness, says: ". . . You have magnified Your word above all Your name!" (AMP).

Paul's conclusion in Romans 11 is his emphatic declaration, "For the gifts and the calling of God are irrevocable"(Rom. 11:29 NASV). Many translations of this passage are just as emphatic, among them Williams' translation, "For the gracious *gifts* (*charismata*) and call of God are never taken back" (emphasis added). The Greek word for *gifts* used here is precisely the same word, *charismata*, which is used to identify the gifts of the Holy Spirit in 1 Corinthians chapters 12, 13, and 14. If our Lord has vowed to keep His promises to Israel, isn't He equally certain to keep His promises (Acts 2:38-39) to all New Testament believers? It is certain, then, our Sovereign God is immutable in His determination to keep His promises—to both Israel and to His Church!

Here, we have examined the significance of Luke's statement, "They continued steadfastly in the Apostles' doctrine." On the basis of our review, it seems obvious that Acts *does include* important doctrines practiced by the early Church. In the process, we have reviewed five of the most dominant. But, it must be said, there are also a number of other doctrines that could have been discussed. However, most of the remaining ones by now have become standard teachings in the various creeds of Christendom.

There are other significant doctrines which are also evident in the teachings of Acts, but space does not allow their inclusion in the full discussion here. However, a few examples are as follows:

(1) The believer's obligation to take the Good News of salvation to those who are spiritually lost.

(2) The inclusion of the Gentiles in God's universal plan of salvation.

(3) The ordinance of water baptism as a public symbol of the believer's commitment to Christ.

(4) The partaking of Holy Communion among believers.

(5) The sharing of the believers' personal income with those in financial need.

And there are more. Even these additional five do not cover all the possibilities. All of the above are cited in the book of Acts, and by now most have become generally-accepted elements of Christian theology.

In conclusion, then, it seems reasonable to restate my thesis for this chapter: the Acts of the Apostles, like the other books of our Holy Bible, *is a legitimate source of sound Christian doctrine.* We are admonished by example, therefore, in Acts 2:42-43: "And they continued steadfastly in the apostles' doctrine and fellowship, in the breaking of bread, and in prayers. Then fear [reverential awe] came upon every soul, and many wonders and signs were done through the Apostles" (NKJV).

Chapter 5

THE HOLY SPIRIT AND THE FEAST
OF PENTECOST IN
OLD TESTAMENT TYPOLOGY

It is exciting to observe that the events surrounding the crucifixion of our Savior fulfilled precisely the details of the Old Testament Passover rituals. Of course, that is evident because Jesus Christ has been identified as "the Lamb of God," providing for the Redemption of mankind. In fact, at the very moment when the Passover lamb was being sacrificed at the Temple, Jesus, the Lamb of God, was surrendering up His life on Calvary's cross.

Since the Hebrew Festival of Passover was fulfilled with such precise timing, what then might be the spiritual significance of the Festival of Pentecost, with its own programmed timing? It should immediately draw our attention to the possibility of spiritual parallels, when we read the opening statement of Acts 2:1, 4: "When the Day of Pentecost had fully come . . . they were all filled . . . with the Holy Spirit" (AMP).

Why was Jesus' command to His disciples fulfilled on the very first day of the Pentecost Festival? And what are the lessons we might learn about our own Christian experience by examining the rituals of the Festival of Pentecost? Obviously, the 120 in the Upper Room were there because Jesus had bidden them to do so. But one still must ask, "What ceremonies had the visitors to Jerusalem been observing that foreshadowed this dramatic outpouring of the Holy Spirit?"

The Apostle Paul alludes to this foreshadowing and fulfillment process when he advised the Colossian believers to avoid bondage to Old Testament rituals (see Col. 2:16-23).

Regardless, in verse 17 Paul does indicate that there is value, albeit residual, for the Christian believers to understand the spiritual implications here: "Such [things] are only the *shadow of things that are to come*,. . . they have only a symbolic value. But the reality the substance, the solid fact of what is foreshadowed. . . belongs to Christ" (Col. 2:17, AMP). It seems obvious, then, that while the Old Testament rituals are not binding upon Christian worship, they do have substantive value because they foreshadow "things that are to come." In addition, they also forecast God's outline for revealing Himself to mankind through the ages. For these reasons it seems profitable to examine the meaning behind the Feast of Pentecost, and additionally the Festivals of Passover and of Tabernacles because they are so spiritually intertwined with Pentecost.

These were, in fact, the three most important festivals in the Jewish calendar. We know this because only for these three Festivals *all* eligible males *were required* to attend. This attendance requirement highlights their importance. In addition, this undoubtedly meant that the fathers' families also were in attendance. No similar attendance requirement applied to the other festivals in the Jewish calendar, although the other festivals were also important. So, the attendance requirements emphasize that these three festivals were particularly important in foreshadowing God's plan for redeeming a people for Himself.

It is certain, then, that these three festivals outline God's roadmap for providing redemption and spiritual fulfillment not only for the Jewish believers but for *all* who believe, Gentiles included. The Jews, however, likely did not fully understand that God's plan was to apply to Gentile believers as well. In any case, while the emphasis of this study has focused primarily on the meaning of Pentecost, it is difficult to review this Old Testament Festival in isolation because there is such an intimate spiritual relationship between Pentecost and the other two.

For example, by general scholarly consensus, from the inter-testamental period to the present, Pentecost for the Jews commemorates the giving of the Law at Sinai. It should be obvious, however, that the Festival of Pentecost would never have been possible without the Passover deliverance occurring first; for in God's eternal purposes, conversion and submission to the Lord must precede every other spiritual experience.

In a similar way, the Festival of Tabernacles, the third of the three mandated festivals, acted as a reminder to the Jews that their life within the relative security of the Promised Land was *still* a temporary experience, always dependent upon God's grace and care until the End. Furthermore, the importance of the Festival of Tabernacles is emphasized by certain Jewish traditions which indicate that Tabernacles is a prototype of the activities of the "last days." Several times in Israel's history, they inaccurately associated a Return of the Jews to their homeland—however temporary it proved to be—with the Feast of Tabernacles and eventually the expected Revelation of their Messiah. Indeed, according to prophecy, that *will* come to pass in our future (Cp. Joel 3).

Thus, the Feast of Tabernacles was widely perceived by the Jews as a symbol of the End of the Age. Christians, too, longingly anticipate the End of the Age, the triumphant Revelation of Christ the Messiah, and the vindication of those He has chosen, both the faithful in Israel and the faithful among the Gentiles. It is very likely, however, that the redemption of the Gentiles was not a high priority in the Jewish understanding of the Tabernacles Festival.

So why were these three festivals emphasized more than any of the others? It seems clear that their celebrations were intended to illustrate a *continuum* of God's magnanimous provisions of grace for all of undeserving mankind. This is illustrated in the following way:

(1) Passover may be equated with Salvation from the bondage of a sinful life.

(2) Pentecost has long been related to the giving of the Law of God at Sinai and subsequently the writing of God's will on the hearts of believers by means of the Outpouring of the Holy Spirit at Pentecost.

(3) Tabernacles represents the time of the full revelation of the King of kings and the Completion of God's great plan of Redemption.

As suggested above, Pentecost is portrayed in prophecy as the writing of God's Laws upon the tablets of the hearts of all who believe instead of on tablets of stone as in the Old Testament (see Ezekiel 36:24-27, Jeremiah 24:6-7). This sequence of God's grace makes the victorious Life of Faith possible because of the Resurrection of the Lord Jesus and His intercessory ministry for us in heaven. Quite obviously, God's ultimate goal was—and still is—to create a holy and sanctified people who are His and His alone.

Before we go further, however, let us consider briefly the symbolism of the Passover. The majority of modern believers seem more knowledgeable about the Passover Festival than they are about either of the other two. Passover was celebrated by the Hebrews—as it is still today—to commemorate their miraculous deliverance from the bondage of Egyptian slavery. It is also perceived as the time when God specifically chose Israel to be His people, who were not really a people while they suffered the humiliation of servitude under their bestial taskmasters in Egypt.

Furthermore, according to the Apostle Paul's analysis in 1 Cor.10:1-2, after they departed from Egypt under God's protective custody, the Hebrews experienced a symbolic water baptism by their passage through the Red Sea and by doing so they were "*baptized* into Moses" (see 1 Corinthians 10:2). Subsequently, *fifty days* later, they were given the Law of God at Mount Sinai. However, still spiritually indolent, they wandered forty years in the deserts until the stagnation of their Egyptian mindset was purged from their thinking. An unbelieving people could not enter the Land of Promise!

Nevertheless, the re-trained second generation finally arrived in the Land of Promise, there theoretically to enjoy a "Rest" from their Wilderness Wanderings (Cp the narrative of Hebrews chapter 4). Of course, human willfulness intruded, as it so often does, into God's symbolical design. For the Israelites failed to fully possess all of the Land God had commanded, all because of their continued unbelief. Hebrews

4:2 puts it this way: "But the message they [the Israelites] heard did not benefit them, because it was not mixed with faith." A sad commentary on the damning effects of unbelief—whether it be theirs or ours!

It should be immediately evident to Christian believers that the symbolism of Israel's historic redemption at the Passover parallels our own wonderful story of salvation from sin and our subsequent water baptism. For we, too, were held in bondage to sin under a cruel taskmaster, the devil. But after a series of events, we were redeemed and given freedom in Christ by His becoming the sacrificial Lamb of God, who willingly shed His blood so that we might live a different life than that by which we once were enslaved.

As has been stated above, Israel's passage through the Red Sea becomes symbolic of Christian baptism, a rite which demonstrates the Christian's commitment to depart from his old, servile way of life to follow a life directed by God day by day—"from faith to faith"(Romans 1:17). These progressive victories lead us, at last, to our own Promised Land. And in this land of faith the Christian learns, step by step, the value of living according to God's promises, rather than by the instincts of his human nature. What is the purpose? It is so that we might at last be "partakers of the Divine nature" (2 Peter 1:4, KJV). The happy result is that we "escape the corruption that is in the world through lust" (verse 4, KJV).

Actually, Israel's experiences in possessing the Promised Land (or perhaps their failure to do so) are themselves symbolic of the Christian's progress in sanctification. Thereby we learn to live from one experience of faith to the next, and thus we grow in grace by claiming the Lord's "exceedingly great and precious promises." By doing so we come to be "partakers of the Divine nature," and, therefore, possess the Land of Faith God promised to us. A bold statement, indeed! For the Christian, the successive steps toward sanctification are described in a wonderfully heartwarming passage found in 2 Peter 1:3-11 (NLT). This translation records Peter's admonition as follows:

> Do you want more and more of God's kindness and peace? Then learn to know him better and better. For as you know him better, he will give you, through his great power, everything you need for living a truly good life: he even shares his own glory and his own goodness with us! And by that same mighty power he has given us all the other rich and wonderful blessings he promised; for instance, the promise to save us from the lust and rottenness all around us, and to give us his own character. *But to obtain these gifts, you need more than faith*; you must also work hard to be good, and even that is not enough. For then you must learn to know God better and discover what he wants you to do. Next learn to put aside your own desires so that you will become patient and godly, gladly letting God have his way with you. This will make possible the next step, which is for you to enjoy other people and to like them deeply. The more you go on in this way, the more you will grow strong spiritually and become fruitful and useful to our Lord Jesus Christ. But anyone who fails to go after these additions to faith is blind indeed, or at least very shortsighted, and has forgotten that God delivered him from the old life of sin so that now he can live a strong, good life for the Lord (Emphases added).

So in one way or another, modern Christians will be the antitype of Israel's Promised Land experiences. Further, if we fail to mature by progressive victories in faith, as the Lord guides us by His Word, we may possibly fall away. However, if we continually grow in grace by claiming God's promises as our own, the Word assures us that we will never fall. This is the declaration of 2 Peter 1:10. In this regard, too, Jesus Himself warned, "For many are called . . . but few are chosen" (Matt. 22:14, AMP).

But there is yet another symbolic dimension to these three Festivals. For the three are represent some phase of the Jewish physical harvest, each related in a symbolic way to God's Final Harvest and the Day of Reckoning for all mankind. For example, the Passover occurs in the Spring, at the time of the barley harvest, which is the beginning harvest.

Fifty days later, the Festival of Pentecost celebrates the middle harvest, which celebrates the harvesting of the grain crops, particularly the wheat harvest. And, lastly, the Feast of Tabernacles—sometimes referred to as the Feast of Ingathering—commemorates the final harvest, or the ingathering of the fruit crops.

As part of the first Festival—the *Passover* worship—green sheaves of barley were waved before the Lord as a thank offering. These were the "firstfruits," and symbolize Jesus' death and resurrection, making Him the "firstfruits of them that slept [died]" (Cp 1 Cor.15:20).

Then, accompanying the celebration of Pentecost after the completion of the grain harvest, yet another wave-offering was offered to the Lord. This time there were two huge loaves of baked bread, prepared from newly ground wheat grain, obtained from the most recent harvest. And why were there two? Many Bible scholars now believe that these represent the Jewish believers on the one hand and the Gentile believers on the other. Perhaps this is relevant to Jesus' statement in John 10:16: "Other sheep have I which are not of this fold."

Interestingly, these two loaves were made of *leavened* dough, rather than unleavened, as one might expect. This middle harvest symbolizes where God's unfolding plan is at the present time. Last of all, the Feast of Tabernacles symbolizes the completion of the harvest cycle, the harvest of the fruit crops, celebrated late in our September or early October, as a kind of Jewish Thanksgiving week. Thus, the ceremonies of the Tabernacles Festival seem to prefigure God's Final Harvest of the believing saints won by His grace during both the Old Testament and the New Testament.

This harvest theme correlates to the prophet Joel's blending of dire predictions about the real causes for Israel's failed harvest—that is, spiritual rebellion. But it must be observed that included with these awesome warnings is an exciting, heavenly promise that God would eventually pour out His Spirit *anyway*, in spite of all the spiritual "mess ups" of humankind. Thus, embedded in Joel's alarming condemnations is God's merciful promise of a history-changing outpouring of the Holy Spirit, which was—and is—to occur in the "Last Days" (Joel 2:28-32).

The context of this promise in Joel, along with Peter's quotation in Acts, cited as occurring in the "last days," emphasizes that this outpouring of the Spirit will precede the

Final Harvest, at the End of Time, just as the Outpouring on the Day of Pentecost introduced the *beginning* of the Final Harvest. This harvesting process continues on, all during the Church Age. Internal evidence for this assumption is that Joel chapter 3—which, of course, immediately follows the promise of Pentecost—outlines the awful judgments God will pour out upon those who persist in their godlessness.

It seems evident, then, that the outpouring of the Spirit just before the End of Time is God's way of strengthening His Redeemed, and perhaps even accelerating the completion of the Final Harvest. The Apostle Peter's inspired quotation of Joel 2:28-32 on the Day of Pentecost adds credibility to this assumption. It cannot be without significance that Peter announced the initial Pentecostal outpouring of the Holy Spirit as the *beginning* of the "Last Days" (Cp. Acts 2:17-20).

It seems reasonable to suggest, therefore, that Joel's reference to the "early rain" and the "latter rain" (Joel 2:23 AMP) includes predictive symbols corresponding to the beginning and the ending of the Age of the Church.

Alexander Cruden, in his *Complete Concordance,* provides this brief, but enlightening explanation of Palestine's "rain" phenomena: "Palestine has its rainy season and its dry season. During the latter the brooks dry up, and the first rains are very welcome. Early *rain* meant the autumn rain, Deut. 11:14, and the latter *rain* that of the Spring, Pr. 16:15" (see Cruden's "rain," p.526).

It may also be helpful here to note that the Autumn rain was called "early" because it was the first to fall during the growing season, sprouting the recently planted seeds in the

Fall. The Spring rain was dubbed "latter" because it brought the growing crops to maturity. As sometimes happened, however, if the latter rain did not come, the crops would be small, or not mature at all.

The spiritual implications here seem obvious: the spiritual *early rain* (which fell on the Day of Pentecost) started the development of the Final Harvest, and the *latter rain* which fell in profusion during the twentieth century (and still continues to this day) is God's provision for bringing the Final Harvest of souls to maturity. These observations will likely prompt Christians to speculate that the time of that Final Harvest, with all of its rewards, both good and bad, is indeed immediately upon us.

Of the three Festivals being considered here, Tabernacles is the most unusual and unique. As Dr. Alfred Edersheim observes (*The Life and Times of Jesus The Messiah*, Vol. II, 156): "We have here the only Old Testament type yet unfulfilled; the only Jewish festival which has no counterpart in the cycle of the Christian year, just because it points forward to that great, yet unfulfilled hope of the Church: the ingathering of Earth's nations to the Christ."

Indeed, the majority of scholars, both Jewish and Christian, agree that this festival has prophetic connotations pointing to the very end of Time, the "Day of the Lord" perhaps. While it is also true that the Tabernacles Feast has numerous other connotations, such as a reminder of Israel's wilderness experiences and/or a celebration of the end of the Jewish calendar year, there can be little doubt that this Festival was meant to be predictive of Israel's final redemption by the physical arrival of their Messiah, the very same Jesus Christ whose Return we Christians look for so longingly.

So the work of the Lord to "call out" a people, to be especially His, will at last be culminated by bringing together both Jew and Gentile as one body. The Apostle Paul anticipated this ideal in Ephesians 2:14: "For Christ Himself is our ... peace. He has made between us Jews and you Gentiles by making us all one family, breaking down the wall of contempt that used to separate us." (TLB).

In addition, certain Jewish traditions provide evidence that their scholars were in an eschatological frame of mind as they sought to interpret the Tabernacles Festival. For example, McClintock and Strong (Vol. X, 149) maintain that the eighth day will be one of four days during this Festival in which God will judge the world. And A. R. Fausset (*Dictionary*, p. 672) writes, "Jewish tradition makes Gog and Magog . . . to be defeated on the Feast of Tabernacles, or [that] the seven-month cleansing [of the land] shall end at that feast" (Cp. Ezek. 39:1-16).

Jesus Himself attended one of the "Tabernacles" festivals, as recorded in the Gospel of John, chapters 7 and 8. It was very likely the one which occurred six months before His crucifixion, in the following Spring. As chapter 7 opens, Jesus was being chided, somewhat disdainfully it would seem, to "go up" to Jerusalem with His brothers so that He might become better known by the people in the capital city. But Jesus absolutely refused to go with them at that time.

There may well have been a symbolic reason why Jesus refused to attend the Feast until it was half completed. The

"Tabernacles" were a reminder to the Jewish attendants of their temporal and dependant status upon God; and Jesus the Messiah was neither temporal nor dependant. When the Festival was approximately half way over, however, Jesus went secretly to Jerusalem to teach the people gathered in the Temple area. There He made several remarkable statements which pointed prophetically to His ministry to believers.

But first we must take note of some of the significant rituals which were a part of the celebration of this Festival. As with the Passover, attendance at Tabernacles was required of all males. It was to be celebrated for seven days, with a somewhat puzzling eighth day added which had its own peculiar solemnities. The major emphasis of this Feast was that every family was required to construct a temporary dwelling, evidently similar to those "tabernacles" the Jewish pilgrims had built during their journeys through the wilderness.

They began building these "booths" or "tabernacles" immediately after the closure of the Day of Atonement, only a few days before Tabernacles was to begin. There seems to have been at least two reasons for the booths being built:

(1) To remind the Jewish people of the Lord's miraculous provisions for their every need during the desert journey.

(2) To remind those now settled in the Land of "milk and honey" that their existence was still only transitory, that they were still dependant on their beneficent God to make their sojourn a success.

This emphasis seems clear when one observes the numerous occasions during the ceremonies that priests and people alike offered long sessions of praises to God for His benevolent provisions. In this regard, then, the Feast of Tabernacles, which was celebrated early during our month of October, was a kind of national Thanksgiving week, similar to—but not the same as—our own Thanksgiving holiday. After the "booths" had served their purposes for seven days, in the afternoon of the seventh day the rustic booths were dismantled, in preparation for the holy ceremonies of the *eighth day.*

In addition to the activities of Tabernacles mentioned above, a daily water ceremony took place as well. As the many morning sacrifices were being prepared at the Temple, an assemblage of priests and people, accompanied by a joyous musical procession, made their way to the Pool of Siloam in the southeastern sector of Jerusalem. There, they fetched water in a golden pitcher which was then returned to the Temple to be poured out before the Lord, at the base of the altar. Many other praises and sacrifices followed. This water ritual was repeated every day during the seven days of the Tabernacles ceremonies, but was not repeated in the activities of the eighth day because—according to Alfred Edersheim—the eighth day is widely considered in Rabbinical literature as a separate holiday, rather than an extension of the Tabernacles Festival More about this eighth day later.

So then, it was on this seventh and final day of the water ceremony of Tabernacles that Jesus cried out with "a loud voice": (The Living Bible records, "Jesus *shouted* to the crowds.") "If any man is thirsty, let him come to Me and drink! He who believes in Me . . . as the Scripture has said, 'From his innermost being shall [continuously] flow springs and rivers of living water" (John 7:37-39, TLB and AMP).

Verse 39 adds that Jesus was referring here to the outpouring of the Holy Spirit, who would come after Jesus had returned to heaven.

Thus, in view of the formalities of this water ceremony, Jesus' bold pronouncement becomes especially meaningful. For, in fact, Jesus was (and is) the eternal Lord who sustained the Israelites in their forty-year journey in the wilderness (see 1 Cor.10: 4). And Jesus became, from that very moment, the ultimate fulfillment of the Festival of Tabernacles.

An additional ritual of the Feast of Tabernacles prompted Jesus to make still another prophetic announcement. That ritual was the lighting in the Temple Courtyard of four huge candelabra—each equipped with four golden bowls. Many scholarly sources, including *Unger's Bible Dictionary*, describe these candelabra as being so massive that when lighted at night they lit up the whole of Jerusalem. Olive oil was used as fuel for the flames, and four young men from priestly families, each attending his own candelabrum, stood on ladders, keeping the lamps well supplied.

These candelabra were lighted each of the seven days of the Tabernacles festival, but were apparently extinguished at the end of the seventh evening, so as to maintain the autonomy of the eighth day. It is believed that this extinguishing of the lamps on that final evening was the occasion of Jesus' second prophetic declaration: "Once more Jesus addressed the crowd. . . I am the Light of the world. He who follows Me will not be walking in the dark, but will have the Light which is Life" (John 8:12, AMP).

Thus, it would appear that on this "last great Day of the Feast"(John 7:37), Jesus twice offered Himself to the House of Israel as their Messiah, first as the "Water of Life," and then as the "Light of the World." And remarkably, according to John 8:30-31, many of the Jews (even "leaders" from among the priests) began to believe that Jesus was really the Messiah. Could this have been because they recognized He was fulfilling the symbolism of the Tabernacles Festival?

But, regrettably, according to the dialogue recorded in the Gospel of John, chapters seven and eight, the malignant unbelief of the religious leaders prevailed for the moment, and thereby Jesus was moved relentlessly toward the crucifixion— although, all in God's Sovereign plan—to occur only when the predetermined time would finally arrive.

Now to return briefly to the subject of the eighth day celebrations, for it too has wondrously prophetic implications. The ceremonies of the eighth day were opened with a prescribed invocation, just as was each of the other important Festivals, seemingly giving this one day equal status with the other Feasts. Moreover, the prescribed rituals are quite different from those of the Feast of Tabernacles. (See Alfred Edersheim, Vol. II, 176 for a list of six differences between the rituals of Tabernacles and those of the eighth day.)

For example, all twenty-four orders of priests were commanded to take part in the seven days of Tabernacles ceremonies, but not so during the eighth day. The priests who served on this eighth day were *chosen* for that honor.

This procedure reminds one of the heavenly scene described in the book of Revelation, chapters 4 and 5. There in chapter 4 describes the absolute magnificence of a heavenly throne room and He who sat on that throne in "crystalline brightness" was surrounded by a halo "like a rainbow of emerald." And around that throne were twenty-four lesser thrones, where twenty-four crowned elders were seated, worshiping—worshiping the magnificent One seated on the central throne! This passage is an absolutely breath-taking scene, which may well be the heavenly fulfillment of the seven-day Feast of Tabernacles, or the heavenly events suggested by the eighth day.

At that point, then, Revelation chapter 5 relates the account of the Scroll over which John wept because no one anywhere—in heaven, on earth, or in hades—could be found worthy to open that Scroll. The result was that John wept "audibly"(AMP), until he was at last informed there was Someone after all: He Who had won the right to break the seven seals. That one Person was, and still is, Jesus Christ, the Lamb of God slain from the foundation of the world. The heavenly ceremony of Revelation 5 parallels the eighth-day ceremonies so strikingly because of the selection of only one order of priests, chosen above all the others, to minister on that eighth day. Significantly, this event also brought the Jewish religious year to a close, which itself also suggests a prophetic fulfillment of the End of the Age.

Furthermore, the eighth day was designated as a day of holy convocation, meaning a Sabbath of rest took place, or as some authorities speculate, a foreshadowing of the millennial reign of the Messiah over all the earth and all people. By way of comparison, in the Creation week of Genesis, God "rested" on the seventh day, His Creation work all completed. Prophetically, the Festival of the eighth day also seems to mark the day God will rest from His supreme work of Re-Creation, that is, His fully completed work of Redemption of all who believe on Jesus the Savior. And, too, this will be the ultimate, joyous Rest for those whom Jesus redeemed through the Ages of Time. No more contests between flesh and the Spirit! Victory will then be sweet at last!

Merrill F. Unger, in his *Bible Dictionary* study of the Jewish Festivals, makes this comment (p.363) about the Feast of Tabernacles and the eighth day:

> The Feast of Tabernacles is thus prophetic of Israel's millennial rest. [It] will be a memorial to Israel, [harking] back to Egypt and forward to millennial rest, [just] as the Lord's Supper now points back to a finished redemption until Christ appears. The eighth day following the Sabbath (Lev. 23:39) points to the new heaven and the new earth following the millennium. . . .

So what have we learned about these three major feasts relative to present-day experiences of Christian faith? First of all, because God emphasized an attendance requirement for all of the men, we can be sure of the relative importance of all that each Festival represented. The warning of Scripture seems pretty clear: Once the Lord has outlined His plans for the procedure, it was expected that those plans would be followed precisely, that is, until God chose to deal with His people differently. It follows, therefore, that nothing can be any more important for the Christian than being "born again," than being set free from the symbolic Egyptian bondage of a sinful life.

And that expectation has never changed since Jesus' admonition to Nicodemus, "You must be born again." So it should be obvious that this beginning, life-changing experience is meaningfully represented by the ceremonies accompanying the Passover. Likewise, it is just as certain that the celebration of the Feast of Tabernacles, or the "Feast of Ingathering," provides prophetic disclosures about how God, in His Sovereignty, plans to close the End of the Age. For instance, in Matt. 13:39, Jesus taught His disciples, "The harvest is the end of the world."

The second of the Festivals is Pentecost, and the declared emphasis of this researched study. It remains, therefore, that we should seek the Lord's guidance in understanding the role of Pentecost in our walk of faith. So let us re-examine, for a moment, the events occurring in the ceremonies of this Festival.

Pentecost represented the mid-point in God's symbolic outline of events, which would eventually conclude in the Festival of Tabernacles, a symbol of the Final Harvest, the harvest to which Jesus referred in Matthew 13:39.

Early in June, when Pentecost usually occurred, the wheat harvest was completed, but not the fruit harvest, which was to be celebrated later, in October. Passover was celebrated with a wave offering to the Lord of a sheaf or bundle of barley, still green but with mature heads. In comparison, Pentecost was celebrated with the two massive loaves of leavened bread—rather than unleavened, as we might expect—each approximately 3 feet x 18 inches x 4 inches deep. These, made of newly harvested wheat, were also waved before the Lord as a thank and praise offering, recognizing the Lord's abundant provisions. The consensus of interpretation here is that these loaves represented the redeemed of both the Jews and the Gentiles.

About this part of the ceremony, Merrill F. Unger writes, "The two loaves are not a sheaf of separate stalks loosely tied together, but a real union of particles making loaves, a homogeneous body. At Pentecost the Holy Spirit . . . formed the separate disciples into one organism, the body of Christ" (Unger, p.363). The Apostle Paul, in 1 Corinthians 12:13, exceeds Unger's observation: "For by one Spirit are we all baptized into one body, whether we be Jews or Gentiles, whether we be bond or free; and have been all made to drink into one Spirit." We can justly conclude from this, therefore, that the Lord was predicting the spiritual blending of two antagonistic races—the Jews with the Gentiles and the Gentiles with the Jews—a miracle that could be accomplished only by the overshadowing presence of the Holy Spirit.

Several other conclusions may also be drawn:

(1) Because of the required attendance of *all* men, the Feast of Pentecost was no less important than the Passover Festival. God demanded it; all were expected to comply. So in the Christian's experience, a Pentecostal outpouring of the Holy Spirit should be the expected norm.

(2) Just as the Festival of Pentecost, occurring just fifty days after Passover, is a separate experience from that of the Passover, so the Christian's experience of being Baptized in the Holy Spirit (as happened on the Day of Pentecost) should be considered a *separate experience* beyond that of conversion. John's baptism in water, as important as it is, was the baptism

of repentance. But the Baptism Jesus offered was in the "fire" of the Holy Spirit, designed for spiritual empowerment to do the work necessary to complete the Final Harvest (Cp. Acts 1:8).

Both Jesus and John the Baptist recognized the important differences between these two baptisms. We cannot read John the Baptist's prophetic announcement of the Baptism in the Holy Spirit (see Matt. 3:11-12; Luke 3:16-17) without noticing that they are unquestionably *two different experiences*. A more studious comparison of the Old Testament Festivals with the New Testament experiences of conversion and Holy Spirit Baptism would undoubtedly only reinforce the assertions of this study. That claim is that the Festivals of the Old Testament are designedly prophetic of God's plan to provide both conversion and the *dunamis* power of the Holy Spirit Baptism.

Chapter 6

THE MINISTRY OF THE HOLY SPIRIT IN CHURCH HISTORY, TO 1000 A.D.

Thus far, we have traced references to manifestations of the Holy Spirit in both the Old Testament and the New. In the chapters which follow, we will be exploring the evidences of the Gifts of the Spirit which have been recorded in history. Can legitimate accounts be verified of the Gifts of the Holy Spirit occurring after the New Testament closed? The answer is, "Yes, without question!"

As a preliminary, it is accurate to say that the claim of the "cessationists," that "there is absolutely no record of the any manifestations of supernatural Gifts of the Holy Spirit after the Apostles died" (or as some state it, "...after the New Testament was finalized") is totally inaccurate. And amazingly, this statement continues to surface in spite of its inaccuracies.

Furthermore, the position of the Apostles and of the early Church believers is definitely not the position of modern cessationists. And the cessationist arguments will not survive the clear evidences of history either—neither secular history nor church history! Indeed, a careful investigation of Church History reveals quite the contrary. So with these thoughts in mind, let us survey what evidences past and current history may provide us.

In his well-documented research, *On the Cessation of the Charismata* (1993), Dr. Jon Ruthven, Professor of Practical

Theology at Regents University, convincingly traces the evolution of the cessationist polemic. He suggests that the negative arguments of today's cessationists appear to have their roots in pre-Christian Rabbinical (Jewish) philosophy. Just as their modern counterparts are doing, Jewish theologians designed a rational explanation for the fact that, after Malachi, no other prophets appeared for 400 years.

In other words, in the centuries after Malachi, the prophetic office was virtually non-existent, and the theologians of the time tried to explain away the embarrassing silence. Apparently, this Rabbinical position was initially designed to preserve biblical orthodoxy during the absence of the supernatural. However, it subsequently deteriorated into a rigid legalism, so that, according to Ruthven, even the authenticity of Christ's miracles were routinely challenged by the very religious leaders who should have been supportive of Jesus. After all, formalized orthodoxy had explained away the lack of God's intervention.

It would seem reasonable to suppose that after 400 years of prophetic silence, these leaders would quickly welcome evidences of the supernatural, such as John the Baptist's prophetic voice and the miracles of Jesus' ministry. Instead, the Pharisees had come to adore their own mistaken theology so much that they were "stuck" in their opinions that Jesus' miracles were of the devil. Sound familiar? And sadly, those Pharisaical theologians who were expected by the populace to be the voices of Scriptural wisdom totally missed recognizing the very Messiah they often spoke about.

There is something terribly tragic about the rationalized reluctance by the self-assured theologians during the revival of those religious experiences from 1550 to the present. When renewed religious experiences became "emotional" as well as logical, many leaders were certain the emotionalism was a sign of getting too close to the devil's territory. How did this come about? For one thing, early in the spiritual decline, when the frequency of New Testament spiritual Gifts began to diminish in the fourth or fifth centuries, arguments began to appear rationalizing their decline. The leaders did not want to suggest that the problem might be a deterioration of their own moral values.

No, it was much easier to suggest, and then to insist, that it was God's plan all along. It is always difficult to admit that we ourselves might be guilty of falling away from the Lord. Furthermore, the Dark Ages took their debilitating toll as well. So in subsequent centuries, when miracles occurred less and less frequently, the New Testament accounts were allegorized, and the allegories were then ritualized, building a superstructure imitating past experiences, a "form of godliness" but "without the power" (2 Timothy 3:5).

And so the rationale slowly evolved that the charismatic *prophecy* of Bible days was really the same as ordinary pulpit "preaching." Similarly, the spiritual gifts of *knowledge* and *wisdom* were equated with scholarly "intellectual accomplishments." In addition, in this environment of deepening moral coldness, physical healings virtually disappeared, so what had previously been prayers for healings, as in James 5:14-15, evolved into the "last rites" given just before the patient died. In his book "Into All Truth," (pp.140-141), Stanley Horton suggests that this is only one of several rituals that evolved out of what was once vital and vigorous supernatural experiences.

Unfortunately, man-made traditions in the Church, once they have become entrenched, take on the nature of official dogmas, and by then are very difficult to correct. And quite frankly, in many cases the great leaders of the Reformation, as they *rediscovered biblical truths*, arrived on the scene still encumbered with doctrinal baggage from their previous church affiliations. Of course, we can recognize that—living as we do under the strong influence of the Reformation—but they could not. We revere them for their courageous stand against erroneous traditions, but they were still very, very human.

For example, Martin Luther correctly declared that spiritual conversion happens only *by faith* in Jesus Christ. But, surprisingly, he strongly opposed the Anabaptists, due to their rejection of Infant Baptism as a flawed doctrine. They accurately observed that infant baptism was not in accord with the Scriptures. The Anabaptists taught that *only* those mature enough to make a decision to serve Christ should be baptized, and then only after a public confession of faith in Christ.

And amazingly, their teaching, once considered radicalism, is now generally accepted as the theological norm by the majority of evangelicals. But in those times everyone lived under the shadow of a thousand years of ritualistic traditions. Thus, Martin Luther remained militantly unconvinced that infant baptism was unscriptural. True, he had rediscovered the truth of rebirth through *faith in Christ* as his personal Savior, but in his dedication to that important premise, he was very reluctant to discard other traditions he had so long believed in.

The Wesleys had similar experiences. Because of the strong ecclesiastical rituals which they had been taught, for some time the Wesley brothers continued to practice the rituals as they had been learned, but which they later discarded. The supposed mystical powers of water baptism is just one example of devoutly held traditions. Later, as the Wesleys matured, they became increasingly aware that a person must experience conversion *before* baptism, and that a life of holiness should follow.

So what is the point to be made here? It is that the "cessationist" polemic has been—and still is—advocated by many honorable and devout Christian leaders. We justly respect them for their dedication to the authenticity of the Bible. But the real truth is that the "cessationist" doctrine is a residual of mistaken medieval theology for which there is no legitimate biblical basis.

Furthermore, the twentieth-century Pentecostal revival has been, and continues to be, of such impressive magnitude—and at the same time so similar in its manifestations in accordance with the New Testament accounts—that the "cessationist" doctrine should, in all honesty, be carefully re-evaluated. Frankly, the cessationist teaching lacks both the historical and the biblical support to substantiate its claims.

In view of the present dimensions of the worldwide Pentecostal revival of the last 120 years, perhaps the time has come to discard the "cessationist" philosophy altogether and recognize that it—like many other medieval doctrines—is a vestige of historical accumulations of mistaken exegeses. Our spiritual forefathers of the Reformation had to alter their well-established theological mistakes. Why shouldn't we alter our position if we are proved wrong?

In fact, motivated by the ever expanding twentieth-century Pentecostal movements, many Bible scholars have searched history and uncovered a wealth of recorded information indicating that the spiritual Gifts (the *charismata*) have indeed continued in every century since the New Testament Church. True, the *charismata* did appear in limited quantities in medieval times because of the serious moral decadence in the Church communities. And furthermore, church history reveals that this medieval "decline" also caused deterioration of virtually all of the other basic Christian doctrines. Conversion by simple faith in Christ alone is a prime example.

In his book, "On the Cessation of the Charismata...," Jon Ruthven provides a very impressive bibliography of scholars who prove that the present-day *charismata* have continued throughout history, showing "a more or less continuous line of charismatic activity throughout the centuries" (see Ruthven, p.18, footnote #1). To provide examples of the activity of post-Apostolic *charismata*, I have chosen two respected scholars—among many others who could have been cited—who have done extensive research in this field.

The two are Stanley H. Frodsham, *With Signs Following* (1941) and Dr. Ed L. Hyatt, *2000 Years of Charismatic Christianity: A 21st Century Look at Church History from a Pentecostal/Charismatic Perspective* (1998). Both men have provided commendable documentation of their search through the annals of history to demonstrate a continuum of Pentecostal manifestations. Likewise, these particular scholars have been selected here because they come from two different generations: Frodsham from the early part of the twentieth century and Hyatt from the threshold of the twenty-first.

It should be noted that Stanley H. Frodsham (1882-1969) is a credible and respected witness to the authenticity of modern Pentecostalism because of his long career as a writer and a scholar in the twentieth-century Pentecostal movement. He was educated in England, and after marrying, he and his wife emigrated to Canada. In 1921 he became the editor of *The Pentecostal Evangel*, a position he held for twenty-eight years. During his career he wrote and published fifteen books. In the book listed above, he has devoted whole chapters to well-documented references from historical sources about the continuance of the biblical manifestations of the Holy Spirit (particularly Chapter 23). Reverend Frodsham was a pioneer Pentecostal and became an early apologist in the Pentecostal revival.

In this same regard, Dr. Hyatt has served as Professor of Religion and Bible at both Oral Roberts University and Regents University. He is now the president of Hyatt International Ministries, Weatherford, Texas. Some significant examples of their investigations are listed below:

1. **Irenaeus** (c.140-202 A.D.): He was born in Asia Minor and became Bishop of Lyon in France about 177 A.D. Thus, his comments on spiritual gifts were made *after* all of the Apostles were deceased. He is especially known for his writings refuting the Gnosticism heresy and his masterful defense of the truth of the Christian faith (see also *Britannica*, 1947, XII). He was a pupil of Polycarp, who was a renowned disciple of the Apostle John. Irenaeus wrote in A.D.V. Her.6,

pg.6: "We hear of many brethren in the Church having prophetic gifts and speaking in all sorts of languages through the Spirit" (derived from Frodsham, p. 253).

2. **Tertullian** (160-240 A.D.): He was born in Carthage, Africa, of a good family and received an excellent education both in Latin and in Greek. His scholarship became well-known because of the accuracy of his historical research. He was converted to Christianity about 190 A.D., and became an apologist of the Christian faith, eventually ascending to the position of Presbyter. Tertullian spoke in his writings of the presence in the Church of "the spiritual gifts, including the gift of tongues" (Frodsham, quoting Smith's *Dictionary of the Bible,* IV, p.3310).

Hyatt concurs regarding Tertullian he writes, "Tertullian became the foremost apologist of the Western Church, gaining the title *Father of Latin Theology.*" Hyatt further observes that "His [Tertullian's] writings also reveal a personal acquaintance with the supernatural Gifts of the Holy Spirit including speaking in tongues" (Hyatt, p.13). In Tertullian's own words, "For seeing that we acknowledge the spiritual *charismata,* or gifts, we too [meaning himself] have merited the attainment of the prophetic gift" (Hyatt, p.13, quoting from Tertullian's "A Treatise on the Soul").

In Tertullian's treatise, "Against Marcion," we are allowed a brief look at the degree of importance the early church fathers placed on the Gifts of the Holy Spirit as God's authentication of their preaching God's message. Herein, Tertullian reasons convincingly against Marcion's heresy, and his basic argument is that the Gifts of the Holy Spirit are the most important evidence of God's continuing approval. And contrastingly, he argues that the absence of such gifts in Marcion's "ministry" is evidence of God's disapproval. In Tertullian's words:

> Let Marcion then exhibit, as gifts of his god, some prophets as have not spoken by human sense, but [instead] with the Spirit of God, such as have predicted things to come, and have made manifest the secrets of the heart; let him produce a psalm, a vision, a prayer— only let it be by the Spirit, in an ecstasy, in a rapture, whenever an interpretation of tongues has occurred to him. Now all these signs are forthcoming from my side without any difficulty (from Hyatt, p. 14).

Although Marcion, referred to above, was the son of a bishop, he unfortunately came under the intellectual influence of the Gnostic teacher Credo. As a consequence, he began teaching that the God of the Old Testament is a different person than is the God of the New Testament. In his view, the Old Testament Deity favored the Jews and, additionally, created evil. By contrast—in Marcion's teaching—the New Testament God is one of love and forgiveness. Of course, Marcion is only partially correct. For this heretical teaching, Marcion was soundly excommunicated from the Church in 44 A.D. (See Bruce Shelley, *Church History in Plain Language*, 1995, pp. 62-64.)

3. **Augustine** (354-430 A.D.) According to Frodsham, Augustine wrote of the spiritual gifts as follows: "We still do what the Apostles did when they laid hands on the Samaritans and called down the Holy Spirit on them by laying on of hands." Augustine continued, "It is expected that the converts should speak with new tongues" (Frodsham, p.254).

Here, Augustine's statement refers to a historical period well beyond the final formulation and acceptance of the New Testament canon, and the "Gifts of the Spirit" were still in operation even then.

In spite of this clear statement by Augustine, modern-day "cessationists" are inclined to focus on an earlier comment by Augustine, when he was quite young, expressing some concern about the declining frequency of manifestations of supernatural Gifts. This has been interpreted by cessationist theologians to mean that Augustine believed the Lord was slowly removing the Gifts from the Church.

But, in fact, this inference is mistakenly derived from Augustine's personal speculations in his more youthful, immature years. However, his views changed as he matured. In the course of his own ministry, he admitted to experiencing many miracles of healing, which he lists again and again. In addition, his more mature views about the Gifts became much more assured that they were necessary for the continued success of the Gospel, as we will observe in a moment.

Thus, if the Gifts were happening less frequently during this time, it is also true that the "godly life-style" of the clergy and their people was in sharp decline, thus seriously distorting virtually every other important doctrine of the Church! The decay of Christendom's moral commitment was unquestionably the real cause of fewer manifestations of the Gifts of the Holy Spirit. After all, one cannot expect the *Holy* Spirit to possess an *unholy* vessel.

Other church historians do verify this positive shift in St. Augustine's position regarding the role of the *charismata* in the ministry. Evidently, it was immediately after his conversion in 387 A.D. that the youthful Augustine entertained questions regarding the continuance of the "Gifts" identified in Acts and the Corinthian letters. At that time he referred to them as "vestiges of the past, adapted to the time and no longer useful in the ministry of the Church." Very likely he was seeking a logical explanation for questions being raised—even by the laity, as historians have observed—regarding the noticeably declining occurrence of supernatural "Gifts" of the Spirit.

But he was mistaken regarding the cause. Augustine's negative position was stated in his homily "The Epistle of Saint John." Unfortunately, it has contributed significantly to the arrival and the survival of the modern-day "cessationist theory." Some moderns are also impressed, I believe, by Augustine's reputation as an intelligent and important theologian. Also, after his death he was canonized by his Church. But, still, we must remember, in spite of his supposed "sainthood," he was still a man subject to errors. In any case, the Scriptures must prevail!

It is regrettable, however, that the people who have relegated the Gifts of the Holy Spirit to the Apostolic era only, seldom refer to Augustine's later statements on this same subject. In "The City of God," pg. 485, he wrote much more favorably about the *charismata*. For example, he observed, "For even now miracles are wrought in the name of Christ, whether by His sacraments or by the prayer. . . of His saints."

Subsequently, in this same document, he provides a long list of healings of which he was personally aware: "healings from blindness, cancer, gout, hemorrhoids, demon possession, and even the raising of the dead." One chapter especially indicates Augustine's change of mind which is given this long but revealing title: "Concerning Miracles Which Were Wrought in Order That the World Might Believe in Christ and Which *Cease Not to be Wrought now* That the World Does Believe" (quoted by Hyatt, pp. 48-49, emphasis added).

Thus, Augustine's lengthy title reveals his assertion that it was necessary that the *charismata* should continue as a confirmation of the authenticity of the Gospel message. And Augustine was absolutely correct in stating this last proposition! For the same reason, it is still important that the manifestations of the Gifts of the Holy Spirit should continue—"in order that the world might believe." Just as important today as then.

In addition to the evidence cited above, Augustine refers to a delightful worship experience which he called *jubilation*. Evidently he was referring to a form of singing in the Spirit in other tongues. Augustine describes this experience as follows:

> And for whom is such jubilation fitting if not for the ineffable [indescribable] God? For He is ineffable whom one cannot express in words; and if you cannot express him in words, and yet you cannot remain silent either, then what is left but to sing in jubilation, so that your heart may rejoice without words, and your unbounded joy may not be confined by the limits of syllables. (Hyatt, p 49, quoting Augustine)

By this statement, Augustine seems solidly in the charismatic camp.

And in remarkably similar language, Rev. Donald Gee, a respected early-day Pentecostal Bible teacher and a theological apologist, describes his own twentieth century Baptism in the Holy Spirit:

> The real Baptism is a bubbling forth of the Spirit within; you are so bursting with joy your ordinary language cannot express the feelings within. I used all the English I could muster, the full extent of my vocabulary and I had more praise in my heart and more worship for Jesus than I could utter. I got against a brick wall, as it were, and I hadn't any words to speak to Him as I had used up all mine; so He gave me His and I spoke in tongues as the Spirit gave me utterance.

Donald Gee was born and educated in England. He traveled widely throughout the world and became a sought-after camp meeting and conference speaker. The above quote is from his book *After Pentecost* (1945, p. 23). So, it seems, a worshipping brother of the twentieth century had much in common with a devoted Christian of the fifth century. If Augustine is to be revered as a theologian, we should be willing to consider, too, his more mature observations about the Gifts of the Holy Spirit.

4. **Gregory the Great** (540-604 A.D.) In Gregory's active years, we can observe that the Holy Spirit was still working miracles among believers at least 550 years after Pentecost. Hyatt lists information about miracles which occurred in the life of Gregory. Some of the miracles in his ministry are recorded in his "Dialogues" (see vol. 39 of *The Fathers of the Church*). Gregory provides accounts of many different

miracles, but perhaps one of the most dramatic is the raising from the dead of a man named Marcellus. According to Gregory's report, Marcellus died on a Saturday but could not be buried on that day, so his sisters requested that their pastor, Bishop Fortunatus, come to pray over the deceased.

Pastor Fortunatus arrived at the home early Sunday morning and knelt by Marcellus, praying for some time. Then Fortunatus arose and sat down, and in a subdued voice called, "Brother Marcellus!" Marcellus opened his eyes, looked at Bishop Fortunatus, and asked in a troubled voice, "What have you done? What have you done?"

Then Fortunatus asked, in turn, "What *have* I done?" And Marcellus explained that on the previous day, two angels had arrived to escort him to heaven. But another messenger intervened, commanding that Marcellus be returned because Bishop Fortunatus was coming to pray over him.

According to Gregory's report, "Marcellus revived, quickly regained his strength, and lived for years after this miracle" (Gregory's "Dialogues," pp. 48-49; cited in Hyatt, p. 52). Dr. Hyatt concludes with this observation, "Gregory obviously believed in miracles (approximately AD 600), and he believed as others did that miracles were to continue throughout the history of the Church. . . he nowhere speaks of a theory of cessation [of miracles]."

In the fourth century, however, an interesting change occurred in the general zeal of the Church, seriously slowing the occurrences of spiritual Gifts. Regrettably, the frequency of the Gifts of the Holy Spirit diminished even further after Emperor Constantine accepted Christianity in 312 A.D. At that time he pronounced Christianity the most important religion of the Roman Empire. And from that point on, subtle changes took place as the Church became more and more institutionalized.

The result? Church monastics and other officials were seen as the only ones worthy to administer the *charismata* of the Holy Spirit. The common people were considered too "common" and too worldly to help others by means of spiritual Gifts, so eventually only the churchmen and the clergy were permitted to do so. This bias toward exclusion became official around the year 1000 A.D. by a number of successive edicts called the "Roman Ritual." These official declarations stated, among other things:

> . . . Speaking in tongues among the common people was to be considered *prima facie* evidence of demon possession. Among the monastics and Church hierarchy, however, it might be considered evidence of candidacy for "sainthood"! Miracles became associated exclusively with the ascetic lifestyle, and any occurrence of miracles among the common people was looked upon as the work of sorcery or witchcraft (from Hyatt, "Saints or Sorcerers?" p. 58).

Rev. Morton Kelsey, an Episcopal priest, also writes about the "Roman Rituals," in his book *Tongue Speaking* (p. 46); there observing that these Catholic documents instructed their priests to consider a parishioner demon possessed if he or she spoke "in a strange tongue or to understand it when spoken by another." (Rev. Kelsey derived his quote from a book entitled, *The Roman Ritual* by Rev. Philip T. Weller, Bruce Publishing Company, 1952, p.169.)

In spite of these "Roman Ritual" edicts, however, in every age following, regardless of how strenuously the establishment might try to stop them, officialdom was not successful in legislating how God should deal with His people, although Church officials—in their zeal to speak for God—very often do try. With this evidence in hand, one point seems very clear: namely that the Church's dogmatic action through the "Roman Ritual" would not have been necessary—*unless* there were a significant number of Holy Spirit manifestations among the common people. After all, why legislate restrictions if the "problem" didn't exist in the first place?

So this abbreviated review of historical evidences has brought us at last to the year 1000 A.D. and obviously by the beginning of that century the Gifts of the Holy Spirit had still not ceased completely. Admittedly, the frequency of their occurrence had diminished. But it seems never to have occurred to the Church leaders in general that the decline of the spiritual Gifts might be caused by the lapse of their own morals. Very serious spiritual apostasy began to be evident. So any diminution of spiritual gifts cannot justly be charged to God changing His plan of giving the supernatural Gifts to mankind. Frodsham also counters this erroneous hypothesis by saying, "During the past nineteen centuries, in times when spiritual life ran high, the Holy Spirit has been received just as at Pentecost, with the accompanying manifestation of speaking in tongues" (*With Signs Following*, p.253).

The conclusion we come to, then, is that *public* manifestations of the Holy Spirit's *charismata* fell out of favor with the Church for two significant reasons:

(1) Any populist manifestations of spiritual gifts apparently threatened the absolute authority church leaders claimed for themselves. This policy, of course, ran counter to God's plan for the use of spiritual Gifts to be available to "all flesh," including common people. As Joel 2:28-29 states, "I will pour out My Spirit on all flesh ... and also on My menservants and on My maidservants" (NKJV).

(2) The second cause was apparently that when most of the Church officials did not themselves manifest the *charismata*, they felt "upstaged" by any "commoners" who appeared to be used of the Lord as they themselves were not. Much later, in the 1700s, John Wesley came to this same conclusion when he researched the history of supernatural manifestations.

So, ever more frequently, the Church officials felt obliged to suppress populist participation in ministry to others. By doing so, however, a ritualistic imitation of the *charismata* gradually evolved into mere ceremonies conducted by the clergy only. As a consequence, an ecclesiastically classed society developed. Increasingly, there was a void between the clergy and the laity, as we shall learn in the next chapter.

Chapter 7

The Holy Spirit Versus "Another Gospel": Church History, 1000 to 1550 A.D.

By the year 1000 A.D., the simple Gospel had accumulated extensive ecclesiastical baggage. No longer was there only one Mediator between God and man. The spiritually Penitent had to seek the intervention of a priest by means of the confessional—whether the priest was a godly, moral person or not. And the priest, as the "representative of Christ," would assume the right to "absolve" the sins of the sinner, or—as an alternative—to require acts of penance, often in the form of monetary gifts to the Church.

Additionally, the spiritually Penitent might also be required to seek the mediation of Jesus' mother, Mary, who by this time was herself characterized, as being god-like, and later was endowed (by Church inventions) with an immaculate birth of her own. Thereby, she herself was deemed worthy of worship. Moreover, there was also an ever-growing number of "saints," canonized by the legislations of the Church, who, because of their formerly exemplary life, could now after death intercede before God for the salvation of the Repentant.

Furthermore, the hopeful Penitent, even then, might not be assured of heaven, so an intermediate abode for the departed was incorporated into Church doctrines, a place called "Purgatory." Supposedly, in Purgatory, those not quite saved as yet could wait for further penitential acts by the living, thereby rescuing them—they were told—from eternal discomfort, or possibly from the eventual fires of hell.

Of course, *if* none of these sacrificial efforts was successful, the Church made no promises of any monetary refund. Any lack of success could easily be assumed as some failure on the part of the supplicant. Later, to this rationale the Church added the provision of "Indulgences—for a substantial price, of course. These mercenary provisions of the Church came to be distasteful to many medieval parishioners, and quite obviously were the practices which finally pushed Martin Luther to break with the Catholic Church.

In addition, other doctrinal inventions added to the already heavy burdens of the commoners. One such non-biblical invention had to do with the ordinance of Holy Communion. An invented doctrine called "transubstantiation" was superimposed onto the original simple ceremony. This was a mystical concept that claimed the elements of the Communion, after being "blessed" by the officiating priest, actually became the flesh and blood of Jesus Christ. This rationalized doctrine, however, posed additional problems later for both the theologians and their parishioners.

For example, the theologians then troubled themselves about what might occur if the "blessed" elements should accidentally fall to the floor. M'Clintock and Strong cite one debate concerning what might transpire if some cathedral pest should happen to partake of the already blessed elements that were carelessly dropped. The implied question, of course, was whether the pest might have some sort of religious experience.

The ramifications of this same concern, however, had larger implications for the parishioners. The Church leaders, now certain that "transubstantiation" was a fact, then concerned themselves about methods to forestall the dropping of communion elements by awkward parishioners. Thus, to avoid the likelihood of any such accidents, the devised answer seems to have been that the officiating priest would himself place the Communion wafer into the mouth of the parishioner; and then the priest would follow this by drinking the Communion wine himself—all of it. That is, none was given to the parishioner at all—which duty the priest very likely did not mind fulfilling.

All of these non-scriptural doctrines, along with issues related to the Church's practice of infant baptism, suddenly became serious doctrinal issues in need of reexamination by all the Church leaders. Of course, the simple biblical teaching, with which later Reformers agreed, was that water baptism was intended only for those who had made a conscious commitment to accept and serve Jesus Christ. As a consequence, huge and sometimes angry debates followed, designed to discredit those who believed the scriptural position was for committed believers only. This medieval controversy was particularly devastating to the Anabaptists of the sixteenth century, who suffered intense persecutions from both the Church and sometimes from fellow Reformers. These and certain other "entrenched" procedures of the establishment Church were eventually universally rejected by the Reformers as unscriptural "traditions," formulated by man rather than by God. And, lo, the dissenters became known as "Protestants."

This disagreement with the Catholic hierarchy became especially intense when the New Testament became available for reading in the language of the people, rather than in Latin, which few commoners understood anyway. Of course, when the Church's liturgy was in Latin and the Bible was also in Latin, the commoners essentially became non-participants. Thus, the eventual availability of the Bible in the language of the people made all the difference between success and failure of most of the Reform movements.

Persecution happened to both categories of Protestants, but only those who maintained a healthy reverence for the Word of God survived. But one must remember with compassion that because the Scriptures were for centuries *not* available to the general population, every major biblical doctrine was distorted sooner or later—including the doctrines of salvation by grace, the real meaning of water baptism, and the significance of Communion. All were insidiously manipulated, or modified, or masked, or mauled into oblivion. Sad, but true!

So it is not surprising that the doctrine of the Baptism in the Holy Spirit and the exercise of spiritual Gifts were particularly vulnerable, given the general moral decadence of the time. And when the Reformation Period finally arrived, these intrusive practices of "another gospel" were changed *only* because some courageous common people and certain brave priests—such as Savanarola, and Wycliffe, and John Huss, and Martin Luther or other brave souls—laid their lives on the line to preach and to practice doctrinal changes already highlighted in the Bible.

Consequently, because of burdensome traditions and the general moral corruption of Church leaders—from the lowliest priest to the Pope himself—as the new millennium of 1000 A.D. approached, most Church historians have observed that there was widespread conviction that things were so bad everywhere that the end of the world must surely be about to occur. This particular medieval uneasiness is interestingly similar to the mystical speculations which prevailed in our own time as the year 2000 approached—and then passed without significant changes.

There were, of course, valid reasons for that medieval society to be concerned, other than the rather vague eschatological suppositions of the Church which existed then. As is implied in Augustine's lengthy title, referred to in the preceding chapter, the theological position of the established Church was that Christianity would eventually win the whole world to the Lord, and thereby the millennial rule of Jesus Christ would be established here on the earth. Fantasy in the midst of Folly!

The medieval Church's eschatological position was terribly ironic, however, for three distinct historical reasons:

(1) The ordained clergy, as we have already stated, were alarmingly corrupt, even to the great dismay of the population to whom the Church was supposedly ministering.

(2) The Church itself was terribly divided in its "evangelizing" efforts, so much so that the Roman Church and the Eastern Orthodox Church had both declared anathemas and excommunication edicts against each other, each supposing they were the official voice of God.

(3) A new, non-Christian religion, Islam, abruptly appeared in Bible lands in the seventh century A.D., systematically supplanting the realm of the Churches.

The general practice of these Moslems was to convert others by one means or another. If personal persuasion failed, the sword proved to be a rather handy device for winning converts, and/or to wipe out those who disagreed, all in one fell swoop. Islam was, and is, at heart an anti-Christian persuasion, because they taught, then as they do now, that Jesus Christ is *not* the divine Son of God. They do, however, recognize Jesus as a prophet, but just the same, one supposedly inferior to Mohammed. This new militant religion quickly made significant inroads into important Christian centers of the Near East: for example, the Holy Land; Jerusalem; Alexandria, Egypt; Constantinople, and other places traditionally Christian.

It seems especially significant that this Islamic religion should appear at a time when the simple means of conversion had been so seriously obscured by the complicated trappings of Church traditions. Furthermore, the weakened influence of the doctrine of supernatural Gifts of the Holy Spirit left a serious vacuum in the continuing warfare between good and evil. In addition, the Church further endangered vibrant Christianity by its declaration that the reading of the Holy Scriptures was off-limits to the populace. Evidently the official concern was that *only* the clergy were qualified to interpret the Bible correctly. It is no wonder, then, that the devil—that supernatural revolutionary—was so successful in inventing many substitutes for genuine Christianity.

Among those reasons for concern about the world coming to an end was a widespread disgust for, and a distrust of, the Church. The failure of the existing Church had continued to become a concern among the laity, and later—in a more influential way—also among some of the progressive clergy. Apparently, almost everyone felt that the fabric of existing society was irretrievably "rotten to the core." Societal corruption and injustice were notably bad on their own, but the more serious problem was that the Church leaders were—according to some historians—even more corrupt than the civil authorities and, consequently, were providing little or no exemplary guidance for the culture they were claiming to represent before God.

Most church historians have prefaced their discussions of the Reformation by identifying one of the central problems leading to the Reformation—the spiritual and moral failures of the existing Church itself. And few have stated the problem more succinctly than Dr. Andrew Zenos of McCormick Theological Seminary of Chicago. He has written as follows:

The marked feature of the age [the medieval period] is the divorce of religion and morals. While piety was externally very great, its root was superstition rather than vital godliness. Fear and not love was the actuating motive in religious life. It was not uncommon for Christians to express their devotion to their faith by building churches, going on [long] pilgrimages, undertaking the [military] defense of the Church against her enemies, and scrupulously obeying her prescriptions in external matters; and yet living immoral lives. The Frankish kings were notorious criminals. Their example could not fail to have its effect on the people. Thus as this age advanced, morals degenerated.

The tenth century particularly is distinguished as the period of the lowest ebb in morals in Europe. It has for this reason been called the Dark Century (seculum obscurum) [or now more commonly "the Dark Ages"]. As the year 1000 drew near the superstitious belief gained ground that the world was coming to its end. This belief had the effect of paralyzing the energies of the Church. Lawlessness prevailed. Piracy, brigandage, and ruffianism became very common. . . But the general decline of morals affected the monastic system [too], and corruption entered here also. The monasteries grew wealthy, and their wealth proved an irresistible temptation to the covetous to enter them for the sake of enjoying, or administering, their property. Many laymen even sought the headship of monasteries for the material gain attached to them. When they did obtain possession of them, they turned them into feudal castles, bringing within these enclosures their wives, their hounds for the chase, and other worldly accompaniments. (Church History, pp. 151-154)

Thus, in the alarming spiritual vacuum at the beginning of the eleventh century, the instinctive response of the general public was to search for avenues of peace and purification other than those so-called "holy" exercises prescribed by the Catholic hierarchy. The people's religious instincts told them there had to be something more fulfilling than the empty activities the Church was offering. With this growing populist dissatisfaction already so far-reaching, the common people began experimenting—with or without the blessings of the Church.

Their unresolved spiritual needs led to the emergence of a variety of so-called "heresies." And it is true that many were heretical, although there were those who pursued genuinely scriptural patterns of life. It is important to note that all— whether heretical or not—represented instinctive efforts to find God's approval. And, it is accurate to say, all sought to bring about reform and to supercede, or to replace, the burdensome and ineffective rituals of the established Church.

Lacking godly guidance, and often with very limited access to the Scriptures, many of these populist efforts developed into fanciful "heresies" which—because of their flagrant deviations from Scripture—did not enjoy God's favor and, therefore, did not survive the onslaught of severe persecutions by the establishment Church. On the other hand, there were some which appeared, however briefly, that *did contribute* significantly to the groundswell of demands for a reformation of religious faith. Generally, those which did survive had the happy circumstance of discovering the real Truth revealed in the Scriptures—even when they had only portions of the Bible to work with.

And another unsettling historical fact is that the Catholic Church, troubled greatly by these "unorthodox" commoners, initially decided to pursue the most plausible (to them at least) counterattack—brute force. As a consequence, all of these so-called "heresies," whether wholly biblical or not, suffered horrendous persecution by the military arm of the Church. As most all historians have observed, it was during this period of religious experimentation that the existing Church established the Gestapo-like Inquisition (c.1100 A.D.), designed to force people either to recant their unorthodox views, or to suffer the most horrible kinds of physical torture.

When intimidation did not effect submission, the usual procedure was to send mercenary troops against these "heretics." And these hired soldiers were almost always artificially emboldened by ecclesiastical promises of exemption—for up to forty days—from Purgatory after death, if only these "sanctified" soldiers would exterminate those "wicked" dissenters forthwith. It is a disturbing story how most of the earliest reform movements were viciously wiped out, usually by the most horrendous kinds of torture imaginable.

For example, "drawn and quartered" is not just some humorous phrase invented in the modern English language. Sadly, it is lodged in modern expression because in medieval times victims were "racked" almost to death—but not quite—and then disemboweled while the victim was still alive. The victim was then meticulously carved into four parts. These quarters were then displayed on a pole in various sectors of the land as a gruesome example of the mortification that awaited all dissenters. The Church of the period used this form of punishment often, if for no other reason than to intimidate those who privately expressed dissatisfaction with Church policy. And these ecclesiastical perpetrators were convinced they represented Jesus, the loving Savior.

One may read numerous graphic accounts of this kind in *Fox's Book of Martyrs,* first published in English about 1563, during the reign of the Catholic Queen of England, Mary I. Fox labeled her "Bloody Mary," an appellation which "stuck" and has been repeated again and again by later historians. It is almost unbelievable that she, like many others in authority at the time, was so sure she was doing God a service, when, in fact, her dedication to preserving Catholicism prompted her to torture and murder at least 300 of the Lord's servants during her short reign in England..

In this spiritually sick culture, then, many of the populace sincerely sought for answers outside the strict boundaries prescribed by the Catholic Church. Indeed, if "hope springs eternal," then the intense longing for spiritual security must have been "screaming" for satisfaction. Without question, the Church of the Middle Ages was not answering the spiritual cry of the people.

If the way to peace was not pointed out by the alleged "ministers of God," then one can hardly blame the Disappointed for searching elsewhere. It is true that some pretty weird teachings emerged from these anxious explorations. Of course, as we have said, the Word of God in the language of the people was generally not available; and even if it were, reading the Bible could certainly prove to be detrimental to the reader's "health," if the Church officials learned it was occurring.

Consequently, the pontifical declarations of the Church, however burdensome they might have seemed at the time, were generally grudgingly complied with as the most pragmatic way to stay alive, even if the people's instincts told them these were not God's ways. It is no wonder, then, that some of the earliest ill-advised efforts to find real Truth were mixed in varying degrees with failed Eastern philosophies, Greek and Roman rationalism, or even grass-root reasoning.

But the compassionate God of heaven did hear the plaintive cries of the Lost, and eventually, the Lord led them into a meaningful relationship with Himself. It seems this is the tale of the godless behavior of medieval history. And mankind did not lose touch with a holy God *overnight*, either. Instead, layer upon layer of accumulated false doctrines eventually obscured from view the compassionate Savior of all mankind. Undoubtedly, many must have wondered how a "loving God" could be so severe. It follows then that just as Jesus' parents searched three days for their Son lost only one day, even so the Restoration of Christian faith took longer to be rediscovered than it did to lose it.

In fact, it now seems clear that the rediscovery of truly biblical Christian experiences is still going on right now. Martin Luther (1483-1546), for example, did not rediscover *all* that had been hidden from believers for centuries, but he did rediscover some—the simple but important truth of salvation by faith alone, being one. And we are immeasurably grateful to the Lord for Luther's courage. The principle which God seems to have employed through the centuries of recovery is "here a little and there a little," lest we be dazzled to consternation by the full revelation of Truth.

And even then, *all* of the reformers—commoners and priests alike—were perceived as radicals and were persecuted unmercifully. So in this flow of rediscovery, the revival of Pentecostal experiences—exactly as they had been experienced in the New Testament—has been blossoming in our own century, though separated from Luther's time by over 500 years. The Revival of Truth has continued into our own period of history.

Indeed, there are records—although somewhat scanty at times—of medieval Christians who manifested Gifts of the Holy Spirit even in that dark, dark period of medieval history: Bogomiles of eastern Europe; the Paulicians, also of eastern Europe; the Cathari (or the "Pure Ones"), originally of Bulgaria, later of southern France; the Waldensians of southern France and northern Italy; and finally, in the last century or more, the various Pentecostal movements—all were a part of that grand rediscovery of biblical Truth.

But one notable survivor of the persecutions of the Dark Ages, for the most part scripturally orthodox, were the Waldenses. Theirs is an exciting story of bravery and dedication to the Truth of scriptural patterns of life! Reading *The Israel of the Alps* (regarding the story of the Waldenses) by Alexis Muston, can give the reader startling enlightenment about this religious group.

But a reform movement appearing long before the Waldenses and before the Dark Ages was the Montanists. As early as the third century these Montanists were greatly concerned about worldly trends and the decline of spiritual dedication they observed in the established Church. Two important reasons stand out:

(1) The obvious moral laxness of the Catholic clerics—a concern cited by the Montanist's most important apologist, Tertullian of North Africa.

(2) A noticeable decline in the occurrences of charismatic gifts in the existing Church. So, they obviously believed the *charismata,* the Gifts of the Holy Spirit, were to continue

beyond the Apostolic Period, since their warnings occurred as late as 300 A.D.

This movement surfaced in Asia Minor about 200 A.D., under the leadership of Montanus, who claimed to possess the biblical Gift of prophesy. In addition, two women prophets, Priscilla and Maximilla, who were associated with Montanus, made the same claim. Among others of their persuasion, this group not only believed in the Gifts of the Holy Spirit, but they were dedicated believers in the imminent return of Jesus Christ, whom they expected to return even in their own time. That end-time awareness seems always to surface in a time of Revival.

However, even Tertullian's scholarly defense of their movement could not save it from error. Probably their limited access to biblical instruction on the manifestation of spiritual Gifts caused the Montanists to develop the erroneous presumption that their prophecies had the same authority as Holy Scripture. Of course, the Catholic hierarchy considered the movement a heresy and vigorously resisted the Montanists. But, in those earliest days of the established Church, they lacked the military strength to destroy the movement—as the Catholic Church was later so prone to do. Consequently, the Montanists survived into the fourth century, in spite of their doctrinal errors. In their defense, however, it is evident that their doctrinal position was distorted by the severe accusations of the Catholic hierarchy.

But in spite of their errors, the Montanists contributed significantly to the Reformation. Indeed, as one reviews their doctrines from present-day perspective, the Montanists are in many ways very evangelical:

(1) They decried the growing immorality of every level of their society.

(2) They vigorously called attention to the Church's diffidence about the manifestations of the Gifts of the Holy Spirit, as they are recorded in the New Testament.

(3) They maintained a strong conviction about the imminent Return of Jesus Christ.

As church historian Bruce Shelley has stated, "The. . . moral fiber in the church [was] weakened. Montanus was not entirely wrong. By the year 220 A.D. it was evident that the Christian churches, together with their bishops and clergy, were no longer what they had been." (Shelley, *Church History*, p.74)

Two other groups, the Paulicians, for example, (from about 700 to 1000 A.D.), and the Bogomiles (from approximately 1000 to 1200 A.D.), reportedly rejected all the external forms of religion practiced by either the Roman Church or the Eastern Orthodox Church. Both of these Reform movements especially objected to the use of religious images, as being idolatrous. For the most part, the Paulicians expressed disgust for the outward ceremonies of ritualized religion, and they sought, instead, to return to the simplicity of Apostolic worship. In addition, they vigorously objected to the worship of the Virgin Mary or any of the "saints." In addition, they objected to any exaltation of the Cross, because it had become an icon of mystical, non-biblical worship.

Furthermore, they refused to partake of the Communion sacraments, objecting primarily to the supposed *material* presence of Christ in the Communion elements (transubstantiation). Severe twelfth century persecutions in eastern Europe eventually drove the Paulicians into the Alpine regions of France and Italy, and it seems likely they eventually merged with the "Cathari," subsequently called "Albigenses" (M'Clintock & Strong, "Paulicians," VII, 835).

Later, also in eastern Europe—Bulgaria, to be precise— the Bogomiles arose, holding many of the same beliefs as the Paulicians. They strongly objected to the empty formalism and ritualism of both the Roman and Eastern Orthodox Churches. But ancient literature also suggests that they may have been guilty of rejecting the divinity of Christ, subscribing instead to the Manichean philosophy of "dualism." However, this accusation may also have been the result of Catholic propaganda.

Stated simplistically, the chief error of "dualism" was that they perceived Satan and God as forces of equal power (Guess who gave them that idea.). This belief—if they really held it— would have caused them to be immediately in opposition to the orthodoxy of the Church. And the story of church history makes one thing certain, the domain of "orthodoxy" cannot long tolerate that which is considered "unorthodox." Thus, severe persecutions in Bulgaria drove the Bogomiles, en masse, first to Bosnia, then to Italy, and finally to the Alpine regions of Italy and France, there to suffer the same fate as other reform movements of that period (*Britannica*, III 1947 and "Micropedia" II, 1980).

The Cathari, too, were a reform sect, the followers of which sought to live a life of sincere holiness. They were active in Europe from about 1250 to 1350 A.D. Amazingly, too, because of their practice of living a holy life-style, and because of the contrasting general moral depravity of the Catholic clerics, the general population—according to historical records—held the Cathari in high regard because of their admirable moral decorum. In fact, it is reported, many of the European upper classes became adherents of this group. These facts, along with other motives, caused the Catholic leadership great consternation, so that eventually the Church's anti-heretical persecution developed into a full-scale military operation. And when these persecutions became ever more vicious, by 1350 the Cathari had supposedly been completely obliterated, at least that was the boast of the Catholic hierarchy.

This reformation group is especially interesting because they believed and taught—as many people believe today—that the infilling of the Holy Spirit was a second definite work of grace, sanctifying them in a special way to be leaders of their congregations, thereby allowing them to be called *Perfecti*, or the "Pure Ones." This experience was identified by them as *Consolamentum,* apparently seen as an experience of sanctification. In pursuit of this experience, they sought to emulate the experience of Christ's baptism in the Holy Spirit after John immersed Jesus in Jordan's waters (see Matt. 3:16-17; Lk. 3:22).

Consolamentum means "Consolation," a word which is linked to the "Comforter," the Holy Spirit. Thus, this experience of "Consolation," among the Cathari was evidently their concept of the Baptism in the Holy Spirit. As among the Samaritans (see Acts 8:17), this experience was accomplished among the Cathari by the "laying on of hands" by the elders of the congregation. It was at that point that the "Perfecti" were admonished to "Go and teach all nations, baptizing them in the name of the Father, Son, and Holy Spirit," as is stated in Matt. 28:19; Mark 16:15-16; and John 3:3. With this ceremony completed, the "Perfected" were expected to manifest the supernatural powers of "binding" and "loosing" both in heaven and on earth, as stated in Matt.16:19 and Matt. 18:18-19 (*Britannica*, 1947, V, 31-32).

Until their demise, the Cathari movement proved to be an increasingly worrisome threat to the established rituals of the Catholic Church, and as a consequence, the Church's persecution of them became ever more militant and vicious. As a result, the Cathari numbers were decimated and eventually "were utterly rooted out in the course of a little more than a century" (Williston Walker, *A History of the Christian Church*, p. 254). Allegedly, the last Cathari bishop (a "Perfecti") was captured in Tuscany of central Italy in 1321 and summarily executed. So by 1350 A.D., the Church claimed it had at last "destroyed" all of Catharism in western Europe. What a murderous accomplishment to boast about!

It is noteworthy that the Cathari reform movement believed in, and practiced, the infilling of the Holy Spirit with accompanying holy Gifts of ministry, even though there is little documented evidence they practiced "speaking in tongues." But the reports of their pursuit of personal holiness suggest the Gifts of the Spirit were an important part of their belief system. Thus, it seems probable that the Cathari were, in fact, an active charismatic group, dedicated to evangelizing the world, as indicated by their invoking on their "Perfecti" the command of Jesus Christ to "Go into all the world. . . and make disciples."

In fact, their aggressive evangelizing, coupled with their general popularity over the Catholic clerics, may have accelerated their demise (see Walker, p. 254). In any case, the Catholic regime could not tolerate for very long the growing Cathari and Waldenses threat to their authority, and as a consequence, the infamous Inquisition was established about 1150 A.D. to accomplish its dark, dark assignments.

It has been alleged, however—whether factual or not— that there may have been other doctrinal issues which weakened the Cathari's spiritual stamina. For example, in spite of the Cathari's devotion to Jesus Christ, church historians of the nineteenth century, after reviewing Catholic documents of the thirteenth century (if prejudiced Catholic appraisal can be trusted) have accused the Cathari of being dualists, perhaps subscribing to the eastern teaching that Satan was the god of evil, equally eternal with the God of heaven. But since most of the Cathari's original writings were burned during their persecutions, and since these accusations were made almost wholly by the Catholic Inquisitors, only God Himself is in a position to judge the truth about the Cathari.

The Catholic Church had plenty of other reasons— mostly political, however—to destroy the Cathari, because the Catholic authorities could not long endure the embarrassment of any group whose pursuit of holiness pointed up the Church's lack of it.

But another flaw has been alleged, namely that the Cathari accepted only the four Gospels and Acts as inspired Scripture, implying that they had rejected the authority of the Old Testament, and even the New Testament Epistles. Some of these accusations cannot be verified, of course, because of obvious Catholic propaganda. Nonetheless, their presence on the religious scene for over a hundred years aptly illustrates the widespread longing for meaningful changes in the practices of the dominant Church.

There is yet another populist reform group that did survive the severest of persecutions: the Waldenses. Unlike the Cathari, the Waldenses began their efforts with no conscious hostility to the Catholic Church. Had they been treated with more diplomacy, the Waldensians might never have seceded from the Church. The movement was started in the late 1100's by Peter Waldo (c.1150–1217 A.D.), a rich merchant of Lyon, France.

One day as he was going about his business affairs, he overheard a traveling minstrel singing about St. Alexis, an early Christian who gave up his wealth to become a preacher of the Gospel. Waldo was greatly moved by Alexis' dedication to the service of others, so Waldo sought the counsel of a parish priest and was advised to do what Jesus had said to the rich young ruler, "Go, sell all that you have and give to the poor and follow me" (Matt. 19:21). Apparently Peter Waldo did exactly that. The year was 1170.

After selling all his possessions, he made provisions for the continued care of his wife and two daughters, and then dedicated himself to a life of mendicant preaching and service to the needs of others. Soon, his unauthorized preaching began attracting many who were already dissatisfied with the ritualism of the Catholic Church. And to his surprise, he soon discovered he had a following for which he was spiritually responsible. Thus, to assist these adherents, he arranged to have the four Gospels translated from the Latin Vulgate into the local French dialect. The results were remarkable! People began observing the glaring differences between the ceremonial demands of the Catholic Church and the spiritual expectations of the Gospels.

Meanwhile, all of this unauthorized religious activity was making the area Church officials increasingly uneasy. So in 1179, when Waldo respectfully asked the archbishop for permission to preach, he was summarily denied the privilege, allegedly because he was not officially trained as a churchman. Waldo responded as the Apostle Peter had responded to the Sanhedrin: "We must obey God rather than man." The result was that Waldo and his followers were eventually excommunicated by Pope Lucius III in 1184.

As might be expected, the Catholic Church instituted increasingly venomous persecution against Waldo's followers. And Waldo, seeking to strengthen his adherents, translated all of the New Testament into the local vernacular, and then required his followers to memorize whole books of the New Testament so that they could encourage one another by means of the Word. The internalized Scriptures strengthened their resolve to remain faithful.

Thus, their reliance on the Word of God gave the Waldensians survivability. It is remarkable, too, to discover that these medieval believers preceded, in point of time, the efforts of those well-known priests who later became Reformers, also challenging the Church's worldliness.

Additionally, it is amazing to discover that even today, Waldensian congregations exist both in Italy—ironically, in the immediate vicinity of the Vatican—and in the United States. It is evident, then, that this group of "Protestants" proved very important to the overall recovery from the moral darkness of the Dark Ages. This fact is confirmed by the following statement from the *Britannica:* "Persecution gave new vitality to their [Waldenses'] doctrines, which [were] passed on to Wycliffe and Huss [and Luther], and through these leaders produced the Reformation in Germany and England" (*Britannica,* 1947, XXV, "Waldenses," p.288).

Another important fact is evident as well, namely that the catalogue of earliest Waldensian doctrines closely parallel those of modern fundamentalism:

(1) The Holy Scriptures are inspired by God, which He intended as an authoritative guide for faith and practice.

(2) They practiced the beliefs expressed in the articles of the Apostle's Creed.

(3) They rejected all external rituals promoted by the Catholic Church, except for water baptism and Holy Communion. They particularly abhorred temples, vestments, images, pilgrimages, the worship of relics, etc., which they considered inventions of Satan.

(4) They rejected the papal doctrines of Purgatory, religious masses, and prayers for the dead.

(5) They rejected the sale of Indulgences and confessions to a priest—although they did teach that confessions to a fellow believer were both biblical and beneficial.

(6) They taught that both water baptism and Holy Communion were only symbols. Thus, they rejected the Church's concept of transubstantiation.

(7) They rejected the Church's complicated hierarchical system of leadership. As for their own organization, they allowed only bishops, priests and deacons as spiritual guides. Further, they taught that the marriage of the clergy was both biblical and *necessary.*

(8) Lastly, they denied any obligation to obey the Pope or any of his officials. Eventually, they went so far as to call Rome "the whore of Babylon" (see M'Clintock and Strong, X, 855).

Some church historians have claimed that the Waldenses did experience the Gifts of the Holy Spirit, including speaking in tongues. This is not at all surprising, since Waldo's followers were so dedicated to living by the rediscovered precepts of Scripture. They were especially careful to follow what the Bible teaches, rather than by the accumulation of invented Church rituals and unscriptural traditions invented by ecclesiastical legalism. Their spiritual adjustment to the Bible standard is admirable, to say the least!

The *New International Dictionary of the Christian Church* states that the Waldenses believed that God gave them visions and prophecies for their instruction and for the direction of their congregations (see "Waldenses," p.1026). Another source claims that they believed in and practiced divine healing, as well as speaking in tongues (Gordon F. Atter, *The Third Force*, p.13). Therefore, based on the testimony of these credible sources, we are justified in stating that the Waldenses were an active charismatic group of the twelfth and thirteenth centuries, noticeably long after the Apostles had gone on to their Rewards, and in addition, long after the New Testament had been formalized.

Furthermore, in view of the horrendous persecutions the Waldenses endured for centuries, the Waldenses were as much in need of the supernatural support of the Gifts of the Spirit as were the persecuted believers of the book of Acts. And since severe persecution is being endured by many Christians in the world even today, the Gifts of the Holy Spirit are equally as necessary in our time as they were then. In fact, whether in Bible days or today, the *consolation* of the Holy Spirit is always a welcome support for those who have to "resist the devil" to maintain a victorious Christian faith. The following admonition of the Apostle Paul to the Corinthians is applicable to today's believers as well:

> It is true that I am an ordinary, weak human being, but I don't use human plans and methods to win my battles. I use God's mighty weapons, not those made by men, to knock down the devil's strongholds. These weapons can break down every proud argument against God and every wall that can be built to keep men from finding Him (2 Cor.10:3-5, TLB).

Last of all, in the interest of fairness, we should observe that although the desire for reform was at first given long and powerful expression by the commoners of the Catholic world, it was the influence of a few *avant garde* Catholic clergy who gave the Reformation energy. The spiritual instincts of both the clergy and laity strongly emphasized that the dogmas and rituals of Catholic traditions were failing to minister to the soul-cry of the people. The medieval Catholic organization was elitist, favoring those adherents of power and position and neglecting—perhaps even enslaving—the ordinary populace. But it was eventually the influence of some of the educated Catholic clerics who at last provided leadership to activate the needed reforms:

(1) One of the earliest was *John Wycliffe* (c.1320-1384), an educator and secular clergyman of England. Motivated by his spiritual discoveries resulting from his own translation of the Greek New Testament, he voiced his opposition to the extensive immoral practices of the Catholic clergy, thereby angering the Church hierarchy. The fact that he resided in England no doubt protected him from martyrdom, for he died a natural death at age 64. But Catholic leaders, later in power and not content that Wycliffe escaped execution, exhumed his bones and burned them to ashes, which were then strewn on the River Wye so they might drift out to the world's oceans, there (they reasoned) to disappear forever.

(2) *John Huss* (c.1369-1415) was a Bohemian educator and religious reformer. Influenced by Wycliffe's translation of the Greek New Testament, Huss spoke out against the general moral depravity of his time, especially the worldliness of the clergy. He urged a return to the godliness emphasized in the teachings of the Gospels and the Epistles. Later, a hundred years before Luther, Huss was tricked into attending a Catholic Church council, supposedly to discuss doctrinal differences between himself and the Church. But in spite of

Catholic promises assuring him of safe passage, when he arrived at the Council of Constance, he was arrested and held in jail for eight months. Subsequently, he was condemned to die by being burned at the stake. According to *Fox's Book of Martyrs*, bundles of firewood were stacked around him up to his chin. He died July 6, 1415, but his dedication to biblical truth lived on in the Bohemian reform movement (Cp Shelly, p.232).

(3) *Girolamo Savanarola* (1452-1498) was a Dominican monk ministering in Florence, Italy. He, too, preached against the moral depravity of the clergy. Consequently, he was eventually hanged by the neck and then burned to ashes in the city square of Florence. Tourists even today can observe a large plaque positioned in the city square, "celebrating" Savanarola's memory—although it was awarded embarrassingly late.

Thus, the courage and commitment to biblical truth cost some of our spiritual forefathers a price beyond description, but their sacrifices coalesced the efforts for reform and influenced others to take a more aggressive stand against the Church's immorality, both physical and spiritual. Some of the later reformers will be discussed in the next chapter, among them Martin Luther (1483-1546), Philip Melancthon (1497-1560), Ulrich Zwingli (1484-1531), and John Calvin (1509-1564).

And so the Age of Spiritual Enlightenment—a Religious Renaissance in its own way—was set in motion. These famous Reformers influenced other clergymen to speak out against the corruptions of the time and in favor of biblical principles. Exposure to the Word of God provided spiritual motivation for the Protestant movements to rediscover the genuine Truths of the Bible—one after another—leading at last, in the nineteenth and twentieth centuries, to the rediscovery of the Baptism in the Holy Spirit and the accompanying ministry Gifts. According to the Scripture, these Gifts were designed for the encouragement of those who maintain a vibrant faith in the Lord Jesus Christ. And we today are the happy beneficiaries of those who courageously insisted on the revival of biblical experiences promised by the Lord—as we shall see in the following chapter.

Chapter 8

THE MINISTRY OF THE HOLY SPIRIT IN CHURCH HISTORY, 1550 TO 1900 A.D.

By the time the sixteenth century was in full progress, a growing number of non-Catholic Reform movements were insisting on expression. Some of these have become watchwords in church history, while many others arched through the night sky of the Dark Ages, meteor-like, and then disappeared forever. After the invention of the printing press in the early fifteenth century (c.1440), the increasing availability of the Word of God dramatically changed the course of all history, including the history of the Christian world.

At last, the public could read the Scriptures for themselves, and those who read were increasingly startled at how much the biblical patterns differed from those "ordained" rituals of the existing Church. True, many counter-Catholic movements had taken place prior to the beginning of the sixteenth century, but many more were to come! And all of these changes, flying in the face of established traditions, were painfully, often tragically, accomplished.

Martin Luther was a German Catholic priest and theologian, and subsequently a reformer, all because of his encounter with the Holy Scriptures. Early in his association with the Catholic priesthood, Luther faced a stubborn spiritual dilemma: he earnestly sought spiritual peace but could not find it in the prescribed penances advocated by his

Church leaders. Reverently but persistently, he continued to try, but with no success.

One day while he was reading the Epistle to the Romans, the Apostle Paul's statement, "The just shall live by faith" (Rom.3:16-17) was suddenly made real to him. At last, he experienced the inner assurance he had been seeking, and this discovery changed his life. But another problem appeared: from that moment on, he began noticing other discrepancies between the practices of the Church and the clear statements of the Bible. Consequently, as the truths of Scripture slowly dawned on him, he began to express publicly his disagreements with the Catholic Church. And so, on October 31, 1517, he nailed his famous 95 theses to the door of the Wittenberg Castle Church. Initially, he respectfully sought only for a dialogue about his objections.

But his action was perceived by most—both among his friends and the leaders of the Church—as a serious confrontation of Catholic authority. As a consequence, Luther was eventually excommunicated by Pope Leo X in 1520. Regrettably, there followed determined efforts to murder Luther, thereby (it was supposed) to benefit both God and the Church by exterminating a "notorious heretic." But German officials shielded Luther from assassination, largely because of their nationalistic loyalties, rather than strong religious convictions of their own.

His innovative theological ideas and his break with the Catholic Church eventually led to his becoming the primary leader of the German Reformation, thereby opening the door for many of Luther's affiliates to reexamine the prevailing theological positions of the Church (see Walker, pp.335-359).

After Martin Luther's ejection from the Church, Lutheranism continued to rush toward a determined "Protestant" ideology, undoubtedly all according to God's design. And this persistent reformation continued even after Luther's death in 1546. The pent-up longing for ministry relevant to the real-life needs of the populace, so long denied them but now at least promised, suddenly came flooding forth, demanding even more. Unbelievably, some of Luther's contemporary reformers even accused him of being only a "half reformer" because of his hesitancy to make major adjustments beyond his own initial rediscoveries.

Nonetheless, in many instances the new Protestant populations grew and grew, often becoming so dominant as to displace local governments, and/or often transforming existing Catholic churches into Lutheran congregations. In incidents of this kind, Catholic icons were usually sidelined politely so that the former Catholic cathedral might function as a Lutheran worship center. The results of this kind of transformation can still be observed today. For example, in Rothenberg, Germany, there are at least two former Catholic churches, both just off the city square, which have undergone the reorientation from Catholicism to Lutheranism, with the traditional Catholic icons still set aside.

But an interesting commentary on Luther's theology continues to surface in the annals of church history. The original source evidently is the German church historian R. Kuntze (1859) who wrote as follows:

Luther was easily the greatest evangelical man after the apostles, full of inner love to the Lord like John, hasty in deed like Peter, deep in thinking like Paul, cunning and powerful in speech like Elijah, uncompromising against God's enemies like David; prophet and evangelist, *speaker in tongues* and interpreter [all] in one person, equipped withal the gifts of grace, a light and pillar of the church. . . (quoted from R. Kuntze, p. 400, 1859 & p. 406, 1882, emphasis added).

It is possible that this statement, implying that Luther might have had some form of charismatic experience, was made as a memorial at the third centennial anniversary of Luther's death, observed on February 18, 1846. But at this point, one cannot be sure of its original intent because of the absence of corroborating testimony. Was it meant to indicate that Luther had actually experienced a personal Pentecost? Or was this statement intended only as a panegyric, lauding Luther's pioneering Protestant convictions? Or could this declaration actually be based on biographical information, not yet fully documented?

Regrettably, there is not enough evidence at this point to be absolutely certain. However, since the Pentecostal experience has historically cut across many "denominational" boundaries, it is not unreasonable to suppose that Luther, in his role as an "apostle" of Protestantism, may have privately enjoyed a Pentecostal experience. Certainly, the terminology used here relating to "tongues," "interpreter of tongues," "prophet," etc., does suggest that the "tongues" experience was not unknown to Luther's biographers—and perhaps even to Luther himself.

Be that as it may, one fact in history is very clear, Luther did have encounters with the Anabaptist prophets of Zwickau who reportedly were experiencing the Gifts of the Spirit in their congregations. Luther, however, seems to have considered them *Schwarmers,* or "fanatics" (So what else is new?) because he believed they were unnecessarily aggressive in their evangelizing efforts (see Walker, pp. 350-353).

Nonetheless, in his book *The Ministry of Healing,* Rev. A. J. Gordon quotes Luther as follows: "How often has it happened and still does, that devils have been driven out in the name of Christ, also by calling on his name [in] prayer that the sick have been healed?" (Gordon, p. 92). To illustrate Luther's belief in divine deliverance, Gordon observes further that healings did occur when Luther prayed for the sick *and* for the possessed:

> In 1541, when Myconius lay speechless in the final stages of consumption, Luther prayed and he was restored to health. Melancthon lay near death of a fever, face sunken and eyes glassy, knowing no one. But Luther sought God and he [Melancthon] began to mend from that hour. "I should have been a dead man," said Melancthon, "had I not been recalled from death itself by the coming of Luther." [Regarding Luther's deliverance ministry, A. J. Gordon continues] When called to deal with a demon-possessed girl, Luther laid hands on her, quoting, "The works [that] I do shall ye do also" [John 14:12] and prayed for her, whereupon she completely recovered" (Gordon, pp. 93-95).

Thus, the long-standing passion for spiritual renewal of meaningful worship led many to explore the Bible with increasing determination, in order to discover God's real intentions among mortals. So while Luther's teachings were dramatically transforming Germany, two other former

Catholic priests were challenging the thinking of Swiss congregations, all of which led to the Swiss Reformation, paralleling that of Germany. One of those priests was Ulrich Zwingli of Zurich; the other was John Calvin of Geneva. Historically, as Luther was guiding the Reformation in Germany, Ulrich Zwingli (1484-1531) was examining similar demands for Reform in Switzerland.

Like Luther, Zwingli was a disenchanted Catholic priest. In fact, early in his priesthood days, Zwingli had experienced his own moral failure—regrettably, not so unusual among the priests then. But after 1516, he began reading the Greek New Testament, translated by Erasmus the Dutch theologian. And, like Luther, he was ever more appalled at the godlessness of his world, and of his own life.

So Zwingli persevered in studying the Scriptures, a practice which eventually transformed his life. Accordingly, he began preaching to his congregations expositorily, directly from the Bible (Shelley, 1995, p. 249), and his innovative preaching style (at least it was innovative then) soon won Zwingli widespread favor with his congregations. As a result of his growing popularity, in 1519 he was invited to pastor the Great Church in Zurich, Switzerland. So by the time Luther was excommunicated in 1520, Zwingli was already being influenced by Luther's teaching. And as a consequence, in 1522, Zwingli himself publicly bolted from the Catholic priesthood.

Zwingli's growing Protestant influence in Switzerland eventually resulted in nine of the thirteen cantons (districts) of Switzerland turning Protestant. Four of those districts, however, remained militantly Catholic, and their Catholic inflexibility eventually led to outright warfare. As a consequence, Zwingli, in the interest of identifying with his people, felt obliged to join his parishioners on the battlefield. Unfortunately, however, in spite of his commendable courage, in 1531 Zwingli himself was killed, the most significant casualty of that conflict. He died at age forty-seven, his work not yet completed (Nichols, 1941, pp. 201-205). But the Sovereign Lord, God of the Swiss Reformation, raised up others to succeed him and to lead the Protestant cause to even greater experiences in the Lord.

But Zwingli was an important Reformer for another reason. His teachings led the "Anabaptists" to be concerned about a number of other religious practices that noticeably did not agree with Scripture. In that day particularly, it was to be expected that anyone examining the Bible for guidance regarding the Lord's "perfect" way would discover a whole trove of inconsistencies not yet dealt with. Once Luther's doctrine of the "priesthood of all believers" had opened the door to widespread Bible reading, others soon discovered additional discrepancies between the Scriptures and the ritualistic traditions of the Church.

In addition, there was a resulting move toward expository preaching of the Scriptures (for example: Zwingli and Calvin) rather than the allegorical method which had been so long fashionable. Researcher William R. Estep makes this enlightening comment in his book *The Anabaptist Story*):

Here for the first time in the course of the Reformation, a group of Christians dared to form a church after what was conceived to be the New Testament pattern. The Brethren [Re. "Anabaptists"] emphasized the absolute necessity of a personal commitment to Christ as essential to salvation and a prerequisite to baptism. The introduction of the believer's baptism [as one example] was not an unpremeditated act. . . Rather it was a culmination of an earnest searching of the Scriptures (p.11).

The "Brethren," as they preferred to call themselves, were scurrilously referred to by their contemporaries as the "Anabaptists," meaning "rebaptizers." This happened because of their highly controversial insistence that commitment to Christ must precede biblical water baptism. This position, of course, essentially negated the established Church's tradition of baptizing children, thus making those children members of the Catholic Church, long before they could choose for themselves. While there were other doctrinal differences which the Brethren considered more important, the nullification of infant baptism became the major touchstone of their controversy with the Church. And, regrettably, with other contemporary Protestants as well. Ritualistic traditions die very slowly!

The Anabaptists had their beginnings in Zwingli's Swiss Reformation, but when they proposed to make changes beyond those Zwingli had advocated—as elementary as those changes might seem to us today—they were considered radicals or fanatics. And as they attempted to adjust to recently discovered biblical patterns, not in compliance with even the Reformation churches, they found themselves at odds with other Protestants, too. Catholic Church ritualism had long prescribed that the little children of Catholic parents should be baptized by sprinkling or pouring in order to make them members of the Catholic faith. The Catholic reasoning, of course, was that water baptism was tantamount to being born again.

But by following the Scriptures, the Anabaptists came to believe that water baptism can only be meaningful if the baptismal candidate is old enough to make a conscious commitment to Jesus Christ. This, of course, would not be possible for a little child who had not yet come to an accountable age. On these grounds, the Anabaptists considered their own childhood baptisms as altogether meaningless, as though they had not been baptized at all— certainly not in the biblical sense.

Furthermore, they reasoned that after a genuine conversion to Christ, in order to be compliant with Scripture, they were compelled to be baptized in water again in order to demonstrate their lifelong commitment to the Savior. Sounds reasonable to moderns, but to those early Reformers the Anabaptists' arguments seemed heretical!

The Anabaptist practice of requiring a confession of faith before baptism may seem inconsequential to modern-day Christians, because most present-day believers readily accept this concept as the intent of Scripture. But not so for the sixteenth-century Reformers, Luther and Zwingli among them. These leading Reformers, not yet fully enlightened as to all the Truths of biblical theology, persecuted the Anabaptists unmercifully. In fact, the Protestant city Council of Zurich decided that in order to punish these "radicals" who had "the audacity" to disagree with traditions, they would first warn them of the consequences of their noncompliance, and if that overture was rejected, the delinquents were then marched out to the local river and pompously "rebaptized" by being held under the water until they were dead.

To some of the mistaken Reformers, it seemed in the realm of reason that "if the 'heretics' want water let them have it" (Shelley, pp. 247-249). The result? Persecutions that martyred thousands nearly wiped out the Anabaptists as a movement. But regardless, the Anabaptist doctrines live on today in their inheritors, the modern-day Mennonites and their Amish cousins.

The second important Swiss Reformer was John Calvin (1509-1564) who was born in France in July of 1509. Benefiting from the reputation of his well-to-do father, he was able to enter the University of Paris in 1523 at the age of fourteen. Very soon he proved himself a brilliant scholar, and he graduated in 1528 with a Master of Arts degree. Calvin's prosperous father had at first intended that his son pursue theology; but when the father had a falling-out with certain royal authorities, Calvin was enrolled at the University of Orleans to study Law. There he later earned a degree Law And his training in Law undoubtedly influenced his method of interpreting Scripture.

But God had ordained that Calvin become a theologian. So after his father died in 1531, Calvin once again turned his full attention to theological studies. During this time the young student had many occasions to read Luther's writings on the subject of salvation by faith in Jesus Christ. As a result, in 1533, at age 24, Calvin experienced what he called a "sudden conversion" because God spoke to him through the Scriptures (Walker, 1918, p.391).

From that moment on, he became increasingly critical of the apostasy he observed in the Catholic Church. His changed attitude was admittedly a dangerous preoccupation, for by so doing Calvin was aligning himself more and more with the Protestant Huguenots of France. Not long after, when his close friend Nicholas Cop gave a public oration in Paris, the speech sounded suspiciously Protestant (Calvin allegedly had written this address for Cop). The consequence was that both of them rather hurriedly decided it was the better part of wisdom to move to safer territory. So they arrived in Switzerland, "posthaste" (see Walker, pp.389-431).

In God's providence, Calvin showed up in Geneva at a time when that city's government was in serious disarray, because of the Genevan disagreements with the authoritarian demands of Catholic leaders. Certainly, the citizens of Geneva were greatly in need of leadership, and Calvin was able to oblige them. In fact, the man then in charge in Geneva pled with Calvin to remain in that city, even though Calvin had fully intended to go on to Strasbourg to teach.

Eventually, under Calvin's leadership, the Genevan canton declared its independence from Catholic rule, and Calvin subsequently established a form of government based on biblical principles, a government called a theocracy. It is of special interest that Calvin's exemplary theocracy later personally influenced John Knox to guide Scotland into the Protestant fold as well. Bernard Bresson, in his extensive historical study of medieval Pentecost, cites sources indicating Calvin's Reformation experiences were a product of his association with the Huguenots, who themselves repeatedly manifested the Gifts of the Holy Spirit in their meetings (*Studies in Ecstasy*, pp.40, 52). In addition, *Britannica* observes that when Calvin was at last well-established in Geneva, he secretly supported, in every way he could, those persecuted Protestant Huguenots in France (*Britannica Macropaedia*, III, 674,1980).

Thus, the Huguenots of France became an important link in the chain of events which awakened the whole Protestant movement of Europe to larger vistas of New Testament doctrine. So while Luther's revival in Germany was progressing, similar convictions began immediately to appear in France. This occurred, at least in part, because of the widespread circulation in France of Luther's writings, even influencing—as has been cited above—John Calvin's "sudden conversion." Officially, of course, France was a Catholic stronghold; and the "royals," the monarchs of that nation, were under great pressure from Rome to keep France in the Catholic camp—at any cost.

But once Protestantism was introduced into France, it grew by leaps and bounds, to the great alarm of both Rome and the Catholic royal families. By 1559, the Huguenots were strong enough to declare their first Protestant Council ("Synod"), in spite of the objections of the Catholic authorities. Indeed, by that time Marguerite of Valois, a sister of the Catholic king, had herself become a follower of the Huguenot teachings. And many others of the ruling noblemen of France had also become believers—among them Admiral Coligny and Henry of Navarre, both men of important political influence.

In 1561 the Cardinal of Sainte-Croix, greatly alarmed, wrote to the Pope, complaining that "The kingdom [of France] is already half Huguenot." Similarly, at about the same time, the ambassador from Venice, Micheli, wrote back to his government that no province in France was free from Protestants (see M'Clintock and Strong, IV, 391). As a consequence, the Catholics, imagining themselves seriously threatened by the Huguenots, contemplated ominous countermeasures, soon to be enacted!

In point of fact, the Huguenots were willing to coexist with the Catholics, but the Catholics were always reluctant. Through the years several compromises had been worked out, but neither the Pope nor the Catholic clerics could endure for very long the prickly presence of—or the aggressive evangelizing by—the Huguenots. Hundreds of nominally Catholic adherents were turning Protestant. Moreover, King Philip II of Spain felt it was his "holy" calling to exterminate Protestants wherever they were found—and by whatever means available. As a consequence, King Philip's shadowy influence was felt in France as it had been in England and other European countries. Since Protestants were usually considered as vermin to be destroyed, agreements could be made and then easily ignored by Catholic factions. In addition, incredibly, murder was often considered a viable option.

Thus, although the Catholic leadership of France initially resorted only to harassment, their tactics soon evolved into martyring the troublesome Protestants. This, in turn, exploded into outright mass murder of the hated Huguenots. The first incident of a Huguenot being burned at the stake occurred in 1523. And, amazingly, the Huguenots' religious freedom was not fully restored until after the French Revolution in 1789, 266 years of persecution with only occasional intermissions (*Britannica*, Micropaedia, V, 189). Brave believers, indeed!

One example of these deceptive intermissions occurred on St. Bartholomew's Day, in 1572. As the day approached, circumstances between the Protestants and the Catholics seemed relatively peaceful. Many Huguenot nobles had gathered in Paris for the festive occasion. In fact, an important wedding was planned for the leading Huguenot nobleman, Henry of Navarre and Marguerite of Valois, King Charles IX's sister (Walker, p.435).

But Catherine de Medici, the mother of the youthful King, had been in connivance with other Catholic leaders to take advantage of the unsuspecting Huguenots gathering in Paris for the occasion. A night-time attack was secretly planned, and executed, which ultimately massacred 8,000 of the visitors to the capital city. Admiral Coligny, the admired leader referred to above, was among those assassinated by the Catholic deception.

During the days which followed this surprise attack, thousands more Huguenots were systematically exterminated throughout the provinces of France. "Open season" had everywhere been declared on the Protestants. It has been conservatively estimated that in the mayhem which followed, over 70,000 Huguenots were unconscionably martyred. Ironically, the Pope, now convinced that all the Catholics involved had at last "accomplished the will of God," "sent congratulations to Catherine Medici, the king's mother. Both thought they were at last done with the Huguenots" (Nichols, p. 212).

Oh, but they were not! Many Huguenots lived on—perhaps to die yet another day—but alive, nonetheless, and still committed to their strong faith in the Lord Jesus Christ! In spite of the supposed demise of the Huguenots, there were survivors of that terrible massacre, and those survivors fled to the Alpine region of the Cevennes mountains, where the troubled remnant cried out to God for grace to endure. And a loving heavenly Father answered by pouring out His Holy Spirit, thereby "comforting" those harassed believers.

This massacre was the origin of the now famous "Cevennes prophets"—to which John Wesley later referred—who were strengthened with Pentecostal experiences by the Holy Spirit. Once again, the heavenly "Comforter," which Jesus had promised His believers, had fulfilled His purpose. In his text, *The Life and Letters of St. Paul* (p. 299), author David Smith observes that in 1685, during this time of severe persecution, as the Huguenots earnestly sought the Lord for consolation, "the spiritual Gifts of the Apostolic Church *reappeared*—miracles of healing, prophecy, and talking in tongues" (p. 299). By 1689, Pentecostal experiences were quite common among the Huguenots of the Cevennes.

James Hastings, in his *Encyclopedia of Religion and Ethics* (VII, p. 480), provides us further valuable information about these retiring, godly outcasts:

> An infectious ecstasy seized people of all ages and of both sexes. They heard supernatural voices. They spoke with tongues. . . uneducated persons gave utterance, when "seized by the spirit," to prophecies in the purest French, when all they knew was the *patois* Romanesque language of the Cevennes.

Some historians claim that "all" of their leaders were "prophets" and that [the Gift of] prophecy was what held them together for two hundred years" (Bresson, 1966, p.41). Bresson's research further claims that when under the anointing of the Holy Spirit, the Huguenots would quote "long passages of Scripture correctly, talked in tongues, prophesied coming events which were to occur a long distance [in time] from them and afterward the event(s) happened as foretold" (Bresson, p.42).

Through the years of persecution, many Huguenots, including members of the "French Prophets" of the Cevennes, fled to England, America, and to other countries, carrying with them the "Good News" of salvation, and of the ministry of the Holy "Comforter," and the Gifts of the Holy Spirit. For example, referring to the "French Prophets" who arrived in England, M'Clintock and Strong call attention to their charismatic and Pentecostal-like activities:

[These "French Prophets"] came over to England about 1706, and brought with them the "gift of prophecy," and soon made converts in England [many from the upper classes of English society]. The great subject of their predictions was the speedy establishment of Messiah's kingdom. Their message was (and they were to proclaim it as heralds to every nation under heaven) that the grand jubilee, "the acceptable year of the Lord," the accomplishments of those numerous scriptures concerning the *new heavens* and the *new earth, the kingdom of the Messiah,* the *marriage of the Lamb,* the *first resurrection,* and *the*

New Jerusalem. . . was *now* even at the door; . . .
(M'Clintock and Strong, III, 661, col. 2).

Further in this report, these Encyclopedists make it clear
that these French Huguenots anticipated having a part in the
fulfillment of their "end-time" prophecies. They expected this
to be accomplished by means of the "inspiration of the mighty
Gift of the Spirit," and that this mission would also be
"witnessed to by signs and wonders from heaven" (III, 661,
col. 2). These pronouncements of the Pentecostal-like French
Prophets will most certainly be recognized as similar to the
present-day   preachments   of   modern   Charismatics,
particularly the Pentecostals.

Near the end of their article, M'Clintock and Strong have
chosen to offer some personal evaluations which reveal their
unfortunate inclinations to scandalize the manifestations of
miracles in modern times; based, it would seem, on the same
philosophy which prompted Dr. Middleton's assertion that
the miraculous no longer occurs, since the Apostles are now
dead. We see this bias in the following passage of M'Clintock
and Strong's report on the "French Prophets":

These prophets also *pretended* [?] to the gift of
languages [tongues], of miracles, of. . . discerning the
secrets of the heart; the power of conferring the same
spirit on others by the laying on of hands, and the gift
of healing. To prove they were really inspired by the
Holy Ghost, they *alleged* [?] the complete joy and
satisfaction they experienced, the spirit of prayer
which was poured forth upon them, and the answer of
their prayers by the Most High (p. 661, col. 2).

"Pretended"? "Alleged"? Oh, Really? Couldn't their own documented report of eighteenth century "Prophets" just as easily been describing events that occurred again and again in the book of Acts? Their theological prejudices—obviously present in their report—do not mean the events they describe did not really happen, although they seem anxious to imply these Pentecostal experiences were imagined. In fact, the M'Clintock and Strong report indicates that some sort of unusual spiritual experiences were happening, evidenced by the fact that people were being changed for the better—even the numerous prominent upper-class believers who became Huguenots. And the theological doubters—like those of Jerusalem in Acts 2—offered rationalistic criticisms, which turned out to be totally false.

But back to the events of Saint Bartholomew's Day. The deception employed then was not the first—nor was it to be the last—of the premeditated and persistently planned extermination of the Protestants. Through the years, although the Huguenots were pacifists theologically, they soon learned that the only possibility of survival was to resort to armed resistance when negotiations had utterly failed. The reason? The Huguenots were willing to arrange coexistence, but the Catholics would never comply!

Because of the Romanists' repeated efforts to expurgate the Protestants from the kingdom, at least eight major civil wars took place in France from 1559 through the late 1700's (M'Clintock and Strong, IV, 391-397). After continued harassment of the Huguenots, "In 1715 King Louis XIV announced that he had [at last] ended all exercise of the Protestant religion in France" (*Britannica*, Micropaedia, V, 189, 1980).

However, during that time, thousands upon thousands of the Huguenots had fled the tribulations of France for the relative security of other countries. But the massive emigration of Huguenot artisans and nobility seriously impacted the French national economy. By the mid-1700s, the general population of France had grown increasingly weary of the meaningless, murderous mayhem caused by the personal prejudices of their rulers. As most are no doubt aware, the French Revolution of 1789 ensued, and the ironic results were the complete restoration of religious freedoms for the Huguenots.

While the Huguenots, elsewhere in Europe, were struggling for survival, the "Quakers" of England were exploring the ramifications of a deeper spiritual life. The word "Quakers" was actually a derogatory label invented by outside observers attempting to describe the unusual behavior of the "Friends" to the moving of the Holy Spirit in their midst. The Quakers, however, preferred to be identified as the "Society of Friends." Nonetheless, their responses as they worshipped were decidedly charismatic; for as they waited before the Lord for "inner light," or inspired direction, they often trembled physically.

They followed the teachings of their founder, George Fox (1624-1691), who abhorred the cold, ritualized worship practices of the dominant Church. They believed, instead, that their worship should be fully directed by the Holy Spirit. Thus, in their meetings, any believer—women as well as men—could sing, or read the Scriptures, or deliver an exhortation impromptu as the Holy Spirit led them. Based on his extensive research of historical sources, Bernard L. Bresson makes this comment about the Quakers:

> A practical mysticism seems to [have] pervaded the entire Quaker Movement. Their literature records visions, healings, prophecies, and a power which they liken to Pentecost. There are many references to the moving of the Spirit (p. 68).

As an example, Bresson provides a primary quote derived from the Quaker literature, as recorded by W. C. Braithwaite and others (see *The Message and Mission of Quakerism*, 1912, p.16). Their record is as follows: "We received often the pouring down of the Spirit upon us, and our hearts were made glad and our tongues loosed and our mouths opened, and we spake with new tongues as the Lord gave utterance. . . " Reports of this kind confirm that the *charismata* of the Holy Spirit continued into modern times, in spite of the sophistical contrary arguments of the "cessationists." It does seem that God insists on being in charge!

Of course, these practices were viewed with great suspicion by the general public of that time, steeped in traditions as they were. As a consequence, the Quaker population suffered much persecution, including martyrdom for some, as they sought to follow their consciences. Our own state of Pennsylvania was established in 1682 by William Penn—himself a devout Quaker—in order to provide the Quakers a haven from persecutions which they had been suffering in both England and America. Somewhat later, according to his own written testimonies, John Wesley and his Methodist followers responded agreeably with the Quakers and eventually some of the Methodists also experienced the charismatic Gifts of the Holy Spirit (Braithwaite, p.16).

The Wesleys, John and Charles, were born into a devout Anglican minister's family of nineteen siblings, although eight died in infancy. John was the fifteenth, born June 17, 1703; Charles was the eighteenth, born December 18, 1707. Both were destined to be co-laborers in the ministry of evangelizing England and other parts of the world, although Charles did not entertain exactly the same deep religious convictions as his brother's.

John Wesley's family life and his theological training tended to reinforce his inclinations to High Church formalism; and as a result, his earliest ministry was largely uneventful—perhaps even unsuccessful. But during his voyage to America to fulfill a church assignment in Georgia, John Wesley became acquainted with Moravian missionaries who challenged the young minister to seek a deeper Christian experience. Indeed, already vaguely conscious of a spiritual void in his life, John Wesley greatly desired just such a deeper experience.

Wesley's two-and-one-half years in Georgia were generally a disappointment to himself, to his brother Charles, and to his colonist parishioners as well. So he and Charles returned to England earlier than they had intended. And at home again in England, Wesley again met faithful Moravian brethren, who by their gentle exhortations led Wesley to a genuine experience of conversion. The Moravians, having experienced the Gifts of the Spirit in their congregations on the Continent and in England, influenced Wesley to recognize the validity of these charismatic experiences, leading to John's later emphasis on the doctrine of entire sanctification. Professor Robert H. Nichols of Auburn Theological Seminary (see *The Growth of the Christian Church*, 1941, pp. 274-275) describes the circumstances of Wesley in 1738:

> . . . At this time he was a man of zealous but rather severe and formal piety. He held High Church opinions, and made much of observance of the rules and seasons of the church. By narrow-minded insistence on this he came to grief in Georgia. There he fell in with some Moravian missionaries, in whom he saw a Christian confidence and a joy which he had never known. Thus began a deep change in his religious life. This went on after his return to England, under the influence of other Moravians. It culminated in his "conversion," which occurred in 1738, during a religious service in London (Cp. Williston Walker, pp. 507-518).

Wesley himself describes the moment of his conversion: "I felt I did trust in Christ, Christ alone, for salvation, and an assurance was given me that he had taken away my sins, even mine, and saved me from the law of sin and death" (Nichols, p. 275).

Wesley was so fascinated by the spiritual power manifested by these Moravians that in less than three weeks after his conversion, he visited their religious center in Germany, called *Herrnhut*, a Moravian village located on Count Zinzendorf's estate. There Wesley spent two weeks in "Marienborn" conferring with Zinzendorf, himself a devout Moravian, and other Moravian believers (see W. Walker, p. 513). These Moravian contacts, and those of the refugee Huguenots arriving in England, influenced Wesley to be very favorable toward charismatic manifestations. Wesley's journals abound with references to Pentecostal-like demonstrations which occurred among his followers during his meetings, and Wesley defended their authenticity, sometimes to the uneasiness of his more formally oriented fellow ministers.

But one of Wesley's most trusted preachers, Thomas Walsh, recorded the following charismatic experience in his journal. The event is dated March 8, 1750: "This morning the Lord gave me a language that I knew not of, raising my soul to Him in a wonderful manner" (quoted by Frodsham, p. 258). Thus, Wesley made it clear that he believed in the continuance of "tongues" and other Gifts of the Holy Spirit referred to in the Bible.

For example, in his sermon entitled "The More Excellent Way" (see Sermon #89, in *The Works of John Wesley*, Thomas Jackson, ed., 2nd series, vol. 7, pp. 26-27), Wesley observed as follows:

> . . . St. Paul has been speaking of the extraordinary gifts of the Holy Ghost; such as healing the sick; prophesying in the proper sense of the word, that is, foretelling things to come; speaking with strange tongues, such as the speaker had never learned; and the miraculous interpretation of tongues. . .

> It does not appear that these extraordinary gifts of the Holy Ghost were common in the Church for more than two or three centuries. We seldom hear of them after the fatal period when the Emperor Constantine called himself a Christian; and from a vain

imagination of promoting the Christian cause . . . heaped riches and power and honor upon the Christians in general, but in particular upon the Christian Clergy. . . The cause of this was not, (as has been vulgarly supposed) "because there was no more occasion for them" because [supposedly] all the world was become Christian. This is a miserable mistake; not a twentieth part of it was then nominally Christian. [No,] The real cause was [that] "the love of many," almost all Christians, so called, was "waxed cold." The Christians had no more of the Spirit of Christ than the other Heathens. The Son of Man, when He came to examine his Church could hardly "find faith upon the earth. . . "

John Emory, editor of *The Works of John Wesley*, cites another very relevant statement from Wesley's journals, as Wesley sought to explain the decrease in the frequency of the charismatic gifts through the medieval period. Wesley wrote:

. . . The grand reason why the miraculous gifts were so soon withdrawn was, not only that faith and holiness were well-nigh lost, but that dry, formal, orthodox men began to ridicule whatever gifts they had not themselves; and to deny them all as either madness or imposture.

. . . There is nothing either in the Old Testament or the New which teaches that miracles were to be confined within the limits of the apostolic or the Cyprianic [post-apostolic] age, or that God hath precluded himself from working miracles of any kind or degree, in any age to the end of time (Wesley, vol. 6, p.556).

As one reads this, it becomes very evident that Wesley had the deepest of convictions that the Lord was still doing miracles in modern times, just as He had done in Bible times. Moreover, Wesley supported this claim for the continuance of biblical manifestations of the Holy Spirit by recording his own experiences of several hundreds of healing miracles during his own itinerant ministry throughout England. So, then, we are justified in agreeing with the Scripture, "Jesus Christ is *the same* Yesterday, Today, and Forever" (Hebrews 13:8). As the Apostle Paul wrote in Romans 3:3-4, "For what if some did not believe? Shall their unbelief make the faith of God without effect? God forbid: yea, let God be true, but every man a liar…" (KJV).

The continuance of spiritual Gifts in the biblical pattern is evident also in the nineteenth century. While there are many reports that could be cited here, a noteworthy example is the powerful charismatic revival in England associated with the Irvingites—so called because Edward Irving (1792-1834) was their leader.

The Irvingites repeatedly experienced charismatic gifts which powerfully stirred London (and all England as well as Scotland) so that a number of that nation's social and political leaders became followers of Rev. Irving. Included among them were Sir James Mackintosh, statesman; Sir David Wilkie, artist; F. D. Maurice, theologian; and Samuel Taylor Coleridge, Thomas DeQuincey, Charles Lamb, and Thomas Carlyle, English authors of renown (see Arnold Dallimore, *Forerunner of the Charismatic Movement*, pp. 46-47).

The principal leader of this revival, Edward Irving, was born in Scotland to Presbyterian parents—his father a Covenanter, his mother of Huguenot background—who ambitiously determined that their son Edward would be a minister. Indeed, Edward willingly prepared himself for that profession by graduating from the University of Edinburgh (1805). Subsequently, he served in minor ministerial roles in his denomination until he was chosen to serve as assistant pastor to Dr. Chalmers of St. John's of Glasgow, where he developed an enviable reputation as a pulpit orator and a pastor.

As a consequence of his success in Scotland, in 1822 he was sent to London to be the senior pastor of the Scottish Caledonian Church on Cross Street, which was slowly languishing into oblivion. Although the Church at the beginning had only fifty members, Irving's anointed preaching was soon attracting large crowds; and in three months his church building, designed for 1500, was filled beyond capacity. At this point, he enjoyed acclaim from many of the important personages of London society mentioned above (Cp. M'Clintock and Strong, IV, 662-665).

So what might have been the cause of Irving's developing successes? One biographer of 1860 stated the following possible *physical* reasons:

> The preacher's great stature, his bushy black hair hanging down in ringlets, his deep voice, his solemn manner, the impressiveness of his action, his broad Scotch dialect, his. . . forcible style, all combined to rivet attention, and made you feel that you were in the presence of a power. Nor did his matter (sic, manner

) belie the impression which was thus created. He was bent upon accomplishing the Gospel ministry in saving souls from death. . . (M'Clintock and Strong, IV, 662, col. 2)

But other biographers have noted what is undoubtedly a more significant reason, the special empowerment of the Holy Spirit. By 1830 Irving was teaching his London congregation that the initial evidence of a believer's receiving the Baptism in the Holy Spirit is his or her speaking in tongues. Furthermore—according to Irving—until the believer speaks in tongues, he has not yet received the Gift of the Holy Spirit. As a result of Irving's teaching, the first public manifestation of the Gift of tongues in his Church occurred on April 30, 1831 (Bresson, p.96). And as one might expect, numerous other spiritual gifts followed.

These charismatic manifestations were generally well received and enjoyed by Irving's parishioners. But, tragically, Irving ventured too far, to the detriment of himself and his congregation. He began teaching that prophesies given under the inspiration of the Holy Spirit should be received as equivalents to the Scriptures. Without question, the Lord of heaven "honors His Word above His own Name"(Psalm 138:2). Unfortunately, however, it is because of this error that too many Bible scholars argue that *everything* which Irving did was heretical—and that is not true. Of course, Irving was very wrong to equate ecstatic speech with God's holy Word. And he suffered a heart-breaking decline because of his mistake. As a consequence, many in Irving's own congregation began to feel uneasy with this latest teaching. This uneasiness grew, and the shortly thereafter the congregation began to object openly.

And, at last, their objections crescendoed into a storm of disapproval.

The unpleasant conclusion occurred in April of 1832, as Irving's own church members chose to relieve him of his pastorate. Finally, in March of 1833, the General Presbytery of the Church of Scotland deposed Edward Irving from the ministry he loved so much. It seems likely that Irving had intruded into God's Holy of holies, and he suffered the most painful consequences. Irving died the next year on December 7, 1834, at the age of forty-two (*Britannica*, XII, 694 and Bresson, p.100).

In spite of his deviation from scriptural doctrines, many of those who opposed him respectfully attended his funeral and praised his selfless ministry to others. As M'Clintock and Strong observed, "Of Irving it may truly be conceded that a more devout or earnest spirit has not appeared on the stage of time in the nineteenth century" (IV, 665).

It would, however, be a monumental mistake to suppose that Edward Irving was the only bright star in the expanding Pentecostal constellation of the nineteenth century. Far from it! There were other powerful revivals led by anointed ministers such as Charles Finney (1792-1875), and Dwight L. Moody (1837-1899), both of whom testified of Pentecostal-like experiences empowering their efforts.

For example, shortly after Finney's conversion in 1821, he was so conscious of his lack of spiritual power that he waited on the Lord, asking for supernatural enablement. One day, as he tarried in prayer, he was mightily moved upon by the Lord. He gives testimony of this in his *Autobiography* (Revell, p. 20) where Finney referred to this experience as the "Baptism in the Holy Spirit" and described the occasion as follows: "I wept aloud with joy and love. . . and literally bellowed out the unutterable gushings of my soul."

The remarkable intensity of Finney's unique experience could just as easily been described in the words of Paul in Romans 8:26-27: ". . . But the Holy Spirit prays for us with groanings that cannot be expressed in words. And the Father who knows all hearts knows what the Spirit is saying, for the Spirit pleads for us believers in harmony with God's own will" (NLT). Here, Paul is obviously referring to the believer's experiences of praying in ecstatic utterances ("tongues"), motivated by the Holy Spirit.

Finney's experience was so intense that he reported he was constrained to ask the Lord to let up a little. But the experience of that anointing was the impetus for Finney's powerfully successful revivals. *Britannica's* biographical sketch of Finney has this to say: ". . . He fomented spirited revivals in the villages of upstate New York. . . His revivals [also] achieved spectacular success in large cities, and in 1832 he began an almost continuous revival in New York City. . . [which] led his supporters to build. . . the Broadway Tabernacle [for him] in 1834"(*Britannica*, Micropaedia, IV, 145, 1980).

Dwight L. Moody was also mightily used of the Lord to bring revival to both America and the United Kingdom. Moody was born in Massachusetts and in 1854 was converted from Unitarianism to Fundamentalist Evangelicalism. During the Civil War he worked with the Young Men's Christian Association (YMCA), and in the 1870s and 1880s he and Ira

D. Sankey conducted evangelistic meetings in Great Britain but with only moderate success at the beginning.

In his disappointment with the results of his evangelistic efforts, Moody began seeking the Lord for the reasons. Perhaps in answer to Moody's prayers, he met two Christian ladies who encouraged him to wait before the Lord for the enduement of spiritual power (reminiscent of Aquilla and Priscilla's instructions to Apollos). Consequently, Moody retreated to his room and did what they advised. Following is Moody's own account of the results:

> I was crying all the time that God would fill me with His Spirit. Well, one day, in the city of New York—oh, what a day—I cannot describe it, I seldom refer to it; it is almost too sacred to name. . . I can only say that God revealed Himself to me, and I had an experience of His love [so] that I had to ask him to stay His hand. [After that] I went to preaching again. The sermons were not different; I did not present any new truths, and yet hundreds were converted. I would not be placed back where I was before that blessed experience for all the world—it would be as the small dust on the balance (See The Life of D. L. Moody, p.149, by William R. Moody; New York: Revell, 1900.).

From that moment, Moody's ministry was noticeably enriched. By his own admission, many, many more people came to the Lord, people were often healed, some prophesied under the anointing of the Holy Spirit, and some even spoke with tongues. Spiritual gifts similar to those recorded in Acts were occurring. Stanley H. Frodsham records the following incident, reported by Rev. Robert Boyd, of one such occurrence at the YMCA in Sunderland, England:

> When I got to the rooms of the Y.M.C.A. I found the meeting on fire. The young men were speaking in tongues and prophesying. What on earth did it all mean? Only that Moody had been addressing them that afternoon. Many of the clergy were so opposed to the movement that they turned their backs upon our poor innocent Y.M.C.A., for the part we took in the work; but afterward, when the floodgates of divine grace were opened, Sunderland was taken by storm. . . The people of Sunderland warmly supported the movement, in spite of their spiritual advisers. There was a tremendous work of grace. (Moody and Sankey in Great Britain, 1875; also reported in Moody and His Work by W. H. Daniels, 1876).

In addition to the examples of Pentecostal experiences listed above, any dedicated researcher will discover that there are many other historical sources describing similar visitations of the Spirit in the nineteenth century. For example, additional accounts can be discovered by perusing Stanley Frodsham's *With Signs Following* (particularly chapters 1, 23 and 24), and other sources, among which is Smith's Bible Dictionary. All of these reports are from a dedicated researcher/author of the modern period under consideration. Likewise, peruse the last three chapters of Bernard L. Bresson's *Studies in Ecstasy*, each of which will provide additional documented information on this late nineteenth-century period of church history.

Finally, several sources, among them the texts listed above, tell of John Wesley's encounter with a noted cessationist, a contemporary of Wesley, named Dr. Conyers Middleton, who published a book entitled *Introductory Discourse and the Free Inquiry into Miraculous Powers* (London, 1749). In this publication, Dr. Middleton argued as follows: "After apostolic times, there is not, in all history, one instance; either well attested, or even so much as mentioned, of any particular person who had ever exercised that gift [the "Gifts of the Holy Spirit"], or pretended to exercise it in any age or country whatever." A very self-assured claim, but remarkably mistaken for someone claiming to be a scholar.

This statement is particularly surprising in view of Dr. Middleton's alleged scholarship, especially when he implies by his statement that he had searched through history and found nothing at all. But the historical records absolutely contradict his claims. His contemporary, John Wesley, also contradicted Middleton, citing as proof the experiences of the prophets of the Cevennes (Huguenots), well-known in England by that time. Evidently, Dr. Middleton was so certain of his hypothesis, that he did not feel it necessary to research the documents of Church History, which would have proven him inaccurate.

Furthermore, because of his supposed scholarship, he has been quoted, virtually verbatim, by subsequent scholars, even into the twentieth century. One example of this can be found in Coneybeare & Howson's classic and otherwise commendable work, *The Life and Epistles of Saint Paul* (1906). Therein Conybeare authored the following statement:

The feature which most immediately forces itself on our notice, as distinctive of the Church in the Apostolic age, is its possession of supernatural gifts. Concerning these, our whole information must be derived from Scripture, because they appear to have vanished with the disappearance of the Apostles themselves, and there is no authentic account of their existence in the Church in any writings of a later date than the books of the New Testament (see chapter XIII, p.372d; also footnote #6, pp. 451-452).

But more recent and more *careful* scholarship, of course, has proven how immensely inaccurate Dr. Middleton and his later cessationist colleagues have been. It is possible that these renowned men felt so secure in their oft-repeated presuppositions that they did not need to research the records carefully for themselves. It cannot be denied that the supernatural Gifts of the Spirit have at times diminished alarmingly. But equally without question, it cannot be denied that there are many verifiable incidents in church history which tell of the Holy Spirit's Gifts being "poured out," even during the medieval church's darkest hours.

However, those "infrequent" sprinkles of blessing in medieval times have become a torrent in the twentieth and twenty-first centuries, a "Latter Rain" downpour of Pentecostal manifestations. These Gifts are helping to mature the Final Harvest, just as was prophesied by Joel to occur in the "Last Days" (see Joel 2:28-29). Think of it! The Master of the Harvest—less interested in preserving denominational names than in gathering the precious harvest—is "paying" workers hired at the end of the "day" just as much as He did those workers employed at the beginning (see Matt. 20:1-16).

The unfolding story of modern-day Pentecost most certainly supports this assertion, as we shall observe further in the chapters which follow.

Chapter 9

"Is This That?":
The Holy Spirit in the
Twentieth Century

Just as our Lord Jesus, the Messiah, was crucified at God's appointed time, fulfilling the Old Testament symbolism of the Passover Lamb, so it was that the initial outpouring of Pentecost in Acts occurred in accordance with God's timetable. The event occurred precisely "when the Day of Pentecost was fully come" (Acts 2:1-2). Significant timing, indeed! Similarly, it seems likely that the timing for the arrival of the twentieth century outpouring of Pentecost was also ordained by God. The present-day Revival of Pentecost began in America on the very first day of the new century, January 1, 1901. Was that just an accident? Is anything occurring under the guidance of a Sovereign God ever an accident? It seems more likely that God was once again signaling His well-ordered plan, this time the conclusion of the prophesied "last days," leading to the "Final Harvest."

In conjunction with this subject of God's timing of biblical prophecy, Joel of the Old Testament provides us with other textual markers. For example in Joel 2:23, Joel cites the metaphor of the "early rain" and the "latter rain." Other Old Testament prophets had also made reference to *rain* and *harvest* as symbols of God's blessings and/or—lacking that—His judgment. The event which occurred at Pentecost in Jerusalem, then, is the fulfillment of Joel's reference to the "early rain," an event which would begin the spiritual harvesting of the "last days."

It seems logical, then, to assume that the "early rain" which fell on the Day of Pentecost opened the period Peter referred to as the "last days." And the "latter rain" would be expected to fall upon believers near the end of the Church Age, as it certainly has in the twentieth and twenty-first centuries. Of course, it is also reasonable to assume the modern-day "latter rain" is designed to mature the world's "final harvest" so that that harvest of the redeemed can be completed before the Revelation of Christ and His final Judgment of the Nations. If this reasoning is accurate—and we believe it is—then there will be a two-fold final harvest, the "harvest" of the Redeemed, followed shortly thereafter by the "harvest" of the Rebellious. With this in mind, compare Matthew 25:31-46, Jesus' parable of the five wise and the five foolish virgins awaiting the arrival of the Bridegroom.

In fact, this concept of completing the harvest in a timely manner seems to be supported further by the concluding narration of Joel's prophecy in chapter 3. Joel 3 provides specific information about those events which will happen during the period after the harvest is completed, that is, after the Church Age closes. Jeremiah also makes reference to a period similar to this by reminding the wayward Jews, "The harvest is past, the summer is ended, and we are not saved" (Jer. 8:20). So Joel chapter 3 apparently describes that which the Lord Jesus had explained to His disciples: "The night cometh when no man can work" (see John 9:4).

Obviously, Joel chapter 3 follows immediately after the prediction of the outpouring of Pentecost in Joel 2:28-32. Chapter designations have never been considered inspired, so it is acceptable for us to remember chapter 3 is a legitimate continuation of the historical events relating to the prophecy of Pentecost in Joel 2:28-32. Chapter 3:1-2 then, provide us additional time-related devices strengthening the hypothesis that the "latter rain" of prophecy is linked to the Pentecostal Revival of modern times, the "latter rain" of modern times just before the second coming of Jesus Christ.

Joel 3:1 reads, "In those days and at that time...." Precise detail is used here, logically connecting the experiences of Israel's Return to their homeland with the promised last-day outpouring of the Holy Spirit. These grammatical/logical signals in chapter 3 become important in our exegesis of Joel, linking the "latter-rain" outpouring of the Holy Spirit, near the end of this Church Age, with the return of the Jews to their homeland and the recovery of Jerusalem by Israel (Ref. Joel 3:1). These events have all happened in the twentieth century, within a few years of one another—and hardly just by accident.

Our effort here is *not* designed to set dates for the Lord's Return! But Jesus did rebuke the Pharisees for failing to discern the "signs of the times," even though they were arrogantly adept at discerning the face of the sky (see Lk. 12:54-56). So, in our time, Israel did gain international recognition in May of 1948, followed later by the recovery of Jerusalem in 1967. Indeed, the passages in chapters 2 and 3 are an essential part of Joel's predictions of the end-of-the-age outpouring of the Holy Spirit. As the ancient prophecy declares: "In the last days I will pour out my Spirit upon *all* flesh. . . ." (Acts 2:17, emphasis added). And when God says He "will," He will do exactly what He said. We can count on it happening! Only, we do not know precisely when.

Amazingly, the modern-day outpouring of the Holy Spirit—paralleling the explosion of Pentecost in the New Testament—has become an important event in modern history. This is particularly true among people living in deprived countries which have not had the spiritual opportunities afforded the so-called "civilized" world. Occasionally, I hear cynical comments by leaders of classical denominations implying that the Pentecostals in the United States are less effective—perhaps even less sophisticated— because the Pentecostals have smaller membership roles in the USA than overseas. The truth may well be because Americans have had their opportunities many times over, and now God is giving others who have not yet heard the Good News a chance to respond. In the harvest-time vernacular among farmers, a "burnt-over field" is understood as a hopelessly tragic event.

But, multitudes *are being won* to Christ in those fields overseas, which have not had the opportunities enjoyed by Americans. For example, on one of my recent travels, I passed through an International airport and was assigned a pleasant, African-born young man to help carry my bags. In fact, he seemed to be bubbling with joy, and as we talked I learned he was both a born-again Christian and a Pentecostal, recently arrived here from Africa. I inquired about his spiritual life and discovered he was joyously converted from Islam. Then, being even more curious, I asked about his church affiliations and was delighted to hear that he was a member of a very energetic African Church of 30,000. I was astonished at the numbers, but delighted at the victories he told me about. It is wonderful to hear that God is winning!

So what are the particulars of the revival of modern Pentecost? At the beginning of the twentieth century, Agnes

Ozman, along with her fellow students were praying that they might receive the Baptism in the Holy Spirit. They reasoned, "Since the Holy Spirit Baptism had taken place in the apostolic church of Acts, why shouldn't it be available for modern Christians?" A heart-warming line of thinking. indeed. At the very beginning of the twentieth century, this group of seekers was a part of a rather widespread interest among "holiness" believers in a renewal of experiences like those in Acts.

Thus, a modern-day Pentecost opened the century, as if by design. Historians generally agree that the beginning year of any century begins at '01. This means, of course, that January 1, 1901, is precisely the beginning date of the twentieth century. And on that date, Miss Ozman "spoke in tongues" she had never learned, as the initial evidence of being Baptized in the Holy Spirit—exactly as believers had experienced in the book of Acts. Significantly, the same initial "tongues" experience had recurred again and again in the book of Acts when the believers received the Holy Spirit, and now it was happening again..

Ozman and thirty-four others had enrolled in Charles F. Parham's Bethel Bible College in Topeka, Kansas. Intentionally, they decided the Bible would be their only textbook. All gathered there in "Stone's Mansion," in the suburbs of Topeka, Kansas for the specific purpose of searching the Scriptures. They "tarried" persistently, praying in three-hour shifts for a fresh manifestation of the Holy Spirit. These events remind us of Jesus' promise in Luke 11:11-13:

If a son asks for bread from any father among you, will he give him a stone. . . . If you then, being evil, know how to give good gifts to your children, how much more will your heavenly Father give the Holy Spirit to those who ask Him!

The widespread longing and praying in the late nineteenth and early twentieth centuries for a fresh outpouring of the Holy Spirit would not—could not—go unanswered for long by a loving Lord who is known for keeping His promises!

Stanley H. Frodsham, one of the earliest twentieth-century Pentecostal historians, has provided a wealth of information in his book *With Signs Following* (1926, rev.1941) among the reports is Miss Ozman's personal testimony of the twentieth-century outpouring of the Holy Spirit:

In October 1900 I went to this Topeka school, which was known as Bethel College. We studied the Bible by day and did much work downtown at night. Much time was spent in prayer every day and all the time.
Like some others, I thought I had received the Baptism in the Holy Ghost at the time of my consecration, but when I learned that the Holy Spirit was yet to be poured out in greater fullness, my heart became hungry. At times I longed more for the Holy Spirit to come in than for my necessary food....
On watchnight [December 31, 1900] we had a blessed service, praying that God's blessing might rest upon us as the new year came in. During the first day of 1901 the presence of the Lord was with us in a marked way, stilling our hearts to wait upon Him for greater things. A spirit of prayer was upon us in the evening. It was

nearly eleven o'clock that it came into my heart to ask that hands be laid upon me that I might receive the gift of the Holy Ghost. As hands were laid upon my head the Holy Spirit fell upon me, and I began to speak in tongues, glorifying God. I talked several languages. It was as though rivers of living water were proceeding from my innermost being.

On January 2, some of us went down to Topeka to a mission. As we worshiped the Lord I offered prayer in English and then prayed in another language, in tongues. A Bohemian, who was present, said I spoke his language and he understood what I said. Some months later, when at a schoolhouse with others, holding a meeting, I spoke in tongues under the power of the Spirit and another Bohemian understood me. Since then, others have understood other languages I have spoken. (Frodsham, p.20)

Another young lady, Lillian Thistlewaite, also attended that meeting in Topeka's "Stone's Mansion," and she experienced similar manifestations of the Spirit. Miss Thistlewaite reported the details as follows:

An upper room had been set aside for tarrying before the Lord. We would spend every spare moment in audible or silent prayer, in song or in just waiting upon Him. The presence of the Lord was very real and there were definite heart searchings.

Through the Spirit I received this message, "Praise the Lord for the Baptism." A great joy came into my soul and . . . I tried to praise the Lord in English but could not. So I just let the praise come as it would in a new language that was given. The floodgates of glory were wide open. The Holy Spirit had come to me, even to me, to speak not of Himself but to magnify Christ. And, oh, what a wonderful, wonderful Christ He revealed. All around me I heard great rejoicing while others spoke in tongues and magnified God. . .

With simultaneous movement, we began to sing together, each one singing in his new language but all in perfect harmony. As we sang "All Hail the Power of Jesus' Name" and other familiar hymns, it would be impossible to describe the glory of His presence in our midst. The cloven tongues of fire had been seen by some when the evidence [of the Spirit] was received.

As we went into meetings it seemed impossible that any one could resist the messages given. Some, understanding the languages spoken, were convinced. But with others the prophecy was fulfilled, "With men of other tongues and other lips will I speak unto this people; and yet for all that will they not hear Me, saith the Lord"(1 Cor. 14:21; Isa. 28:11-12) (Frodsham, pp. 21-22).

Additionally, among those students at Stone's Mansion were twelve credentialed ministers of various denominations, who subsequently received the same experience. One of these twelve was Howard D. Stanley, who wrote of his experience in a letter to Superintendent E. N. Bell, dated January 17, 1922. This letter is detailed in Carl Brumback's book, *Suddenly From Heaven* (1961):

About 10 o'clock while in one of the upper rooms cloven tongues like as of fire came down into the corner of the room (I saw them), and suddenly our vocal cords and tongues changed so that we began to speak in other tongues and praise . . . And those who could speak English stood to their feet and sang the old song: "The Comforter Has Come!" (Brumback, p. 25)

In the few days which followed, at least half of the thirty-five students also received this same *glossalalic* experience, among them the leader of the group, Rev. Charles Parham himself. All of these participants had previously been actively involved in Christian work but had never received the Gift of the Holy Spirit's empowerment. That night Parham had ministered at a Free Methodist meeting, and although he arrived back at the prayer meeting somewhat late, he too received this same Spirit Baptism. Carl Brumback records Parham's testimony in Parham's own words:

> Those days of tarrying were wonderful days of blessing . . . and with ever-swelling tides of praise and thanksgiving and worship, interspersed with singing, we waited for the coming of the Holy Spirit.
>
> On the night of January 3rd I preached at the Free Methodist Church in the city of Topeka, telling them what had already happened, and that I expected upon returning the entire school to be baptized in the Holy Spirit. On returning to the school with one of the students, we ascended to the second floor, and passing down the corridor, heard the most wonderful sounds. . . . Twelve ministers who were in the school were filled with the Holy Spirit and speaking with other tongues. Some were sitting, some still kneeling, others standing with hands upraised. There was no violent physical manifestations, though some trembled under the power of the glory that filled them. . . .

When I beheld the evidence of the restoration of Pentecostal power, my heart was melted in gratitude to God for what my eyes had seen . . . I fell to my knees behind the table unnoticed by those upon whom the power of Pentecost had fallen. . . . All at once they began to sing, "Jesus Lover of My Soul," in at least six different languages carrying the different parts with a more angelic voice than I had ever listened to in all my life. (Brumback, "Suddenly..." pp.24-25). [Brumback obtained this testimony from Parham's periodical, "The Apostolic Faith," December 1950—January, 1951.]

At the time of the outpouring of the Holy Spirit in Topeka, Miss Ozman was 30 years of age. In the years which followed, she became an active evangelist across America, and in 1911 she married Philemon LaBerge. The two continued to hold evangelistic meetings around the country. From 1917 she held credentials with the Assemblies of God as an evangelist. Mrs. Ozman-LaBerge died in Los Angeles in 1937, at the age of 67 (Burgess, *Dictionary of Pentecostal and Charismatic Movements*, 1993, by E. L. Blumhofer, p.657.).

At the time of the Topeka outpouring, Miss Lillian Thistlewaite was 28. She subsequently traveled as an evangelist, and in about 1930 she wrote a detailed account of the Topeka revival in an article she entitled, "The Wonderful History of the Latter Rain." She passed away in 1939. Additionally, after his Pentecostal experience in Topeka, Rev. Howard D. Stanley opened a Pentecostal chapel in October 1901, in the university city of Lawrence, Kansas. (Brumback, "Suddenly...," p.25 and *Dictionary of Pentecostal . . . Movements*, p. 657).

The other important participant in the Topeka revival, Rev. Charles F. Parham (1873-1929), was born in Iowa, and at five years of age moved with his parents to southeastern Kansas where, in his mature years, he conducted most of his ministry. In his early teens he was converted to Christ and became active in the local Congregational Church. At twenty he withdrew from college to serve as a supply pastor of a Methodist church. Unfortunately, he was beset by persistent attacks of rheumatic fever, for which he repeatedly sought the Lord's healing.

Philosophically enamored by the doctrines of the Holiness movement, he resigned his pastorate in 1895 to dedicate himself to an independent ministry. This decision eventually led him to establishing Bethel College in Topeka when he was twenty-seven. Four years later, in 1905, Parham established a Houston Bible School in Texas. There, William J. Seymour, a black Holiness evangelist, was trained under Parham's teaching before Seymour was invited to Los Angeles to become the pastor of a Holiness congregation. In 1929, at age fifty-six, Rev. Parham passed away in Baxter Springs, Kansas (*Dictionary of Pentecostal Movements*, pp. 660-61).

As for William J. Seymour, the Los Angeles Holiness congregation immediately objected to Seymour's Pentecostal emphasis which he had brought with him from Texas. So having been invited to *come*, he was soon invited to *leave*. But Seymour had Holy Spirit "fire" burning in his soul and would not be stopped. He was invited to continue his preaching in the Richard Asberry home on Bonnie Brae Avenue, in Los Angeles.

Continuous prayer meetings and powerful preaching from the Asberry front porch led to large crowds that soon could not be contained in the Bonnie Brae residence. As a consequence, Seymour found larger accommodations in a two-story, barn-like building located at 312 Azusa Street which eventually gained fame as the "Azusa Street Apostolic Faith Mission." So in spite of Seymour's previous rejection, the Lord led him to become the Pastor and Leader of the history-changing Los Angeles revival of Pentecost.

In the course of the Azusa Street revival, many were wonderfully converted, and many miraculously healed of numerous diseases. Multitudes were Baptized in the Holy Spirit, accompanied by the initial evidence of speaking in other tongues just as occurred in the book of Acts.

As the revival continued, Frodsham records another remarkable personal testimony of a Hebrew named Maurice Kullman, who had come to know Christ in the Baptist Church. Initially, Kullman was very opposed to modern-day Pentecostal manifestations. Maurice Kullman's own account is as follows:

> [My] wife and I were conducting a mission among the Jews of St. Louis, Missouri. We were backed by some wealthy people in whose eyes Pentecost was a shame and a disgrace. [My] wife, like most women, was more susceptible to spiritual things than I was, and so in [the] course of time she received the precious Baptism in the Holy Spirit. I thought she had lost her mind and I became bitterly opposed to the precious truth. She conducted prayer meetings at our home and I remember how I used to walk out of the house in

anger over her inviting Pentecostal workers into our home.

One night I thought I would stay to hear them pray and try to pray with them. Now my wife is a converted Roman Catholic. I have thanked the Lord many times for inducing me to stay at home that night. As my wife prayed she began to lose her natural language and began to speak in the pure Hebrew tongue. She quoted Deuteronomy 6:5, 6: "Thou shalt love the Lord thy God with all thine heart, and with all thy soul, and with all thy might. And these words, which I command thee this day, shall be in thine heart." I thought she had picked up the quotation. Later I asked her to repeat it, but try as she would she couldn't repeat those two verses in Hebrew. I asked her if she knew what she said, and she replied, "No." I quoted it to her and have asked her to repeat it a hundred times or more since then and she has never been able to say it after me till this day.

I remember as she quoted it [in tongues] she emphasized the Hebrew word 'bekol' which means 'all' in our English language, just as if she were giving me an admonition for not loving the Lord as I should. She articulated the Hebrew guttural sounds perfectly which none but a Hebrew can.

This heavenly message convinced me, a converted Jew and a Baptist preacher, that God was still doing the supernatural in this day and time. Not very long after that I also spoke in tongues when I received the Baptism in the Holy Spirit, and many are the times that the Spirit has spoken through me in the same marvelous manner as He did through my wife that night" (Frodsham, pp. 233-234).

In addition, the other Gifts of the Spirit, as enumerated in Acts and 1 Corinthians, were also evident in meetings throughout the United States. The nationwide publicity connected with this Azusa revival attracted many from across the States, some just to observe, but most to find answers for their own personal needs.

Furthermore, many from foreign countries also visited the meetings, found the Lord's blessings not only remarkable but life-changing, and returned to their own countries, taking the Pentecostal message with them. In addition, those already in Christian work, when they were Baptized in the Holy Spirit, found their ministries revolutionized as never before. And those newly converted and then Baptized in the Holy Spirit became dynamic messengers of the Lord, always anxious to win others to Christ. Many ministers and believers in today's societies are still experiencing the same phenomena of the Holy Spirit.

Remarkably, all participants discovered that the experiences described in the book of Acts do still happen today. It soon became apparent that the supernatural Gifts of the Spirit had not "vanished" after all. Thus, although some theologians have alleged that when the New Testament Apostles passed on to their reward, the Gifts of the Holy Spirit disappeared, modern-day seekers have found it to be dramatically the opposite. Indeed, the God of all grace is still benevolently meeting those who earnestly call on Him for the Holy Spirit Baptism. Praise His Name!

A Pentecostal historian and Professor of Church History at Fuller Theological Seminary, Dr. Cecil. M. Robeck, Jr., summarizes as follows the impact of the Azusa Revival on the Christian world:

> Azusa was typically described by the press as a "colored" congregation that met in a "tumbledown shack" and made the night "hideous" through the "howlings of the worshipers," yet it was [in fact] a church where whites, blacks, Hispanics, Asians, and others met together regularly and where from their own perspective the "color-line" was virtually nonexistent. Clearly, Seymour may be credited with providing the vision of a truly "color-blind" congregation. . . .The significance of the revival is equally related to its teachings about baptism in the Spirit and in the gift of tongues. . . .
>
> While tongues speaking played a significant role in the life of Azusa, it was the emphasis on power for ministry that most frequently sent people to the evangelistic [field] or mission field. . . .the experiences of tongues, healings, and other spectacular gifts tended to underscore the immanence of God.
>
> The significance of Azusa lies also in the testimonies of those whose lives were transformed by an experience of an [all-pervasive] God, through the Holy Spirit. Many found their intellectual orientation transformed. Their own ministries suddenly gained new direction of power, their personal spiritualities were enriched, and their vision of the church's task immeasurably broadened. Thus, the significance of Azusa was [that] those who were touched by it took their experiences elsewhere and touched the lives of others. Coupled with the theological threads of personal salvation, holiness, divine healing, baptism in

the Spirit with power for ministry, and an anticipation of the imminent return of Jesus Christ, ample motivation was provided to assure the revival a long-term impact ("Azusa Street Revival," p. 36, Dictionary of Pentecostal and Charismatic Movements, Stanley Burgess and Gary McGee, eds.,1993).

Undoubtedly, there will be those who think this story of twentieth-century Pentecost cannot be quite complete without a detailed review of the flaws, the faults, and the failures of the Pentecostals, both then and now. We do not deny that there were some excesses and inconsistencies. It is the very nature of mortals. There are those who do fail to respond as they should, especially when they are exploring new spiritual territory—yes, even when it is the Lord Himself Who is leading them into a fuller spiritual life. The Bible narratives provide us with numerous examples of persons who responded to God's revelations in an overly reactive way, but excesses do *not* make the Lord's blessings any less real.

One biblical example is Peter's overreaction on the Mount of Transfiguration. Commenting on this very subject, the Apostle Paul wrote to the charismatically troubled Corinthian Church, "We hold these [heavenly] treasures in earthen vessels"(2 Cor. 4:7), thereby underscoring the innate weaknesses of mortals. We do not, we *cannot*, excuse fanatical failures, but we must remember that *failing to seek* the Lord is also a serious error.

Again, take the Corinthian Church as an example. Paul had "fathered" the Corinthian Church (see Acts 18:9-11; 1 Cor. 4:15, TLB), and without question he had introduced them to the Baptism in the Holy Spirit, accompanied by the ministering Gifts of the Spirit. But he later had the unpleasant task of disciplining them by making several "house calls" on this congregation, and by means of the two Corinthian letters. But in spite of their unwarranted behavior, Paul admonished by writing, "Let everything be done decently and in order, *but forbid not to speak with tongues*" (emphasis added).

Paul had no intention that his efforts at correction should bring an end to the experience of speaking in tongues, either as the initial evidence of being Baptized in the Holy Spirit," or as the operational Gifts in the congregation of believers. This is clearly the admonition in God's Word and should stand as the final authority on the matter!

It should also be immediately evident, however, that it is more than disastrous when "nervous" Christians reject any of the blood-bought provisions of the Lord, just because they have heard that some other believers have failed to appropriate God's Gifts in an orderly and scriptural manner. But consider this analogy: We all know people who will *not* attend church, nor will they give their hearts to the Lord, all because they claim "there are too many hypocrites in the Church." What a shame for any person to lose his or her eternal soul because of some hypothetical "hypocrite," who actually may not exist at all.

And even if there are hypocrites, they—and the squeamish objectors—are very likely to meet again in some more hellish abode, together for all eternity. Horrible the thought! It is, however, a widely recognized psychological principle that mortals are prone to find fault with what they really do not want to respond to anyway, especially so when there is a hint of spiritual obligation involved.

The above excuse related to accepting Jesus as Savior is analogous to the modern criticisms which have been leveled at twentieth-century Pentecostals, alleging that they have indulged in fanaticism. By means of this kind of fallacious reasoning, some excuse themselves from pursuing a deeper walk with the Lord. It is true, some fanaticism has occurred. We do not deny that! But foolish behavior also happened among the sixteenth-century Reformers, as the Lord introduced them into new territory. Of course, the implied, but faulty, argument here is that because there has been some fanatical behavior, therefore none of the Pentecostal manifestations are worthy of consideration. Erroneous reasoning, especially when related to Bible doctrines, is spiritual thievery, robbing others of God's wonderful provisions.

By hiding behind flawed reasoning such as that cited above, many modern Christians have robbed themselves—or have been robbed by mistaken theologians—of God's bountiful blessings. Or, it is also possible that by so doing, they have sought to excuse themselves, content to remain spiritually apathetic, resorting to man-made ritualism rather than the leading of the Holy Spirit.

Our first clue to seeking more from a beneficent God should be the scriptural accounts—as in the book of Acts, for example—portraying the richness of the Lord's grace. Indeed, since the Holy Spirit's Baptism and the *charismatic* Gifts are unquestionably occurring in at least the first two centuries of the Church, why not expect as much in our own century? God spoke through Isaiah to unbelieving Judah: "Is My hand shortened at all, that it cannot redeem? Or have I no power to deliver?" (Isa. 50:2, KJV). It is *not* God who changed! No, but mortals have! (Cp. Hebrews 13:8).

The Apostle Paul wrote only moments before he was to be executed, "If we believe not, [even] yet He abideth faithful: He cannot deny Himself" (2 Timothy 2:13, KJV). This statement harks back to God's own statement about Himself, found in Numbers 23:19: "God is not a man, that He should lie, nor a son of man that He should repent [or "change His mind"]. Has He said, and will He not do it? Or has He spoken, and will He not make it good?" (NKJV).

So what is the status of Pentecost today? Statistics indicate the Pentecostal movements are still healthy and well. Yes, as of today, there are many Pentecostal groups both inside and outside the major denominations. The modern Pentecostal outpouring has been, from the beginning, a worldwide evangelistic movement and it continues to be so.

After all, Pentecost is not a denomination! It is an experience, just as "getting saved" is an experience that crosses denominational lines. It is a provision by our Sovereign heavenly Father, designed to empower His workers to become "Conquerors." Increasingly through the years since 1901, new doors of ministry have opened, new mission fields have been cultivated, and new revivals have broken out. Our God is still managing the reaping of the Final Harvest, and all of us are rejoicing in the Lord's modern accomplishments by means of His *last day* Pentecostal outpourings.

Amazingly, too, miracles of all kinds have occurred, and are continuing to occur, just as in the book of Acts: documented healings of many diseases, people delivered of demon possessions or demonic oppression, even some raised from the dead. One such example of this has just recently come to my attention. In a recent Missionary Convention at People's Church in Salem, Oregon, African missionary Rob Shipley told of the experience of some of his students, Ethiopian Pentecostal seminary students who had been moved to act on the Lord's "Great Commission." After praying about this conviction, they decided to go and preach the Gospel to one of their neighboring tribes.

As a result, twelve or more of these Ethiopian nationals were impressed by the Lord to go to a neighboring Moslem tribe to share the Good News of Christ as Savior. During their ministry in that community, a young Moslem girl, who was being cared for in the local clinic, succumbed to her afflictions and was officially pronounced dead. Consequently, she was wrapped in burial garments and was being carried by the usual parade of local mourners to be buried nearby.

As was locally customary for all to show respect and sympathy for the deceased and for the mourning family, these Ethiopian national Christians joined the procession to help carry the bier. One of the Christian brethren suddenly felt impressed to pray for the deceased little girl. However, his Christian partners were alarmed at his proposal and warned him of the dangers of violence if the little girl was not revived. But this Ethiopian brother's impression persisted, as from the Lord, so he proceeded to pray for the deceased child, even while she was being carried toward the cemetery by these Moslem mourners. Suddenly, the little girl's cloth-draped arm began to move, and she was immediately resurrected from death.

According to Rev. Shipley's report, she remains alive to this day. The surprised Moslem mourners asked, "How did you do that?" Of course the Christians explained, and several Moslem mourners responded by accepting Christ as their Savior. Others are enquiring further about who this "Jesus" is. No amount of intellectualized theological denials can convince those Africans that God no longer works miracles. Praise be to our God!

So, at this point in time, as a consequence of over a century of worldwide Pentecostal missionary efforts, conversions, with miraculous signs following—as in the book of Acts—have caused a dramatic growth in numbers of Pentecostals. This growth has been so dramatic that it has multiplied the number of Pentecostal believers in the world exponentially. It has been delightful to read of the surprise expressed by various Pentecostal historians at the exploding number of believers who have come to Christ since 1901.

For example, before 1940, Evangelist Donald Gee, expressing some amazement at his discovery, estimated there were at least 30,000 Pentecostals. Then, by 1980, Dr. Vinson Synan, a Professor at Emmanuel College in Franklin Springs, Georgia, claimed 50,000,000 classical Pentecostals existed in the world. But more recently, professionally gathered statistics compiled by Dr. David Barrett's survey team indicate that the number has now surpassed 700,000,000 (as of 2005 A.D.), and the numbers are still growing exponentially each year.

At the present rate of growth, Dr. Barrett and his statistical colleagues project that there will be one billion Pentecostals in the world by 2050 A.D. We do not glory in numbers, but these statistics give strong indication that our God is accomplishing something *big*, right here in our own time. (Dr. David Barrett, ed., *World Christian Encyclopedia,* 2nd ed., Oxford University Press, 2001)

Also, to the amazement of many of the nay-sayers, this twentieth-century resurgence of New Testament Pentecost not only has continued from 1901, but it has blossomed—even ballooned—into the astounding numbers of people who have become participants in the modern Pentecostal revival. And the widespread denominational participation in present-day Pentecost has led some observers to refer to this phenomenon as the "Pentecostalization of the modern Church." For just as the outpouring of the Holy Spirit in Apostolic times resulted in multitudes being won to Christ, so it is that in the twentieth century Pentecostal outpouring, multitudes of souls have been garnered into Christ's kingdom.

The sense of Scripture, then, is that Pentecostal experiences were to be a significant factor in Christendom, at least until "the great and terrible day of the Lord" arrives. This sequence of events is supported further by the fact that Joel 3:1 predicts that at least two of the signs of these "last days" would be (1) the return of the Jews to their homeland, and (2) their eventual recovery of the city of Jerusalem. And as already stated above, these two events did actually happen midway into the twentieth century, giving even further credibility to the outpouring of the Spirit in the twentieth century. This subject will be visited more specifically in chapter 11 of this book

As for these new Pentecostals, documented records reveal that miracles of healings, deliverances from demonic oppression and possession, and other miracles, have followed their preaching, leading to the salvation of many—just as is recorded in the book of Acts. Unfortunately, it is also true that some modern churchmen—as in Bible days—when confronted by these supposedly "new" spiritual experiences, have denied the miraculous powers of the Holy Spirit. This is probably because these skeptical leaders have themselves not yet experienced the Baptism of the Holy Spirit. In addition, some have gone further, even beyond *doubting,* and are now openly *resisting* this modern move of the Holy Spirit—just as their religious counterparts did in the narratives of Acts.

But still, many have recognized these miraculous events as the genuine work of God, and they have committed themselves anew to the cause of Christ—just as multitudes did in the narratives of Acts. The people of Acts—and of today—proceeding cautiously at first, but then in ever-increasing numbers, have recognized the accuracy of the Scriptures: "Jesus Christ [is] the same yesterday, and today, and forever" (Heb. 13:8).

Unquestionably, the ministry Gifts of the Holy Spirit—the *charismata*—have *not ceased* to be operational, after all! In spite of those who have chosen to defend their own systematized, man-made theologies, the Spirit Himself has continued to move with dynamic power among those who believe in the literal interpretation of the Apostle Peter's prophecy: "The promise [of conversion and the Baptism in the Spirit] is unto you, and to your children, and to all that are afar off, even as many as the Lord our God shall call" (Acts 2:39, KJV).

In conclusion, Frodsham refers to an interesting statement by Rev. Thomas B. Barratt (1862-1940) of Oslo, Norway, the long-time pastor of the Filadelfia Church of that city. Rev. Barratt summarizes the doctrinal position of the Pentecostals as follows:

As regards salvation by justification, we are Lutherans. In baptismal formula, we are Baptists. As regards sanctification, we are Methodists. In aggressive evangelism we are as the Salvation Army. But as regards the Baptism in the Holy Spirit, we are Pentecostals (Frodsham, p. 274).Indeed, this comparative statement gives credibility to the theory expressed in an earlier chapter of this study regarding the progressive restoration of biblical doctrines seriously obscured—indeed, well-nigh lost—during the medieval Dark Ages (Cp. Stanley Horton, *Into All Truth*, Chapter 10; also Cp. chapter 7 of this study). Without a doubt, the modern-day Pentecostal movement is a significant part of the mighty river of rediscovered biblical truths.

So now that we all have been thrust, with some trepidation, into the twenty-first century, Christians worldwide suddenly have opportunity to inspect and reevaluate the events of the twentieth century. Because of documented evidences of the work of the Holy Spirit through history—from the awe-inspiring events of Acts, through the dark Ages, and into the twentieth century—it is manifestly clear that the New Testament Gifts of the Holy Spirit did *not* cease, as the "cessationist" theologians mistakenly claim.

Furthermore, because modern-day believers are experiencing the outpouring of the Holy Spirit as the believers did in the book of Acts, this fact, in and of itself, should prove that the supernatural Gifts of the Holy Spirit have not ceased after all. The huge explosion of Pentecostal activity in the twentieth century should be enough to silence forever the flawed claims of the "cessationists."

As in the accounts found in the New Testament, people in modern times have been filled with the Holy Spirit, have spoken in other tongues when baptized in the Holy Spirit, and have subsequently manifested those supernatural gifts identified in the Scriptures. In addition, there has been a renewed emphasis on the redemptive purposes of the Lord Jesus Christ as is expressed in the "Great Commission" (see Matt. 28:19; Mark 16:15-18). And we can participate in God's ordained plan for the ages by earnestly praying that it will be completed exactly as He intended!

Chapter 10

PENTECOST, THE PROPHET JOEL, AND THE FINAL FULFILLMENT

By way of introduction to the brief review of prophecy, which follows, it is generally understood that the Jewish people have a deep respect for those prophets represented in their Old Testament canon. But, it must also be said, they often were not so reverently disposed toward those very same prophets while those prophets were alive. The role of the prophets of God was often to name the sins of the nation and then to call the Jewish people to repentance and a change of lifestyle. History reveals that the Jews often resented this call for a change of behavior.

As a consequence, most Old Testament prophets were badly mistreated—some even martyred—while they were delivering God's message.[1] It is too often an unpleasant experience to be a prophetic voice for the God of heaven! During the final week before His crucifixion, Jesus Himself chided the leaders in Jerusalem regarding their deplorable reputation. He reminded them, "O Jerusalem, Jerusalem, *you who kill the prophets and stone those sent to you*, how often I have longed to gather your children together . . . but you were not willing" (Matt. 23: 37, NIV).[2]

Although there is no sure record that the prophet Joel was persecuted in the manner of some of his fellows, he, like other prophets, did declare a message of reprimand that would probably not have been very popular with the residents of the Southern Kingdom. And yet, his warning of coming judgment proved to be so painfully accurate that he was given a respected place among the great prophets of Holy Writ.[3]

But, in addition, the long-term importance of his message was further emphasized by the fact that a significant portion of his prophecy was quoted by Peter on the Day of Pentecost (see Acts 2), just to prove the authenticity of the Pentecostal experiences in the Upper Room.

And the way Peter phrased his message indicates the Baptism of the Holy Spirit was intended to be available until the end of the Age when Christ Returns. Thus, in view of the significance of Joel's prophecy to both the Old and the New Testament believers, it seems reasonable that Joel's message should be reviewed and examined more carefully for its relevance to our own period of history. Few today will question that we are now living in the "last days" to which Joel refers, and Paul reinforces this in 2 Timothy 3. Joel's proclamation is essentially God's master plan for the birth of the Church and the subsequent restoration of Israel.

With reference to Joel's historical background, the exact date of his prophecy cannot be determined with accuracy because of the limited scope of both internal and external evidences. As a consequence, scholars differ about exactly when he prophesied. Still, there are allusions in his message which provide us some clues. Therefore, based on the available evidence, most conservative authorities hold the position that Joel's was one of the earliest of the prophecies, most likely before the invasion of Judah by the Babylonians under King Nebuchadnezzar, who captured the country and leveled Solomon's Temple about 588 B.C. Consequently, if

Joel's message was, indeed, a prophecy, it would have been necessary for Joel to make his declaration prior to that date.

Supporting the hypothesis that Joel was one of the earliest of the minor prophets is the fact that Joel makes no mention of a king; and—so the theory goes—King Joash, being a minor, was for some time under the regency guardianship of the high priest, Jehoida (see 2 Kings 11:20-12:2). If this theory is accurate, then Joel probably made his declarations of impending judgment about 836 B.C., perhaps during the reign of Judah's King Joash (835-796 B.C.). Some modern scholars, however, are inclined to date Joel's prophecy about 450 B.C., but the evidences cited by these later scholars are not a bit more credible than those referred to by their predecessors.

What is certain, however, is that he was a prophet to the Southern Kingdom, Judah, and that the time of his prophecy is pre-exilic. Joel's name means *worshipper of Jehovah*, and this fact, coupled with his frequent references to the leadership responsibilities of the priests, along with his more classical literary style, have led some to suppose that he himself may have been a priest of the Temple in Jerusalem. If these hypotheses are accurate, then in his youth he probably would have known Elijah, and he certainly would have been a contemporary of Elisha.

The occasion for Joel's message was the trauma caused by the devastating plagues of locusts, which in several waves had ravished the crops of the Southern Kingdom. This physical crisis caused Joel to focus his message on the real cause of the devastation, which was the spiritual and moral decline of the Jewish culture. Moreover, he predicted even more severe consequences of their spiritual decline to occur in some future era of God's dealings with the Jews.[4]

But in the midst of the rampant Jewish Apostasy and the resulting apocalyptic predictions, there are those declarations of God's intended mercy and His promise eventually to restore the fortunes of His chosen people. The most memorable of these predictions, of course, is Joel 2:28-32, that of the outpouring of the Holy Spirit on the Day of Pentecost (see Acts 2:1-2). This matter of promising restoration underscores the Lord's wonderful generosity!

With these considerations in mind, the book of Joel may be analyzed as follows:

I. Reproof of the Jews and the Ruination of their Land 1:1-2
   A. Remember Forever these Ruined Harvests 1:3
   B. Rapacious Reaping by Swarms of Locusts 1:4
   C. Results Reviewed1: 5-2:11
      1. Ravishment of the Food Chain 1:5-20
      2. Ruination by Invading Armies 2:1-11
II. Revocation of God's Judgment Requires Repentance . . . 2:12-17
   A. Repentance Rituals Recommended 2:12-13
   B. Reminders of God's Mercies 2:13-17
III. Reply from the Lord: Restoration and Renewal 2:18-32
   A. Restoration of the Land and of Judah's Honor 2:18-19
      1. Removal of the Invading Armies 2:20
      2. Rejoicing and Recovery in Judah 2:21-27
   B. Revitalization of the Spiritual Life of the People 2:28-32
      1. Return of the Early and Latter Rains . . . 2:28(Cp.v23)
      2. Revival of the Prophetic Experiences 2:28-29
      3. Related Signs in the Heavens 2:30-31
IV. Reproachment of the Nations and the Revenge of God 3:1-16
   A. Return of Judah and Jerusalem: "In that Time" 3:1
   B. Revenge of God in "Valley of Jehosophat" 3:2-16
      1. Recounting the Records of Abuse 3:2-8

(Outline by Lynn Kanaga)[5]

In the New Testament, when false accusations were made against the rejoicing believers because of the "outpouring of the Holy Spirit, the Apostle Peter—with surprising boldness—declared the phenomenon as being from God Himself. He quoted the prediction of Joel 2:28-32 as verification that "this is that" which God had promised long before. While his admirable assuredness must largely be attributed to the recent anointing of the Holy Spirit, his immediate reference to Joel's prophecy leads one to speculate that Jesus' previous instructions regarding the coming of the "Other Comforter" may have included an exposition of Joel 2:28-32. If this theory is a probability, then rereading Acts 1:2-4 seems worthwhile:

> He returned to heaven after giving his chosen apostles further instructions from the Holy Spirit. During the forty days after his crucifixion he appeared to the apostles from time to time, actually alive, and proved to them in many ways that it was really he himself they were seeing. And on these occasions he talked to them about the Kingdom of God. In one of these meetings he told them not to leave Jerusalem until the Holy Spirit came upon them in fulfillment of the Father's promise (TLB).

Whatever the precise teachings Jesus may have shared with His apostles during these private sessions, on the Day of

Pentecost Peter, with remarkable boldness, quoted Joel's prophecy concerning the arrival of the Days of Restoration foretold by the Holy Spirit. Of course, Joel 2:28-32 fairly sparkles with the atmosphere of God-sent predictions, and Peter covered these predictions in detail in Acts 2:14-21. A careful review of the prophecy's implications leads us to several important observations:

(1) Joel's predictions were given in the context of awesome pronouncements of judgment upon the harvests of the Jewish Southern Kingdom; that is, that wave upon wave of locusts were to bring successive devastation to the harvests. And the chief causes were the Jews' spiritual arrogance and their lethargy toward God. But there is an important transition observable at this point: Joel is obviously characterizing *more* than just the four stages of destructive locusts. He indicates that the four stages of locusts are symbols, or foreshadowing of future invasions of pagan armies that were to ravish and ruin the Jewish land.

According to the Jameson, Faussett, and Brown commentary (vol.1, "Joel"), Hebrew scholars apparently believed these invaders were the four successive occupations of their land by the Assyrian-Babylonians (588-538 B.C.), the Medo-Persians (538-330 B.C.) the Greco-Macedonians (330-190 B.C.) and finally the Roman oppressors (38 B.C.-70 A.D., and beyond).

The four periods of domination actually began with the destruction of Solomon's Temple by Nebuchadnezzar in 588 B.C. Seventy years later, the Temple was reconstructed by order of the Persians. But these two oppressive overlords were succeeded by the Greeks under Antiochius Epiphanes, who shamelessly desecrated the Holy of Holies about 165 B.C. However, there was still another Temple to be built, one built by Herod the Great just before the birth of Christ, which was subsequently razed to the ground in 70 A.D. by the ambitious but frustrated Roman general Titus.[6]

In addition to these historical facts, according to *Fausett's Bible Dictionary*, some Hebrew scholars also believe that the letters used to name the four different kinds of locusts precisely represent the number of years each of these four invading armies held control over the Jews of Palestine. It must be added, however, that this numerological interpretation is not given much credibility among modern Bible scholars.

Nonetheless, amidst these dark and awful predictions of judgment, a sudden explosion of Hope is evident, a promise with specific details of mercy and restoration. God in His inclination to extend mercy to the undeserving, promised to intervene, that is, to provide eventual deliverance from both the terrestrial and the spiritual Ruination of Jewish life.

(2) Precisely in this regard, Joel's Old Testament pronouncements of the Ruination of the Harvests may be observed as a contrast with the New Testament fulfillment at the Feast of Pentecost (see Acts 2). Significantly, this Feast was also harvest-related, and it celebrated the outpouring of the seasonal latter rain which the Lord provided in order to mature on time the Jewish natural harvest. Thus, this Festival of Pentecost is symbolic of both the "early rain" and the "latter rain," which the Lord provided to prepare the world for the Messiah's Final Harvest.

It follows, then, that on the Day of an important Jewish harvest Festival, the outpouring of the Spirit came to them in the Upper Room, signaling the beginning of God's promised Restoration. Furthermore, Joel's prophecy portends that once this phenomenon was set in motion, it was to continue until the arrival of the Messiah, as King of kings.

As the narrative in Acts indicates, it was "when the Day of Pentecost was fully come" that Peter quoted Joel's famous prophecy. It is certain, then, that the outpouring of the Spirit at Pentecost initiated the Lord's preparation for a *Final Harvest* of souls, wonderfully designed to include the Gentiles in His great plan of salvation.

(3) It should also be noted here that although it is strongly implied in Joel's prophecy—without specifically being stated—the promised Restoration would indeed usher in the "Church Age," that period which made it possible for Gentile believers to be included in the listings of "God's chosen people." In retrospect, we now better understand this fact by comparing Joel's prophecies with the events recorded in the book of Acts. Cornelius (Acts 10) must have been as delighted about this wonderful miracle of God's grace as are the rest of us Gentiles whom the Lord has called to Himself.

(4) In addition, Joel used a number of time-related transitions: for example, "afterward" (verse 28), "in those days" (verse 29), "before" (verse 31), and "in those days and in that time"(3:1), So that it seems certain that Joel himself had some understanding of the sequential events occurring in the development of his prophecy.[7] It seems fitting, therefore, to analyze carefully Joel's implied timeline. For one thing, it is obvious that the period during which this "outpouring" is to

be in force was intended as a continuum to the end of the Church Age, and therefore unto "the coming of the great and terrible day of the Lord." In other words, this magnanimous and miraculous "outpouring" of God's grace is expected to continue unabated (at least, God intended it that way) until the Lord's Return and the Final Judgment, cited in Joel chapter 3.

Furthermore, in this regard, it is important to note that there is not the slightest hint herein of some "period of cessation" which would interrupt the promised *last day* phenomena of the Holy Spirit's visitations. In fact, every reference in the Bible—Old Testament or New—to the Holy Spirit's Restoration of Faith implies that the Restoration of biblical doctrines will continue until the Lord Himself returns. For example, in Romans 11:29, the Apostle Paul, while discussing God's promise to restore the Jews to faith, reminds us that "God's gifts [*charismata*] and His call can never be withdrawn; He will never go back on His promises" (TLB). Compare this with the promise of Pentecost cited by the Apostle Peter in Acts 2:21.

In any case, why would the Lord of the Final Harvest limit the harvesters' effectiveness by decreasing the provisions to accomplish the task? Such a theory does not agree with the portrayal of the Lord's renowned generosity to those who believe in Him and to those who faithfully labor in bringing in His Harvest.

The *Quest Study Bible*[8] makes this comment about Joel 2: "With the coming of the Holy Spirit on all believers [at Pentecost], the last days began (Acts 2:14-21). At the end of the last days, God will judge the earth . . . signaling the end of human rule on the earth and the subsequent rule of Christ [as outlined in] Matt. 24:29-30."

(5) Joel 2:28, "I will *pour* out my Spirit" (emphasis added), emphasizes a greatly abundant supply, that is, "without measure, a profuse outpouring, the *malkosh* of a physical 'latter rain'" (Cf. James 5:7), which in seasons of plenty concluded the Jewish growing season. These "latter rains" insured sufficient precipitation for an abundant harvest at the end of the summer. Most Bible scholars believe this reference to "the latter rain" is a symbol of the promised outpouring of the Holy Spirit, just as the preceding reference to locusts was a symbol of the four eras of invading armies. Pentecostal believers of the early twentieth century often referred to their Pentecostal experiences as the "Latter Rain." [9]

6) "Upon all flesh" (Joel 2:28) is an amazing prediction because it indicates, too, the vast scope of God's intended restoration. Here again is an indication of the Lord's gracious generosity. During the Church Age, "all flesh" is given opportunity to participate in the benefits of accepting the Messiah as Savior! So the "outpouring" of the spiritual Gifts (*charismata*) is to extend the Renewal experience to men and to women, to boys and to girls, to the young and the old, to both slave and to master, to Jews and to Gentiles, yes even to all the nations. It is doubtful, however, that orthodox Jews understood the extent of God's grace expressed here. How magnanimous for an offended God to include everyone in His outpourings of Grace and Salvation.

The prophet Joel then specifically announces a restoration of those Old Testament prophetic activities cited by Moses in Numbers 12:6, which is that the authenticity of prophetic revelations would be identified by means of supernatural "dreams" and "visions"—in addition to the usual predictive declarations. Of course, we learn in the New Testament that the manifestations of the Spirit are abundantly more numerous and profound than only these three components of dreams, visions and prophecies. And through the centuries, these are precisely the experiences which Pentecostal groups have experienced.

(7) Let us observe further, from Joel 2:30 through 3:21 that there is a startling catalogue of events as the Church Age blends into the Final Judgment period upon all those nations who have tormented the Jews and/or their tormenting of Christians through the Ages. And through all the time they have sought to recast Christ's doctrines into their mold, they themselves have resisted God's invitation to receive the Messiah/Savior. Verses 2:30-31 predict, "And I will show wonders in the heavens and in the earth, blood and fire, and pillars of smoke. The sun shall be turned into darkness, and the moon into blood, *before* the great and terrible day of the Lord come" (emphasis added).

In this passage, the transition word "before" indicates that unusual signs, in the heavens and on the earth, will most likely occur near the end of the Church Age, most likely the result of cataclysmic world wars, as Jesus predicted (Matthew 24). These horrendous events will eventually blend with increasing intensity into that time when all nations prepare themselves for the Battle of Armageddon.

Some Bible commentaries are inclined to list these cosmic catastrophes as occurring *after* the Lord returns. These people are inclined to project prophesied earth-shaking catastrophes as impossible for *now,* always sometime in the distant future, when–in fact—the prophesied events are currently happening all around us, even now. Mortals are so inclined to provide a shallow, scientific explanation for the phenomena God Himself caused to happen. Witness the current efforts of some scientists to *re-write* the history of biblical events—for example, the Exodus of the Hebrews from Egypt. Generally, the biblical account is never quite accurate, and *"the hypotheses of the 'expert scientists' have once again discovered inaccuracies in the biblical account."* Personally, I would much rather risk believing the Bible's version!

But is this really an accurate interpretation of Joel's end-time list of events? Or have some of these signs already been occurring in our own time? One hermenuetical fact must be taken seriously: the word "before" is significantly attached to this prophecy. It is a signal to prayerful readers to be alert to historical events which are precursors of the Lord's triumphant Return. So, let us ponder Joel's predictions carefully, because they are irrevocably bound to one of the most important doctrinal statements of the Church, Joel 2:28-32.

In the next chapter, we will examine some of the significant events of the last 100 years, and examine them in light of Joel's larger prophetic outline, especially since those prophetic events relate to chapters 2 and 3 of Joel. By using this method, we may discover where we are in God's prophetic timetable.

One fact is self-evident: the twentieth-century outpouring of the Holy Spirit is itself a prophetic phenomenon of awesome proportions, and very obviously a precursor of the Lord's grander intentions. Whether we are fully aware of it or not, God's Final Harvest is now in full progress. The garnering of those who have been "called out" is occurring worldwide at this very moment. Our God is redeeming His people, those from every tribe and nation under the sun.

Endnotes

[1] Biblical accounts and Jewish traditions make reference to the cruelty of the Jews to many of the Lord's prophets. For example, Jeremiah 27:7-8 records the account of an angry Jewish mob attempting to "kill" Jeremiah. In addition, Unger's Bible Dictionary refers to a "credible" tradition that Isaiah was "sawn asunder" (Heb. 11:37) at the beginning of King Manasseh's reign (See p. 534, col. 2).

[2] See also Luke 13:34.

[3] The organization of the OT canon is almost certainly intentionally arranged chronologically. For example, the major prophets appear in the order of their ministries both before and during the period of Jewish Exile. In a similar manner, the minor prophets seem to have been arranged according to the time of their ministries before the 400 years of silence and the later appearances of John the Baptist and Jesus the Messiah. Thus, if Malachi is the last of the minor prophets and Hosea is the first of this group, then Joel must have prophesied very early in the sequence, more than likely in the ninth century BC.

[4] This information was derived from A.R. Fausset's Bible Encyclopaedia and Dictionary and from The New Bible Commentary: Revised, D. Guthrie and J.A. Motyer, editors.

[5] While this outline may be similar to others, here the organization and vocabulary are entirely my own.

[6] "Joel," <u>A Critical and Explanatory Commentary</u>, Vol. I, R. Jamieson, A.R. Faussett, and D. Brown.

[7] I am indebted to Professor Ronald Wright of Vanguard University for calling this fact to my attention.

[8] See <u>The Quest Study Bible</u>, notes on p. 1254.

[9] For example, review <u>Three Pentecostal Tracts</u>, Garland Publishing, New York, 1985 and <u>Azusa Street</u> by Frank Bartleman, Bridge Publishing, Inc., 1985.

Chapter 11

JOEL'S PROPHECY CONCERNING THE "LAST DAYS" AND THE EVENTS OF MODERN HISTORY

We have observed in the preceding chapter that there are very important hermeneutical indicators in Joel's prophecy, particularly in chapters 2 and 3, that the "last-day" outpouring of the Holy Spirit is actually a precursor of very serious judgmental events which will follow, either as the "Church Age" closes or immediately thereafter. The "Church Age" is, in fact, the miraculous inclusion of the Gentile believers, along with the Jews, in God's plan of redemption.

So have any of these predicted events happened in recent history? The answer seems obvious if we have at all been alert regarding world events! So, of course, we must answer "Yes." Events which are fulfillment of prophecies have been occurring again and again, decade after decade. And virtually all of these have happened inside the twentieth century—the "Century of the Holy Spirit," as it has been referred to in recent years.

This so-called "Century of the Holy Spirit" definitely had humble beginnings, for in a Topeka, Kansas, Bible school, Agnes Ozman first spoke in tongues on January 1, 1901, an indication she had been baptized in the Holy Spirit exactly as the 120 had been in Acts 2. Others enjoyed the same experience. As a result, a revival broke out which continued in the Azusa Street mission of Los Angeles, spreading, by means of evangelism, to many, many countries of the world.

The modern Pentecostal outpouring has been, from the beginning, a world-wide soul-winning movement, and it continues to be so to this day. It has been delightful to read of the surprise expressed by Pentecostal writers through the century—surprise at the burgeoning numerical growth of Pentecostal believers. For example, expressing some amazement at his own observations, Donald Gee cited an estimated 30,000 Pentecostals by 1940, only thirty or so years after Topeka and Azusa. Then by 1980, Dr. Vinson Synan (also Frank Bartleman's biographer) claimed 50,000,000 classical Pentecostals.

In recent years, however, verified statistics gathered by Dr. David Barrett's professionally trained survey team of 400, indicate that the number has now surpassed 700,000,000, and the number is still growing exponentially each year. We do not glory in numbers, but these statistics give strong indication that our God is up to something grand and glorious, right here in our own time.

Question: *If* the Lord, throughout the twentieth century, has actually been fulfilling an ancient prophecy of spiritual Restoration, would Satan, the old "destroyer"—as he is named in 1 Peter 5:8—accept this restoration without resisting, perhaps even reacting in a violent way? No, not very likely!

It is fascinating to observe that just fourteen years after the initial twentieth-century outpouring of Pentecost in 1901, a devastating World War erupted. There had never before been a war of such destructive magnitude, nor one that would be identified as a "world war." And, horror of horrors, only twenty-one years later, another world war followed, beginning anew in 1939 and progressing devastatingly through 1946. World War II was even more destructive than the first. Indeed, the carnage of these two world wars is almost unbelievable. According to *World Book Encyclopedia*, these two successive wars caused a total of 82,769,826 military casualties, of which 23,407,079 were killed outright. And sadly, these figures, as terrible as they are, do not account for the inestimable loss of life among the world's citizenry, nor for the horrific costs of destroyed public property.

So the question remains: Was all this only incidentally linked to the outpouring of modern Pentecost, or has the demonic "destroyer" also been at work during the "Century of the Holy Spirit"? The answer seems obvious! And yet perhaps an even deeper question is this: Were the two devastating World Wars the devil's "countermovement" to the latter day outpouring of the Holy Spirit? The early-day Pentecostals pondered this very same question; and many, after searching the Scriptures, made the claim that these international events were without a doubt "signs" of the "last days."

Perhaps we who have stumbled so awkwardly into the twenty-first Century are better prepared to answer this prophetic enigma. It seems especially significant, since the twentieth century is now been labeled by Church Historians as the "Century of the Holy Spirit." At the same time, it is very ironic that modern political historians are now marketing the same period as "The Century of Warfare." Perhaps the two camps are observing the terrestrial manifestations of the age-old battle between Good and Evil.

Indeed, even since the above observations were written several years ago, we are now hearing every night on the

International News of people being beheaded or bombed, or otherwise brutalized day after day—and all in the name of a heartless, murderous religion of fanatical "martyrs" claiming to be doing the destructive will of their god!

Is it possible that the evil one, the "Old Destroyer," is seeking to imitate in reverse, God's "Harvest of Souls" by means of the ministry of the Holy Spirit? If this speculation regarding the enemy is accurate, then Satan is ushering many, many souls into hell without their having the opportunity to know Jesus the Savior, and doing so in a profoundly more devilish, more deadly, and ever more merciless devices. The World Wars of the last 100 years—and other regional wars since—have ushered millions into hell without their having a chance to prepare themselves to meet the God of heaven!

With reference to the World Wars, it is worth noting that both Peter and Joel made reference to awesome wonders which would occur "in the heavens and in the earth" (Joel 2:30-31), before concluding with the now famous promise, "And it shall come to pass, that whosoever shall call on the name of the Lord shall be saved" (Acts 2:21). The biblical descriptions of the culmination of this present Age, as in Joel 3 and Zechariah 14, are so fearsome that some Bible scholars are inclined to identify these phenomena as occurring during the Lord's final judgment on the nations. And, in fact, there may very well be *more* incidents in the future of still more horrific proportions. Mankind has for centuries "sown to the wind," and they will be "reaping a whirlwind" (Hosea 8:7).

But many suppose these events will be so terrible that they could not possibly happen in our period of history. It is important to note, however, that these "wonders in the heavens and earth" are listed by Joel *before* God's promise to "those who call on His Name." The signs described so vividly in these passages seem to be an integral part of the prophecy of the "last-day" outpouring of the Holy Spirit, as though they are to occur before the actual Revelation of Jesus Christ.

It seems reasonable, therefore, to consider that these images are the prophet's way of describing the effects of two World Wars, and others like those of the twentieth century, for example, the massive bombings which occurred, particularly in the course of World War II. "Blood and fire and pillars of smoke" (Cf. NLT and AMP) stir horrific memories of the "fire bombings" of London, England; Tokyo, Japan; and Berlin and Dresden, Germany, among many others, during WWII.

And the reference to "pillars of smoke" (or "columns of smoke," AMP) is an apt description of the awesome "pillars of smoke" which are etched in our memories as a part of the explosions of the atomic bomb. Is it possible that we moderns have been observing the conflagrations of the *eschaton*, or "last days," virtually unaware of their relationship to Bible prophecy?

As significant as these considerations are, there are more—perhaps equally important ones—to be considered carefully. These are found in the opening verses of Joel chapter 3. It is certain that chapter 3 is largely given over to descriptions of the preparations for the final World War, the Battle of Armageddon. However, Joel 3:1 identifies in general *when* the Lord Jesus will Return and when the Final Judgment is near. And Joel 3:2 identifies the *what* that will happen. For God had said, "I will gather all nations into the Valley of Jehosophat (i.e. the Valley of 'Judgment'). Next, verses 3:2-6 reveal the *why,* the real reason for God's wrath: "I will judge them for harming my people, for scattering my inheritance among the people [of the world], and for dividing up my land."

In addition, verses 7-16 answer the *how* of God's plans to accomplish this judgment of the nations. The terminology used here is startling, shocking, even frightening, to say the least ! The imagery used in this passage is that of an irate Father, moved from patient toleration of the pesky antagonists of His children, to outright retaliation on those who have mistreated His well-loved children. Indeed, to paraphrase this passage, it might read, "It's not nice to fool [with] Father God!"

Let us take a moment, though, to evaluate the *when?* question a little more precisely, measuring it against twentieth century events of history. In fact, this comparison of Scripture with historical events may help us to discover where we are in God's grand schematic for the ages.

Joel 3 deals primarily with the Final Judgment and the final Triumph of the Messiah. However, it has another important message: it also predicts events which, when they occur, will mark the beginnings of the End of Time. This passage employs another—perhaps the last—of Joel's frequent use of time-related markers. But here it is seemingly doubled for special emphasis. Verses 1-2 of chapter 3 read: "For behold [i.e., 'watch carefully'], *in those days* and *at that time,* when I shall reverse the captivity [of Judah] and restore the fortunes of Judah and Jerusalem, I will gather all nations...."(AMP). So, *when* will the Lord begin calling the offending nations to account? The answer: He will begin this "gathering of nations" when we observe the return of the Jews and the restoration of Jerusalem to Jewish administration. Of course, anyone who reads the news and history knows full well that those events have already happened. So we are prompted to ask, "What then is to happen next?"

We ask again, then, have any of these predictive events happened in *recent* history? Of course they have, and in the twentieth century, too; the so-called "Century of the Holy Spirit." Notice that as devastating as the two World Wars are known to have been, the political ramifications were, after all, instrumental in returning the Jews to their ancient homeland; and, of course, not without startling dimensions of violence and bloodshed. A brief review of this remarkable history seems relevant to our subject.

After the largely unsuccessful medieval Church Crusades into Palestine, the Moslem Ottoman Turks became the dominant power in the Holy Land from 1291-1917. But in World War I, the Turks, seeing opportunity to exploit the vicissitudes of the war in the eastern Mediterranean, and anxious to extend the boundaries of their empire, joined forces with the Axis Powers (then called the "Central Powers").

As a consequence, British forces, to protect their flank, invaded Palestine under the command of General Allenby. And the British were soon successful in routing the Ottoman forces. Among many other reasons was the fact that their Muslim minds allegedly translated the name "Allenby" into "Allah Bey." As a result, their armies became disheartened because they supposed they were warring against the "Son of Allah." (This information from Dr. Henrietta Miers, Gospel Light Press.) The upshot of this phase of the war was that the

British became the official administrators of Palestine when the Armistice was finally signed on November 11, 1918. Then on April 24, 1920, the year-old League of Nations granted Great Britain a mandate to govern Palestine, an immensely uncomfortable "gift," as it turned out, to those victors over the Ottomans.

In fact, a Zionist movement designed to return the Jews to their homeland had long been their nationalistic dream. As early as 1870, European Jews, weary of widespread persecution in their European homelands, began to trickle into Palestine. This meager migration, however, was about to change dramatically; for during the course of WWI, a Jewish chemical scientist named Chaim Weizmann had so greatly assisted the British war effort that he was rewarded by British Parliament with the "Balfour Declaration" of November 2, 1917.

This Declaration endorsed the creation of a national homeland for the Jewish people in Palestine. But subsequent Arab militancy against this Plan caused the British to restrict sharply the number of Jewish immigrants allowed into Palestine. Just the same, the Jews, undaunted, came on anyway, in ever greater numbers—all this in spite of British efforts to control their arrival. The Jews seemed to sense that ancient prophecies about their Return to their homeland were being fulfilled, regardless of the immense opposition.

Then, World War II opened in September 1939, eventually bringing about even more hellish persecution of the Jews. For, as early as the 1930's Adolph Hitler instituted a plan to exterminate 11,000,000 European Jews, a plan he called "The Final Solution." Actually, however, Hitler succeeded in murdering only (?) 6,000,000 of the 11,000,000, even though the Nazis had planned to destroy every last one. And those who died suffered horrible deaths in the German prison camps.

Although there were many alleged reasons for Hitler to pursue his insane plan, it was supposedly because the Jews had caused the humiliation of the German people in WWI, and because Hitler taught that the Aryan race was the only "pure" people. But when WWII finally closed, and the horrors of the German prison camps were fully revealed, Jewish people from all over the world converged at the shores of their new country, literally by the hundreds of thousands.

Increasingly alarmed at this nationalistic "invasion," in 1948 seven angry Arab nations formed a military alliance in a campaign designed to haze the Jews "back into the sea." However, after seven months of intense fighting with the Israelis, the Arab alliance was astonished to find themselves backed into the desert, soundly defeated by the Jewish Defense League. Miraculously triumphant, the Jews declared themselves the "Nation of Israel" and were promptly recognized officially in May of 1948 by both the USA and the USSR.

At last the Jewish people realized their ancient dream of returning to their Promised Land. Seemingly, the first part of Joel 3:1 had been fulfilled. But there was still another chapter to be written. In addition to the Return of the Jews to their homeland, God had also promised, through Joel 3:1-2, "to restore the fortunes of Jerusalem." For according to the prediction of Joel 3:1, two signs, rather than one, are cited as preceding the calling of all Nations to the "Valley of Decision" (3:14).

It is true that Israel had decisively won the 1948 seven-month conflict, but one all-important prize had been denied them—Jerusalem. Jerusalem remained in the hands of the Jordanians. The Jews had fought tenaciously to liberate that city in the 1948 war, but crack British-trained Jordanian troops had kept them at bay. Nevertheless, with the '48 war won, the Israelis achieved political independence in May of 1948.

But the nations of the Arab Alliance, deeply embarrassed by their resounding defeat by the Israelis, courted the USSR's assistance in rearming for yet another try at destroying those "pesky" Jews. Persistent military skirmishes continued all around, and within Israel's borders, foreshadowing the huge conflict that was to come. So Israel, under constant threat from her Palestinian neighbors, launched a preemptive strike on all fronts in June of 1967. Those Hebrews took a deep breath before the Lord, then shook themselves as in Old Testament times, and proceeded to decimate their enemies— in only six days. This has since been identified in history as "Israel's Six-Day War."

And as for Jerusalem, this time after severe hand-to-hand fighting in the streets, the Jewish people at last claimed the "City of Peace" for their God! As one historian described the drama of that moment, "Israeli soldiers, with Uzi submachine guns slung over their shoulders, wept—bowing their heads in victorious reverence at the foot of the Wailing Wall." (see *Israel*, p. 55, George Melrod, ed., Houghton Mifflin, 1995).

After so long a time, the Jews were at last in possession of their Eternal City. Was Jesus' prophecy at last being fulfilled? "And they [the Jews] will fall by the edge of the sword, and will be led captive into all the nations; and Jerusalem will be trampled underfoot by the Gentiles *until* the times of the Gentiles be fulfilled" (Luke 21:24, emphasis added, NASB). No one would deny that through the Ages, the Jews have fallen by the sword. No one can deny that they have suffered as captives in all nations. Neither can we deny that Jerusalem was possessed for centuries by Gentiles. But now, in our day, Jerusalem is under control of the Jewish people. So what now are we to conclude about God's predicted timetable? Are these historical events indicators of the accuracy of God's predictions? And is the twentieth century outpouring of the Holy Spirit one of those markers?

With all these historical events in mind, it is next to impossible to deny that Joel 3:1-2 has been fulfilled in our own time. But if the argumentation offered in this study in any way implies that the Jewish occupation of the City of Jerusalem in 1967 was a benchmark event, ushering in a period of peace and security, that is a grossly mistaken assumption. Indeed, as editor Melrod has observed, the triumphant Israelis were initially euphoric, enjoying a period of celebration "within what were thought to be secure boundaries" (p. 55).

And, indeed, that ultimate experience will one day be afforded them—sometime in the future—after Jesus Christ, their Messiah, returns to Earth to complete the predicted Restoration. Zechariah 14 discusses this same future event, but in even more shocking detail.

As for the present, however, the Israelis are continuing to struggle for a peaceful settlement of the militant Palestinian resistance to the Jewish presence in the country. In an effort to achieve peace, the Israelis even have offered to surrender land which they had won during their several wars. On the other hand, the Palestinians claim they have been unjustly disinherited from the land on which they once lived.

Meanwhile, the Jews maintain that they are simply taking possession of the land that was inherited by their forefathers, land promised to them by God long, long ago, land to be Israel's forever. Meanwhile, the governments of the rest of the world—still very uneasy in the aftermath of two World Wars—see the Palestinian issue as extremely dangerous, a probable catalyst for yet another world war.

It is certain, if we take Joel's prophecy seriously, that chapter 3, verses 2-16, portray God as the Sovereign of Sovereigns beckoning *all* nations to the "Valley of Decision" for a time of reckoning justice. Why? The Scriptures declare that it will be because of the long history of mistreatment of God's chosen people, both unwarranted and unnecessarily cruel!

Is it possible, then, that we of the twenty-first century are living at the very threshold of the long-anticipated Armageddon? Zechariah 14:1-14 and Revelation 16:13-16 provide us a more detailed accounts of the tragic events associated with the Return of the Lord with His Saints and the ensuing final battle of all time. Zechariah 14:12-14 provides us a very dramatic description of a future war involving a strange, debilitating "plague" which will cause people's flesh to "rot away," making them "walking corpses." The biblical description here is not unlike the descriptions we have heard of victims of atomic bomb fall-out in World War II. Is that catastrophe in the immediate future of those who continue to defy the God of heaven? Perhaps we shall know the answer sooner than we think.

Chapter 12

CONCLUSION:
THE REASONABLE IMPLICATIONS
OF THIS STUDY

In this study, our concentrated review of Scripture, our extensive examination of Church History, and the argumentation of the New Testament Patriarchs all indicate that the New Testament believers—most importantly, those who personally listened to the teaching of Christ Himself— were convinced that the supernatural Gifts of Pentecost would continue to be a part of their spiritual heritage until Jesus returned at the end of the Age. They gave every indication that Pentecostal experiences were to be their "birthright" until Jesus returns as King of kings.

There is, in fact, no hint in their interpretation of prophecy or in their understanding of the teachings of Christ that the spiritual Gifts, which were so much a part of their ministry, would someday "vanish," or even to decline, as some "cessationists" have claimed. Never! If anything, they seem to have had a sense of being "disarmed" when they were without the miraculous power (*dunamis*) of the Holy Spirit. And, by contrast, they acted fully armed *only* when they ministered under the *dunamis* power of the Holy Spirit. In the words of Paul, "The weapons of our warfare are not of flesh and blood, but they are mighty before God for the overthrow of strongholds"(2 Corinthians 10: 4, AMP).

The Promise of the Word was (and still is), "This Promise is unto you ... and to all who are afar off, as many as the Lord our God shall call" (Acts 2:39). There is enormous life-giving power in the Word of the Lord! And it is the Word of the Lord God we deal with here. Indeed, to illustrate, "We understand that the worlds were framed by the Word of God, so that the things which are seen were not made of things which are visible"(Heb. 11:3, NKJV). But when professionals try to explain this phenomenon of Creation, the closest they can come by means of their secular mindset is to refer to the event known as "The Big Bang." But the Creation event is much bigger than trying to determine *What* happened.

To be much more accurate, the issue revolves around the *Who,* not the *What.*" It was the *Who—that is God Himself—* who spoke the worlds into existence. And additionally, the Gospel of John, chapter 1, adds further pertinent information indicating that believers are included in His great creation Plan: "All things were made through Him, and without Him nothing was made that was made. In Him was life, and the life was the Light of men....But as many as received Him, to them He gave the right to become children of God, even to those who believe in His name"(John 1: 3 - 4, 12, NKJV). How marvelously gracious of the Lord to include mankind in His creative plans. The Psalmist, too, expresses his awe at this phenomenon: "What is man that You are mindful of him, and the son of man that You should visit him?" (Psalm 8:4, NKJV, see margin).

I am persuaded that our minds, for the most part, have great difficulty understanding the extent of God's love and His provisions for those who believe. The Apostle Paul observed that He (speaking of Jesus)"gave gifts unto men"(Eph.4:8; Ps

68:18, NKJV). W. E. Vine, in his *Expository Dictionary*, indicates this passage is referring to "the gift of the Holy Ghost Himself" (see Eph. 4:7-8, NKJV). In this life, we will likely never fully understand the extent of His "giving," *agape* Love. No other idolatrous god in all the world is known for its compassion, mercy, and love, but our God is. And by participating in the Gifts of the Holy Spirit, we can at least partially understand.

In addition, our study of the Feasts of the Old Testament indicates these Feasts are actually God's roadmap of His intended dealings with mankind until the end of time. Jesus, as the Lamb of God, was crucified on the significant day of Passover, emphasizing that Jesus was God's Passover Lamb. Similarly, the outpouring of the Holy Spirit occurred "when the Day of Pentecost was *fully come*"(emphasis added), indicating the Lord was once again delivering His Gifts on **His** schedule. Likewise, we have discovered that Pentecost is one of the three Jewish Festivals related to the Harvest cycle. Pentecost represents the "middle" harvest and is a preliminary to the "final" harvest. And at the conclusion of the "final harvest" the matured fruit crops are gleaned during the Feast of Tabernacles, also known as the "Ingathering."

The Passover Festival is representative of Christian conversion. Pentecost, a completely separate Festival, is symbolic of God's empowerment for workers laboring in the harvest field. And finally, the Feast of Tabernacles (the" Ingathering") concluded the three-part harvest cycle. Thus, the Feast of Tabernacles or the "Ingathering" represents the "Final Harvest" at the End of Time, when the spiritual harvest is at last completed, and the Lord of the Harvest, Jesus the Messiah, is finally revealed. In the Jewish culture, only these three Festivals were made preeminent by God's requiring every Jewish male to attend. Thus, the Feast of Pentecost, also having the mandated attendance requirement, is endowed with a distinction revealing the Lord's unfolding plan for completing the "Final Harvest" of souls.

It is important to observe, too, that the Festival of Pentecost occurred fifty days after Passover, indicating it was to be observed as a *separate experience* from that of conversion—prefigured, as has been noted, in the Passover Festival. So, Pentecost was celebrated in the Jewish society as a *separate experience*. Also, Pentecost had its own distinctive rituals. "And when the Day of Pentecost was fully come, they were all filled with the Holy Spirit." Once again, this statement indicates that God was following His pre-arranged timetable that extended to the time of Jesus' Return.

While "speaking in tongues" and other Gifts of the Spirit continued for centuries after the Day of Pentecost, the prevailing moral depravity of the Dark Ages (c.500 A.D.-1500 A.D.) also caused the evidences of the *charismata* to decline steadily. Equally, every other major biblical doctrine suffered a similar fate during the Dark Ages. However, the reports of spiritual gifts totally "vanishing" is not supported at all by the records of Church History. Rather, Church History discloses that, in spite of the widespread decline of morals, the manifestations of these supernatural Gifts continued to occur, both from inside the Church, as well as among groups of independent believers.

So the God of heaven did not change His mind, after all. People and the Church that led them were the ones who had changed, retaining "a form of godliness but denying the power thereof"(2 Timothy 3:5). But as time progressed, when those who were spiritually deprived began to read the Bible for themselves, the spiritual atmosphere slowly improved, and the *charismata*, the Gifts of the Spirit, once again were experienced more and more frequently. This general restoration of biblical doctrines led to the revival of Pentecostal experiences, such as we have seen occurring in the twentieth, and now the twenty-first centuries.

As a matter of fact, the ancient prophecy of Joel, quoted at length by Peter on the Day of Pentecost, seems to verify not only the *beginning* of the "last days" but the *conclusion* of the "last days" which we are presently observing. Joel and other Old Testament prophets predicted those very events we are hearing in today's international News Reports. And because of the seriousness of the News, we are almost forced to contemplate the times in which we live and to wonder what is going to happen next!

So, in spite of the claims by some theologians that the Gifts of the Holy Spirit "vanished" after 300 years, a more careful study of Church History reveals that they *did not* and *have not*, even though the occurrences of *charismatic* Gifts did suffer limitations as did other doctrines.

So, during the infamous Dark Ages, *all* of the important doctrines of the Bible suffered an eclipse. But rather than it being God's plan to change New Testament practices, the real cause was the deterioration of moral values. And it is certain, too, that Gifts of the Holy Spirit continued in every century from the Day of Pentecost to the present. In addition, the modern explosion of Pentecostal experiences in the twentieth century—and now in the twenty-first—is further emphatic proof that the Gifts of the Holy Spirit have not disappeared at all. In fact, they continue to abound in our own time!

Furthermore, a closer study of Joel's prophecy, chapters 2 and 3, indicates this twentieth through 21st-century revival of Pentecostal experiences may very well be a significant precursor of the imminent Return of our Savior Jesus Christ. The abundance of fulfilled prophecies in our own time gives this rationale further credibility. Yes, the "Comforter" has come, "and He will *remain* with us!" just as Jesus promised. John 14:16-17 assures us that the power of the Holy Spirit's Baptism will continue "forever" to confirm the truthfulness of the Word of God: "And I will pray the Father, and He will give you another Comforter, *that He may abide with you forever.*"

Epilogue

MY REFLECTIONS ON THE IMPORT OF THIS STUDY

As I have researched and written about this subject over a three-year period, the experiences of New Testament Pentecost have become very dear to me. Increasingly, as the evidence has accumulated, I am more assured than ever before that the continuation of Pentecost, as it is portrayed in Acts, is God's answer to the waves of godless Apostasy occurring in our own time. Godless behavior was predicted in detail by the Apostle Paul in 2 Timothy 3:1-7. The believers of New Testament times needed the Gifts of the Spirit *then* so that they could minister with the God-given Authority more than equal to the task.

Indeed, those Gifts of the Holy Spirit are needed just as much *now* as then, and for the same reason: so that the Word of God being preached might be authenticated as being genuinely from the Lord! The world to whom we minister is, if anything, more corrupt, more filled with evil, more godless than ever before. And yet, in the midst of that godless, unbelieving cesspool of wickedness are multitudes of souls who desperately need to be made aware of a miracle-working God who cares enough to meet the pains of real, live people.

As a result of my research, and desirous to share my discoveries, may I respectfully suggest that all those reflecting on prophecy, now being fulfilled,— prayerfully and thoughtfully—read at least a couple of passages of Scripture. First, read Joel 2:28-32, and all of Joel chapter 3, all at one sitting. Notice the logical connection between the outpouring of Pentecost in chapter 2, and the horrifying events predicted in Joel 3, especially verses 1 and 2.

This logical connection is accomplished by means of time-related adverbs in Joel's narrative. For example, verses 1 and 2 read, "For behold *in those days and at that time,* when I shall bring again the captivity of Judah and Jerusalem, I will also gather all nations. . . into the valley of Jehoshaphat [meaning 'Jehovah is Judge']." Second, as we read the Apostle Paul's prophecy in 2 Timothy 3:1-9 for the details of the surge of evil during the end-time, it becomes evident that Paul's prophecy reads like today's news reports. This investigative exercise will provide the reader an important perspective on the sequence of events that have occurred since the "latter rain" outpouring of the Holy Spirit in the early decades of the twentieth century.

A serious question results: Is it possible that we have seen—and are still seeing—some of the very same events which both the Old and the New Testament prophets said would occur in conjunction with the "last day" outpouring of the Holy Spirit?

More and more, as I have studied the Scriptures on this subject and have perused the annals of Church History, I have experienced a growing awe, a holy reverence in my spirit, as though I were standing at the edge of a vast arena observing an ongoing drama of fulfilled prophecy. My own sensation is particularly meaningful in view of the fact that we all have watched the phenomena of modern-day Pentecost, poured out on believers around the world, very much like (and I could say "exactly like") those experiences recorded in the New Testament.

Remarkably, this tidal wave of modern Pentecost was predicted in the prophecy of Joel, and by the Apostles Paul and Peter, as a part of the unfolding events of the "*last days*," just "before the great and terrible Day of the Lord come" (see Joel 2:31; Malachi 4:5-6).

And this is all the more remarkable, it seems to me, because of the immensity of the present-day ecumenical dissemination of Pentecostal manifestations, which we are observing in many countries around the world. In the past century and a half, this biblical phenomenon of Holy Spirit gifting has long since breached denominational lines. And regarding this twentieth century Pentecostal phenomenon, I have come to believe its impact on all the major denominations was really the Lord's intention all along! Why? Because God originally promised this outpouring of the Holy Spirit to be "upon all flesh"(Joel 2:28).

But in the early days of the twentieth century, the established churches, for the most part, would have none of it, claiming either that Pentecostal experiences were "off-beat cults," or "manifestations of the devil." As the century has progressed, however, Pentecostal experiences have been (and still are) being manifest in many of the major denominations and in many different countries. Coupled with this fact are the numerous other current events which have proven to be impressive fulfillments of Bible prophecy. Many of these predicted events are by now history, yet very much "alive" in our own memories.

As an example, because I lived during WWII, I remember—as many of you can also—the painful difficulties the British had honoring the "Balfour Declaration" to return the Jewish people to their homeland, as the British had originally promised.

But it happened just the same, because God promised it would happen (see Joel 3:1). All this leads one to suspect that God is up to something grand and magnificent—as though we were watching the slow but determined closure of "the time of the Gentiles." And current events are important signs which the Bible has predicted would precede the *Parousia*, the final Revelation of Jesus Christ as King of kings. Accompanying that final event will be the ultimate, universal Recognition by everyone of Jesus Christ as the Messiah—but especially so for the Jewish people. What a beautiful moment it will be to experience the final Triumph of our Savior and Lord!

However, since both good and evil coexist in the world, there is yet another side of this culmination of prophecy: the predicted "Great Tribulation" and the Final Judgment. Thus, the way modern history is developing makes one wonder if we are about to observe another segment of fulfilled prophecy. As we hear in the News everyday about the terrible turmoil in the Middle East, if we are sensitive to God's prophecies, we cannot help wondering if we are observing the very beginning of "Jacob's Trouble," the time often referred to as "The Great Tribulation."

Joel certainly seems to be predicting that event in chapter 3. And will our Savior soon appear to "rapture" His Church—as we fully expect Him to do—"catching away" those who have already believed on Him as their Savior and are exhibiting the Fruits of the Spirit? Is the Rapture of the Church the next event on God's agenda? We live in momentous times, indeed! I find my own spirit stirred with joyous excitement, wondering what our God is going to do next!

Regardless of possible differing philosophical positions on this matter of interpreting prophecy, we are obliged to recognize that God Himself identified the importance of prophecy. It becomes a matter of His honor. He stated His purpose for prophecy, speaking through Isaiah in chapter 46: 8-10, TLB as follows:

> Don't forget this, O guilty ones . . . don't forget the many times I clearly told you what was going to happen in the future. For I am God—I only—and there is no other like me who can tell you what is going to happen. All I say will come to pass, for I do whatever I wish.

One point seems certain as we consider Joel's prophetic outline: we are marching with dramatic inevitability toward the "gathering of all nations" into the "Valley of Decision" (or "threshing," see Joel 3:14, KJV, margin). For many, that final Revelation of the Lord Jesus will not be a happy time. Consequently, we are admonished in Scripture to take full advantage of the "Today" of salvation! "Even so come quickly, Lord Jesus!"

TEXTBOOKS

Atter, Gordon F. *The Third Force*. Ontario: The College Press, 1982.

Bartleman, Frank. *Azusa Street: The Roots of Modern-day Pentecost*. (Reprint) South Plainfield: Bridge Publishing, Inc.,1980.

Blumhofer, Edith. *Restoring the Faith*. Chicago: University of Illinois Press, 1993.

Bresson, Bernard L. *Studies in Ecstasy*. New York: Vantage Press, 1966.

Brownville, C. Gordon. *Symbols of the Holy Spirit*. London: Revell, 1945.

Brumback, Carl. *What Meaneth This: A Pentecostal Answer*. Springfield: Gospel Publishing House, 1947.

_____*Suddenly. . . From Heaven*. Springfield: Gospel Publishing House, 1961.

Bruner, Frederick Dale. *A Theology of the Holy Spirit*. Grand Rapids: Eerdmans, 1970.

Conybeare, W. J., and J. S. Howson. *The Life and Epistles of Saint Paul*. Hartford: The S. S. Scranton Company, 1906.

Dayton, Donald W., ed. "The Higher Christian Life." In *Three Early Pentecostal Tracts*. New York: Garland Publishing, Inc.,1985.

Dunn, James D. G. *Baptism in the Holy Spirit*. London: SCM Press, LTD, 1974.

Edwards, Jonathan. "Christians a Chosen Generation, a Royal Priesthood." In *On Knowing Christ*. Reprint, Edinburgh: The Banner of Truth Trust, 1997.

Estep, William R. *The Anabaptist Story*. Grand Rapids: Eerdmans, 1963.

Fox, John. *Fox's Book of Martyrs*. Edited by William Byron Forbush. Philadelphia: John C. Winston Company, 1926.

Frodsham, Stanley H. *With Signs Following: The Story of the Pentecostal Revival in the Twentieth Century*. Rev. ed. Springfield: Gospel Publishing House, 1941.

Gee, Donald. *Concerning Spiritual Gifts*. Springfield: Gospel Publishing House, 1972.

_____. *The Fruit of the Spirit*. Springfield: Gospel Publishing House, 1975.

_____. *The Ministry Gifts of Christ*. Springfield: Gospel Publishing House, 1930.

_____. *Spiritual Gifts in the Work of the Ministry Today*. Los Angeles: LIFE Bible College, 1963.

Gordon, A. J. *The Ministry of the Spirit*. Grand Rapids: Baker, 1964._

Grudem, Wayne A., ed. *Are Miraculous Gifts for Today?: Four Views*. Grand Rapids: Zondervan, 1996.

Horton, Harold Lawrence. *The Gifts of the Spirit*. 3rd ed. Shreveport: The Voice of Healing, 1949.

Horton, Stanley M. *Into All Truth: A Survey of ... Divine Revelation*. Springfield: Gospel Publishing House, 1955.

_____. *What the Bible Says About the Holy Spirit*. Springfield: Gospel Publishing House, 1976.

Hunter, Harold D. *Spirit-Baptism: A Pentecostal Alternative*. Lanham: University Press of America, 1983.

Hyatt, Eddie L. *2000 Years of Charismatic Christianity: A 21st Century Look at Church History*. Dallas: Hyatt International Ministries, 2001.Linzey, Dr. Verna M. *The Baptism with the Holy Spirit: The Reception of the Holy Spirit as Confirmed by Speaking in Tongues*. Xulon Press, 2004.

Matthews, David. *I Saw the Welsh Revival*. Chicago: Moody, 1957.

McDonnell, Kilian, and George Montague. *Christian Initiation and Baptism in the Holy Spirit: Evidence from the First Eight Centuries*. Collegeville: The Liturgical Press, 1994.

Morgan, G. Campbell. *The Analyzed Bible*. Westwood: Fleming H. Revell, 1964.

Nichols, Robert Hastings. *The Growth of the Christian Church*. Philadelphia:Westminister, 1941.

Robeck, Cecil M. Jr., ed. *Charismatic Experiences in History*. Peabody: Hendrickson, 1985.

Ruthven, Jon. *On the Cessation of the Charismata: The Protestant Polemic on Postbiblical Miracles*. Sheffield, England: Sheffield Academic Press, 1997. rev.,

Sherrill, John L. *They Speak With Other Tongues*. Westwood: Revell, 1966.

Stronstad, Roger. *The Charismatic Theology of St. Luke*. Peabody: Hendrickson, 1984.

Synan, Vinson. *The Century of the Holy Spirit: 100 Years of Pentecostal and Charismatic Renewal*. Nashville: Thomas Nelson, 2001.

Reference Sources

Barrett, Dr. David B., et. al. *The World Christian Encyclopedia*, second edition. Oxford: Oxford University Press, 2001.

Burgess, Stanley M. and Gary B. McGee, eds. *Dictionary of Pentecostal and Charismatic Movements*. Grand Rapids: Zondervan, 1993.

Cruden, Alexander. *Cruden's Complete Concordance*. Grand Rapids: Zondervan, 1968.

Douglas, J. D., ed. *The New Bible Dictionary*. Grand Rapids: Eerdmans, 1979.

Encyclopaedia Britannica, 1947 edition.

Encyclopaedia Britannica, Macropaedia and Micropaedia, 1980 edition.

Edersheim, Alfred. *The Life and Times of Jesus, the Messiah*. (2 volumes) New York: Longmans, Green and Company, 1906.

Fausset, Andrew R. *Bible Encyclopaedia and Dictionary*. Grand Rapids: Zondervan, n.d.

Guthrie, D. and J. A. Motyer et al. *The New Bible Commentary*. Grand Rapids: Eerdmans, 1971.

Halley, Henry H. *Pocket Bible Handbook*. Chicago: Henry H. Halley, 1946.

Jamieson, Robert et al. *Commentary, Critical and Explanatory.* vols. 1 and 2. Hartford: The S. S. Scranton Co., (n.d).

Leeser, Isaac. The Holy Bible., Hebrew and English, New York: Hebrew Publishing Company, 1926.

M'Clintock, John, and James Strong. *Cyclopedia of Biblical Theological and Ecclesiastical Literature.* 12 vols. New York: Harper Brothers, 1894.

McMichael, George. *Anthology of American Literature*, vol.1. New York: Macmillan, 1980.

Melrod, George, ed. *Israel: Including the West Bank and Gaza Strip.* Boston: Houghton Mifflin, 1995.

Muston, Alexis. *The Israel of the Alps: A History of the Waldenses.* Translated from French by Rev. John Montgomery. 2 vols. Glasgow & New York: Blackie and Sons, 1857.

Nichols, Robert Hastings. *The Growth of the Christian Church.* Philadelphia: Westminster, 1941.

Schaff, Philip. *History of the Christian Church.* 8 vols. Peabody: Hendrickson, 2002.

Shelley, Bruce L. *Church History in Plain Language.* Dallas: Word Publishing, 1995.

Tenney, Merrill C., ed. *The Zondervan Pictorial Dictionary.* Grand Rapids: Zondervan, 1970.

Unger, Merrill F. *Unger's Bible Dictionary.* Chicago: Moody Press, 1957.

Vincent, Marvin R. *Word Studies in the New Testament,* 4 volumes. Peabody: Hendrickson, n.d.

Vine, W. E. *Expository Dictionary of New Testament Words.,* 4 volumes. London: Oliphants, Ltd., 1943.

Walker, Williston. *A History of the Christian Church.* New York: Charles Scribner's Sons, 1929.

World Book Encyclopedia. Vol. 19, 1963.

Zenos, Andrew C. *A Compendium of Church History.* Philadelphia: Presbyterian Board of Education, 1938.

Comments on the Progression of Pentecostal Scholarship

A few comments may be in order here regarding the improving sophistication of Pentecostal scholarship since 1901. At this point in time, there are many authors who have investigated this explosion of Pentecost. But only a representative few of those can be cited here, cited in order to illustrate the progressive improvements in scholarly efforts. In addition, the Bible scholars and theologians listed below have been chosen because their research efforts have spanned the whole century of Pentecostal activities.

Frank Bartleman (1871-1936) is important because he was probably the first to chronicle the Azusa Street revival in his book *How Pentecost Came to Los Angeles* (1925). His emphasis was largely *experiential,* although occasionally he ventured into biblical interpretation. His book is historically important because it provides *eye-witness* accounts of the Pentecostal Revival from 1905 through 1911, events in which he himself participated.

Bartleman arrived in Los Angeles in December of 1904, wholly committed to the holiness cause, but at that time he had not yet personally experienced Pentecost. However, about 1906 he came under the teachings of William J. Seymour concerning the Baptism of the Holy Spirit, and he, too, experienced New Testament Pentecost. Subsequently, Bartleman wrote six books and numerous articles and tracts, all related to the biblical relevance of the Pentecostal Revival. (C. M. Robeck, Jr., "Frank Bartleman," See *Dictionary of Pentecostal. . . Movements*, 1993, pp. 50-51).

Stanley H. Frodsham (1882-1969) has already been quoted several times in this study. His book *With Signs Following* has now become a classic. It was researched prior to 1926, approximately twenty years after Topeka and Azusa, and was first published in 1926, with revisions and re-publications presented later. Frodsham's research was designed to answer the disdainful chorus of "cessationists" warning that miracles and tongues were "of the devil" because (as they claimed) "the Gifts of the Spirit ceased when the Apostles died." Frodsham saw that it was necessary to compare history with experience, to see which of these counterclaims were accurate. As a consequence, Frodsham sensed the importance of his text focusing on the experiences of believers throughout history, and in the twentieth century.

Frodsham's conclusion seems obvious: history proves that Pentecostal experiences *did not cease* after the Apostles were gone. Neither did they cease when the New Testament canon was finally completed. Unfortunately, however, the frequency of their occurrence did diminish during the Dark Ages. But more likely this diminution occurred—as it did to many New Testament doctrines—because the moral tone of medieval "Christianity" seriously declined at the same time, and—it should be obvious—the Holy Spirit does not fill, will not fill vessels which are determined to live self-centeredly.

Thus, the decline of spiritual gifts cannot be perceived as the will of the Lord, if mortals have not met the conditions! Even the Apostles had to meet the Lord's conditions in order to receive the Holy Spirit Baptism. But in spite of medieval failures, the Lord has always remained faithful to His promises. Indeed, His very Name is "Faithful"! And He has always had a "remnant" who have joyfully experienced not only genuine conversion, but the Baptism of the Holy Spirit with accompanying spiritual gifts.

In this regard, Carl Brumback (1917-1987), while pastoring in Florida, also felt the need for a rational historical and biblical defense of Pentecostalism because of the repeated argumentative statements by the "cessationist" theologians. In an effort to meet this need, Rev. Brumback implemented a series of radio messages, presented from 1942 through 1944. Brumback's series of scholarly studies were so effective that in 1947 they were compiled and published in his book, *What Meaneth This?*.

This publication is especially significant because it is one of the earliest efforts to marshal biblical argumentation for the continuance of the *charismatic* gifts. Later, in 1961, Brumback completed another publication, *Suddenly . . .From Heaven*, which specifically employs the historical approach in order to detail the development of the Assemblies of God. (Cp. *Dictionary of Pentecostal. . . Movements*, p.100).

And finally, the late twentieth century publication of Jon Ruthven, *On the Cessation of the Charismata: The Protestant Polemic on Postbiblical Miracles*, published in 1993/1997, is a masterful and scholarly defense of the credibility of the modern Pentecostal Revival. Dr. Ruthven observes in his "Preface" what his detailed study subsequently affirms: ". . . the amazing world-wide growth of the Pentecostal-charismatic movement and the increasing sophistication of its apologists have also prompted a widespread re-evaluation of cessationism" (p.7).

The research of these scholars, and the efforts of many others not mentioned here, developed with greater precision as the twentieth century progressed. The earliest—such as Bartleman and Frodsham—recorded a plethora of personal experiences exactly like those portrayed in the book of Acts. However, more recent theologians—such as Carl Brumback and Jon Ruthven—have emphasized the scriptural arguments for the rise of modern Pentecost. Both emphases were necessary because of the unsubstantiated claims that the supernatural gifts had ceased to be operational after the demise of the Apostles. Subsequently, however, the most elementary historical research has proved the sweeping assumptions of these "cessationists" to be biblically and historically inaccurate.

Permissions

The Scripture cited from "THE NEW TESTAMENT," by Charles B. Williams, published by Moody Press of Chicago, in 1958, is hereby gratefully acknowledged.

The Scripture taken from "The New Testament: An American Translation" by Edgar J. Goodspeed and published in 1924 by The University of Chicago Press, Chicago, Illinois, is hereby gratefully acknowledged.

Amplified Bible. Vol. I, II, and III, 1964, 1987. (AMP) Scripture quotations taken from THE AMPLIFIED BIBLE, copyright 1954, 1958, 1962, 1964, 1964, 1987 by The Lockman Foundation. All rights reserved. Used by permission. (www.Lockman. org)

King James Bible. (KJV) New York: American Bible Society.

The New King James Version. New York: Thomas Nelson Publishers, 1983.
Scripture taken from the New King James Version. Copyright 1982 by Thomas Nelson, Inc. Used by permission. All rights reserved.

Leeser, Isaac. The Holy Bible (Hebrew and English), New York: Hebrew Publishing Co., 1926.

The Living Bible: Paraphrased. "Christianity Today Edition" (TLB) Wheaton: Tyndale House Publishers, 1976. Scripture taken from THE LIVING BIBLE, copyright 1976.

Used by permission of Tyndale House Publishers, Inc., Wheaton, Illinois. All rights reserved.

New American Standard Bible, 1977. (NASB)
Scripture taken from the NEW AMERICAN STANDARD BIBLE, Copyright 1960, 1962, 1963, 1968, 1971, 1972, 1973, 1975, 1977, 1995 by The Lockman Foundation. Used by permission.

The New Living Translation, 1996. (NLT)
Scripture quotations marked (NLT) are taken from the *Holy Bible*, New Living Translation, copyright 1996. Used by permission of Tyndale House Publishers, Inc., Wheaton, Illinois 60189. All rights reserved.

The New International Version, 1984. (NIV)
Scriptures taken from the HOLY BIBLE, NEW INTERNATIONAL VERSION (NIV) copyright1973, 1978, 1984 by the International Bible Society. Used by permission of Zondervan. All rights reserved.

The Quest Study Bible, (NIV), 1983.

The Message, A Free Translation by Eugene H. Peterson, 1995. (Message)
Scripture taken from THE MESSAGE. Copyright by Eugene H. Peterson, 1993, 1994, 1995. Used by permission of NavPress Publishing Group.